AF608382

ELGER ESSER MORGENLAND

ELGER ESSER MORGENLAND

2004 – 2016

SCHIRMER / MOSEL

Ich pflücke keine geknickten Blumen.

Søren Kierkegaard

Contents

لبنان LEBANON

2004—2005

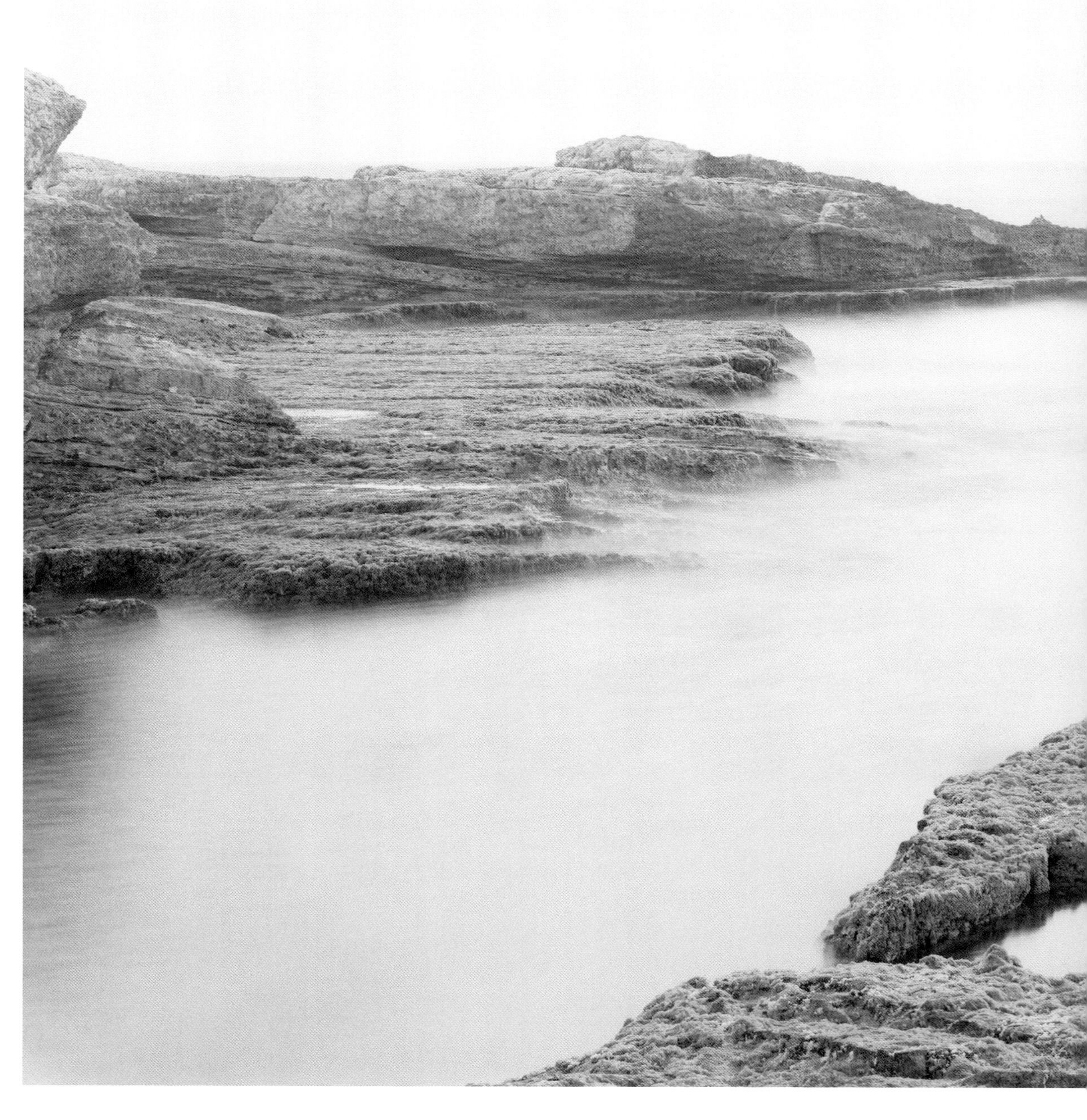

Raouché II 2005

Λ

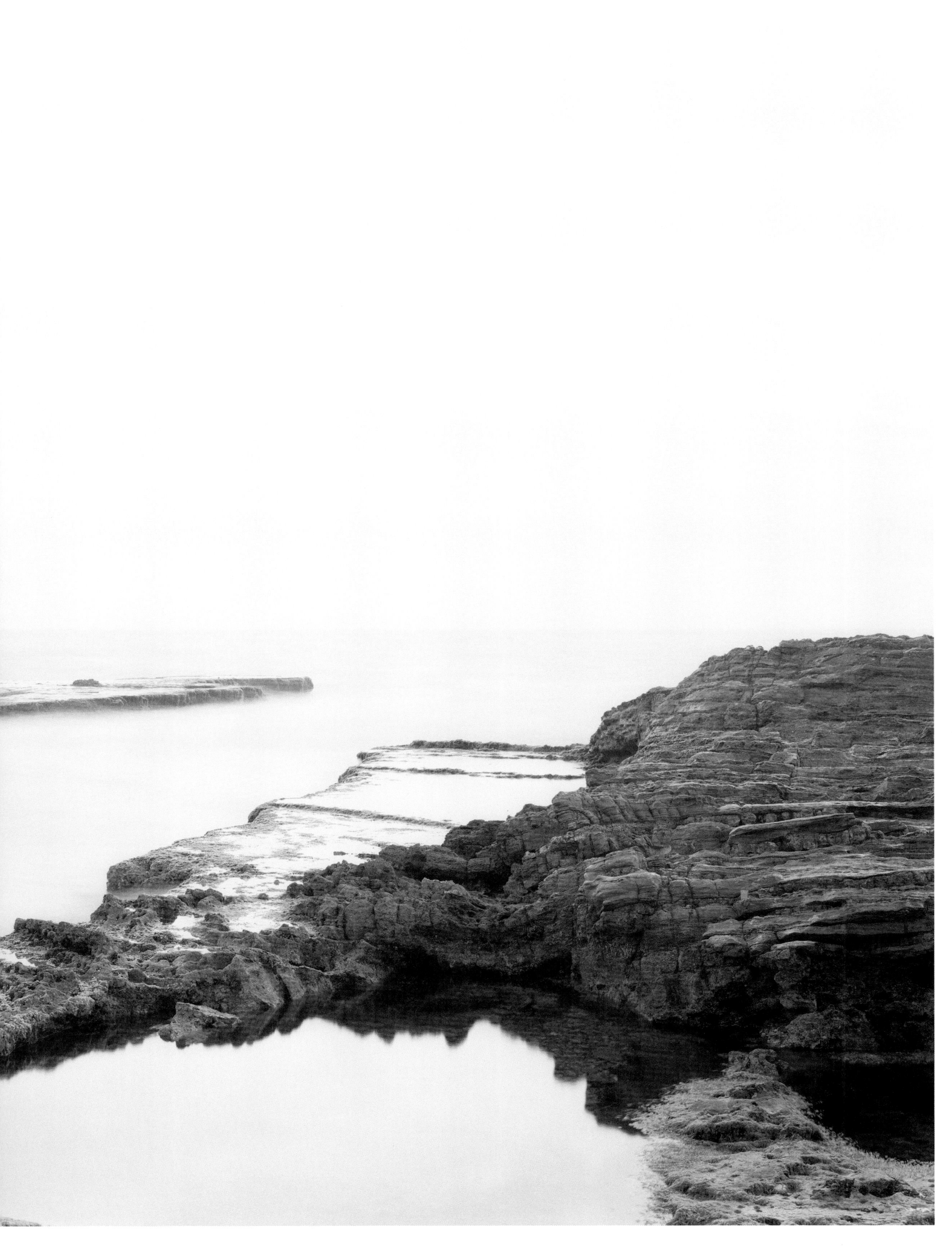

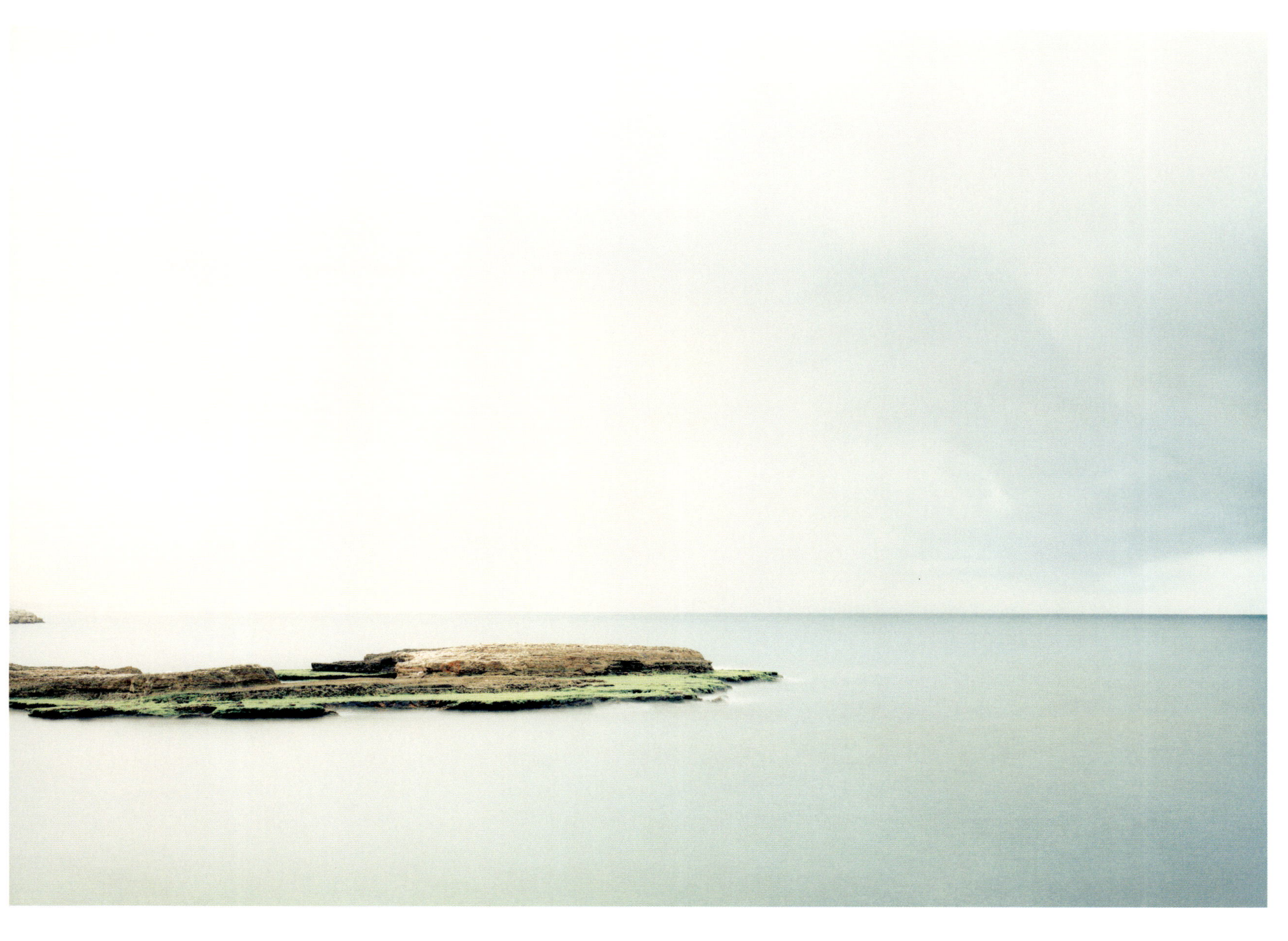

Jbail 2005

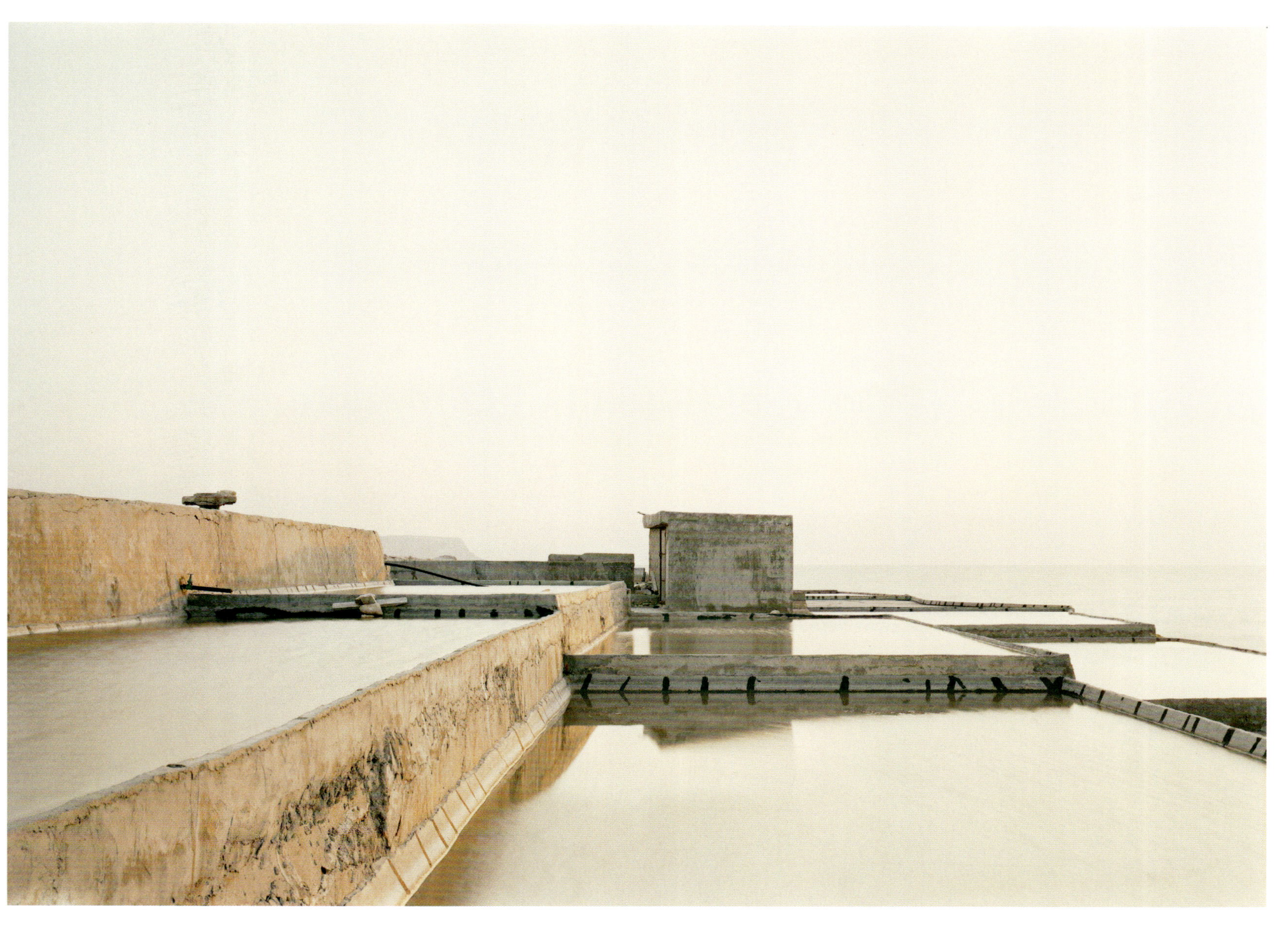

Enfeh I 2005

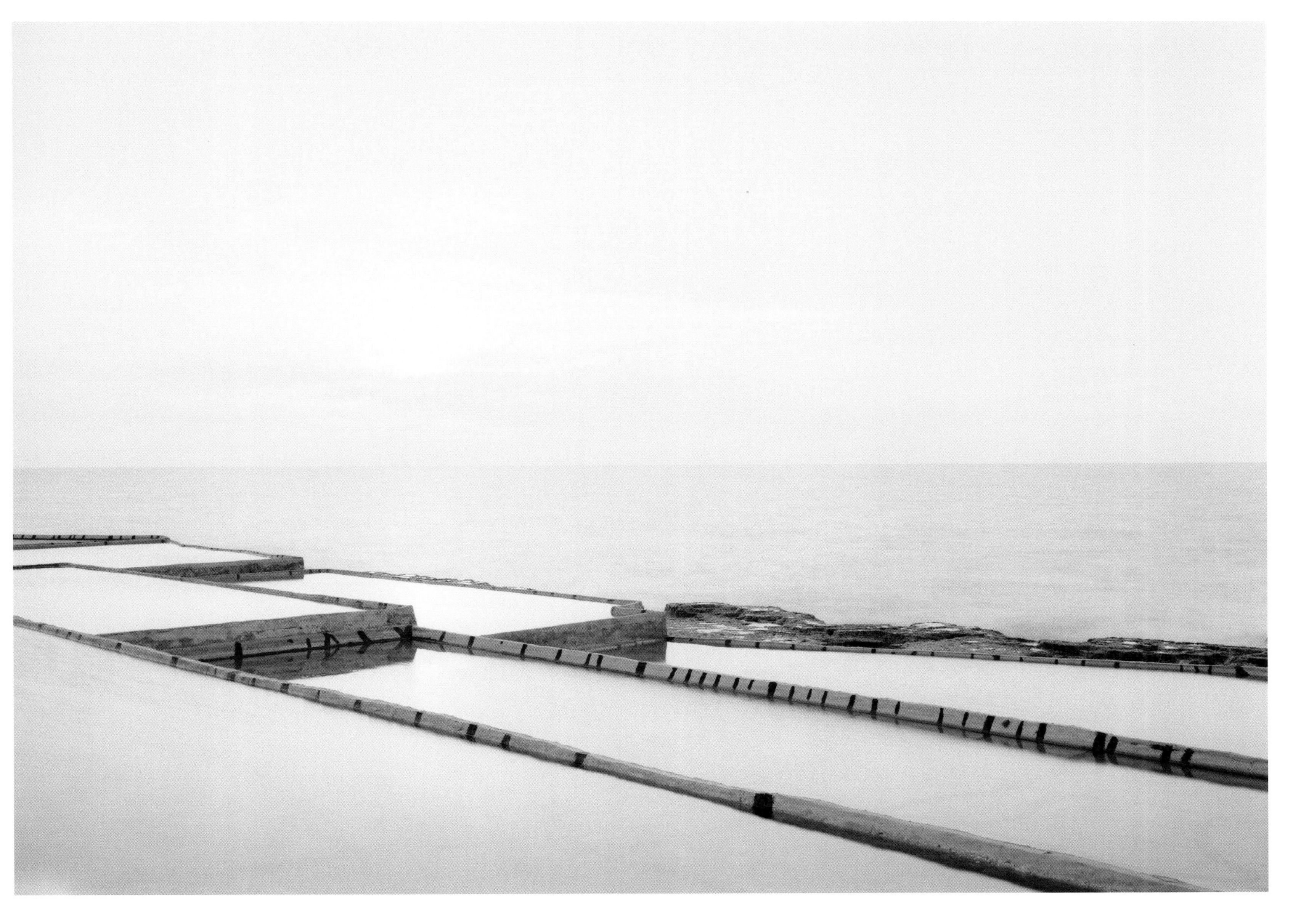

Enfeh II 2005

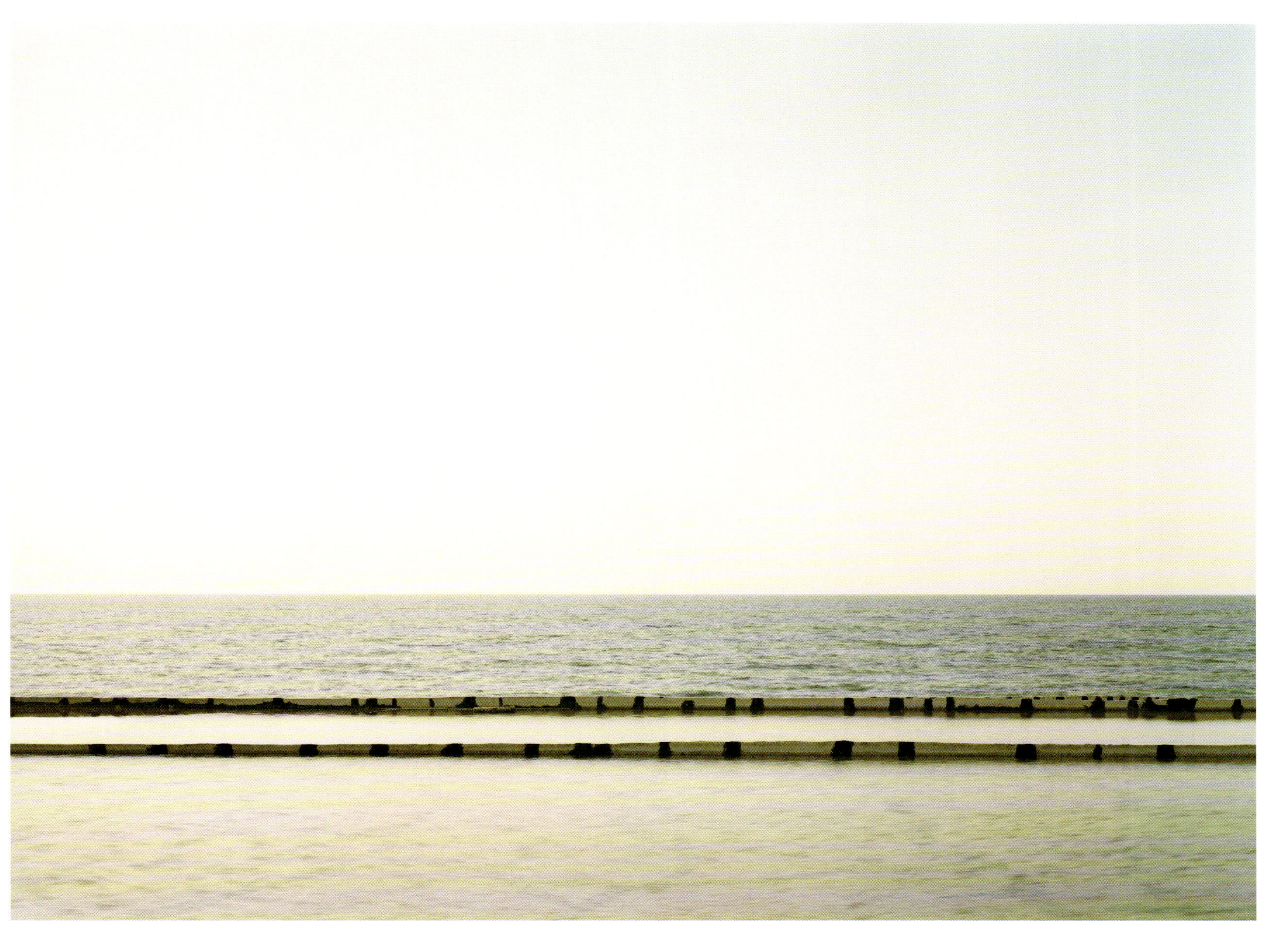

Enfeh III 2005

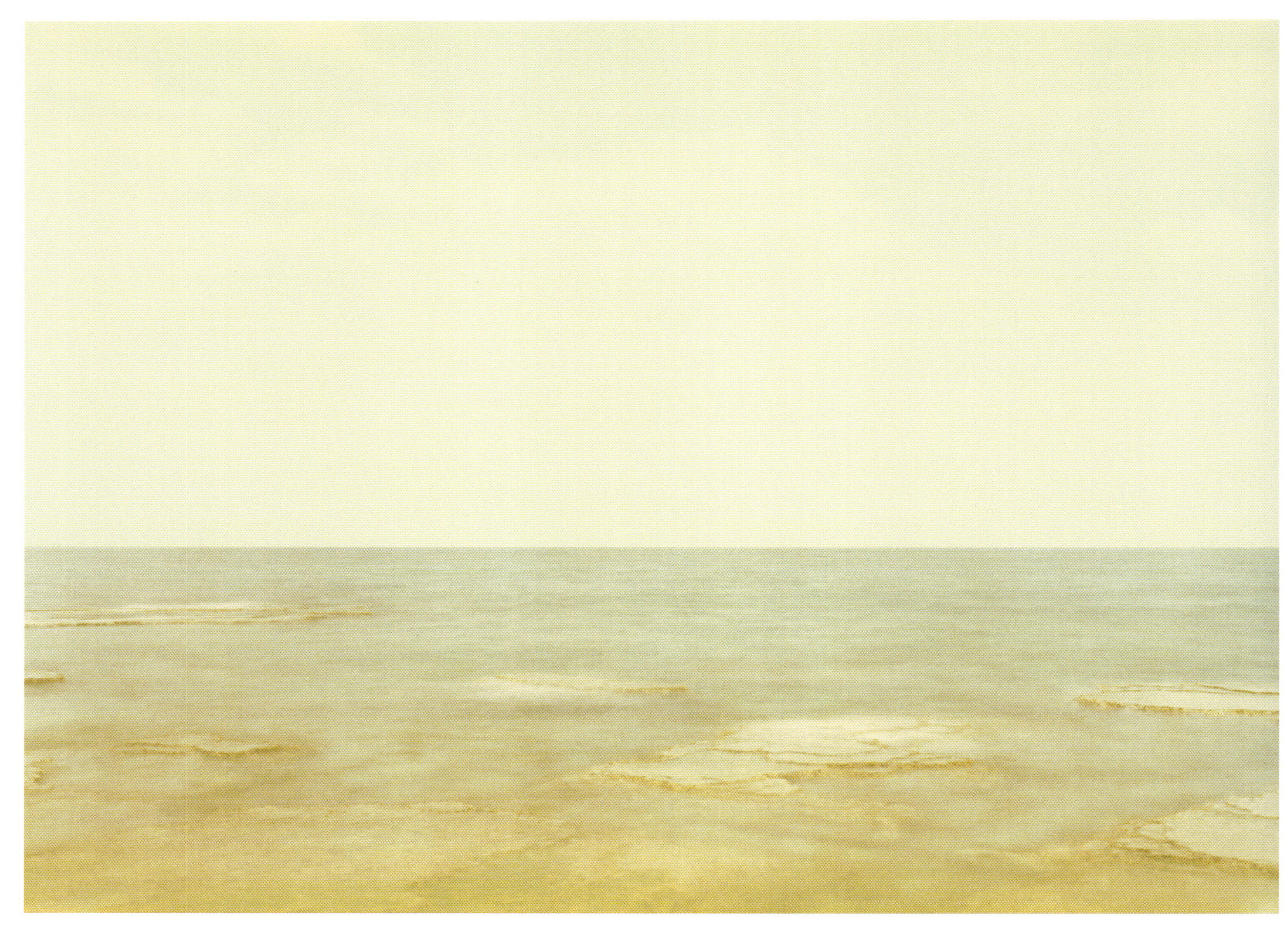

En Naquora I 2005

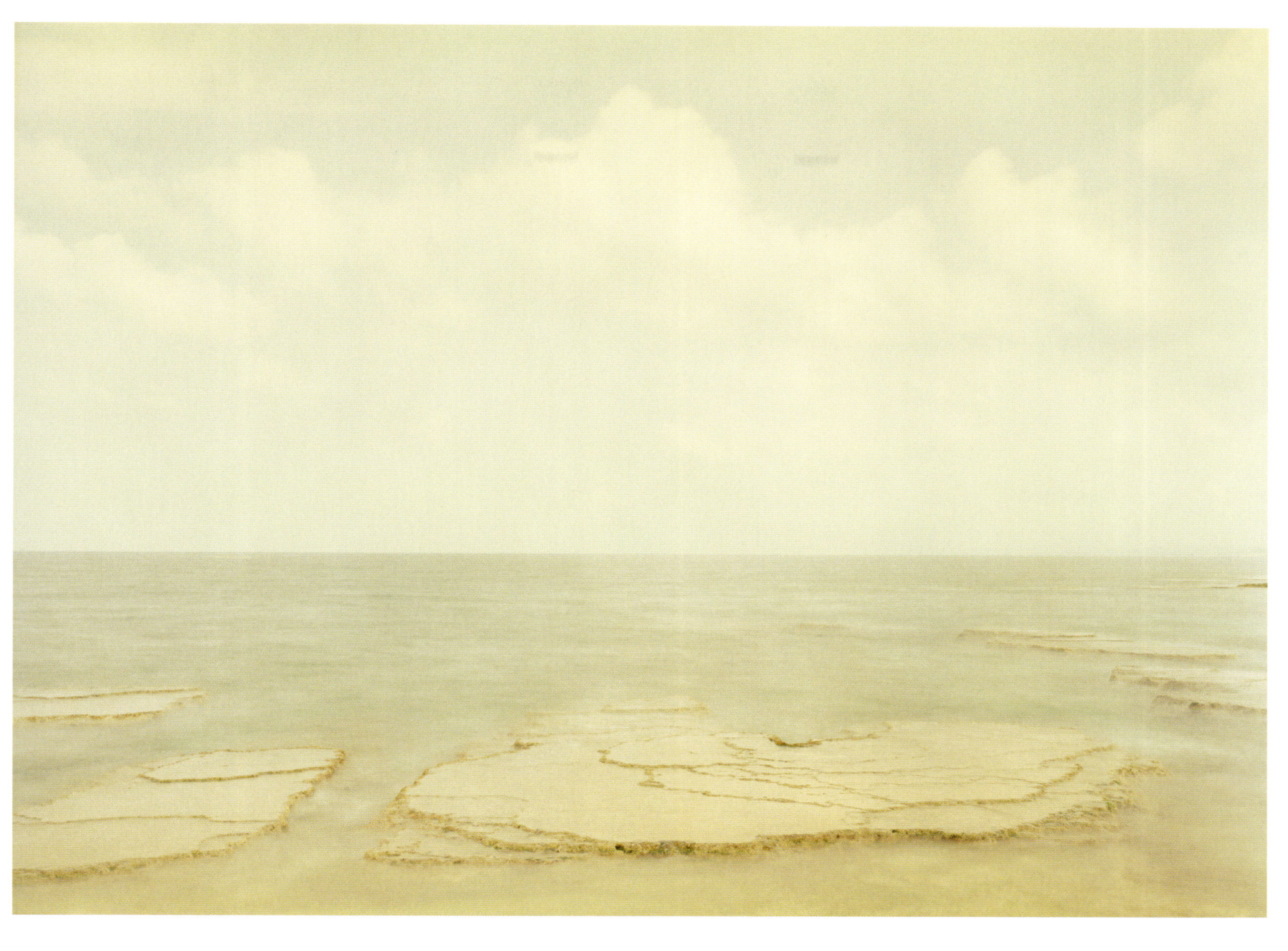

En Naquora II 2005

Saida II 2005

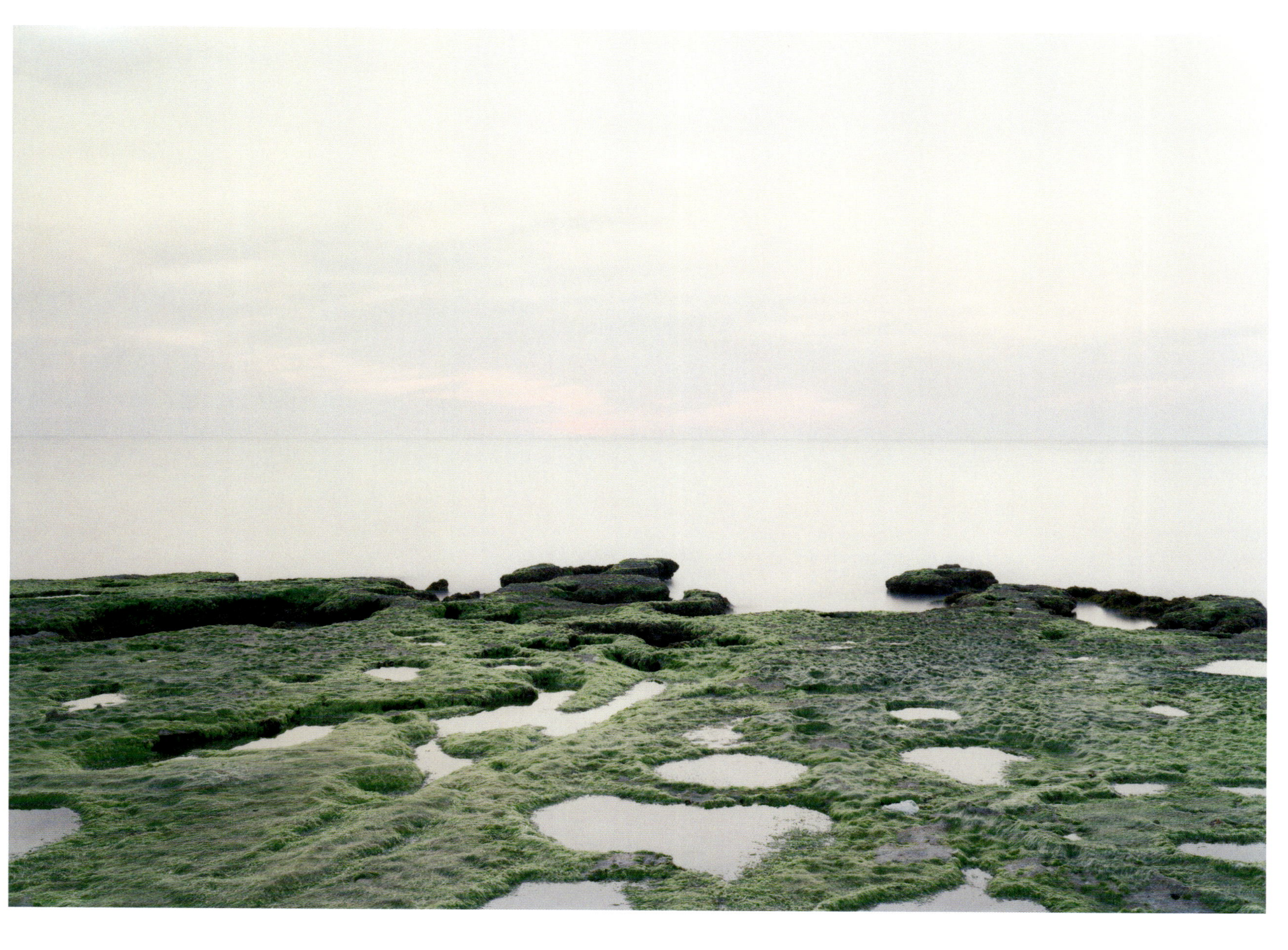

Raouché 2005

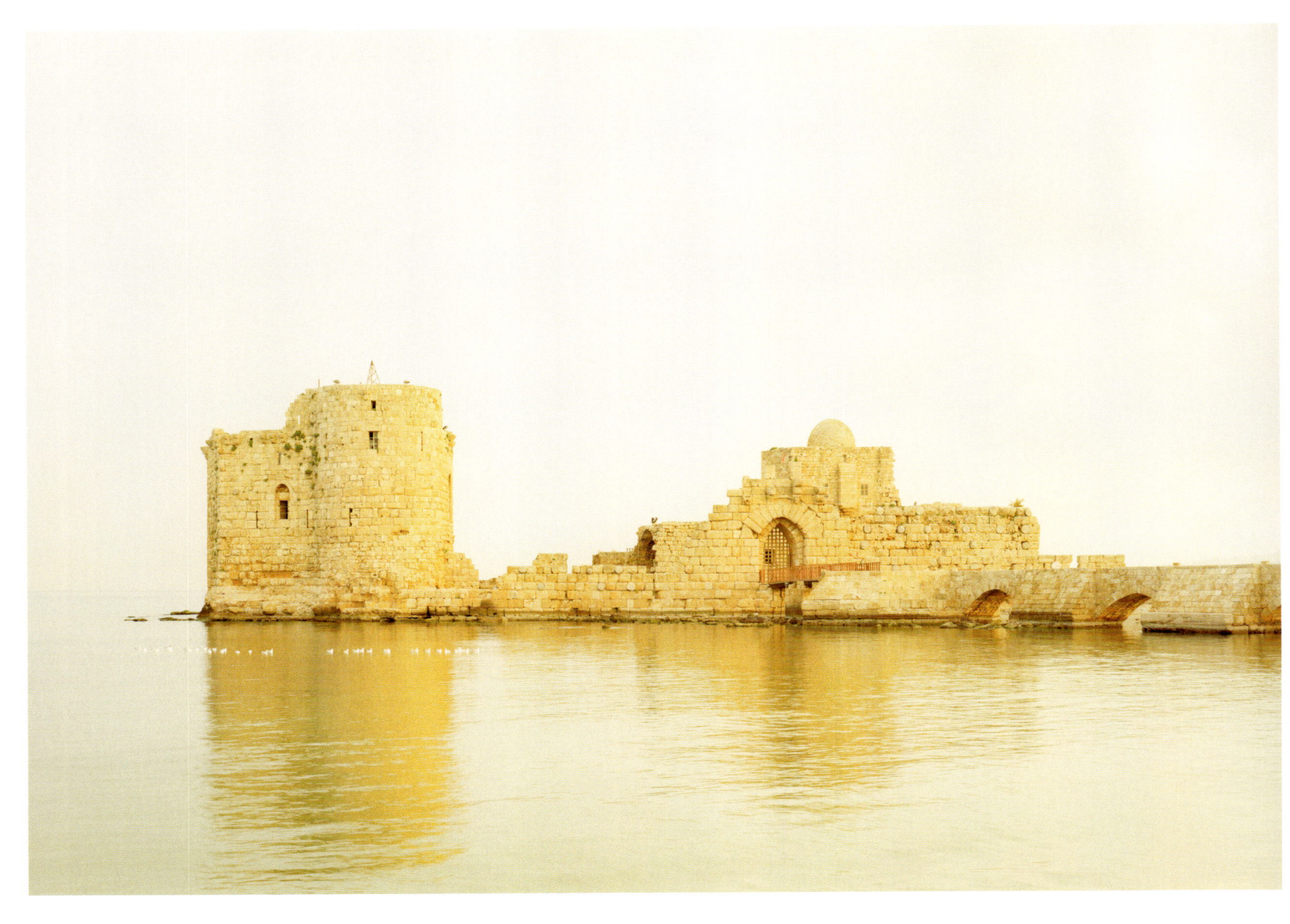

Saida I 2005

The Orient in the Orient.

Elger Esser's and Gustave Flaubert's Perspectives in the Near East

ÖZKAN EZLI

"[...] I try Arab bread, partly baked dough in large galettes. I watch myself as much as I can so as not to commit any improprieties. After the meal, walk to Abū-Mandūr on the left bank of the Nile. – Garden and reeds (the only place on the Nile where I have seen any; otherwise they hardly appear on the banks of the Nile) – large sun on the water.
At Abū-Mandūr the Nile makes a bend to the left (right bank) and on this side there are high banks of sand.
A canja boat in the tartane style passes by; that is the true Orient, melancholic and sedating effect; you sense already something of the immense and pitiless in the middle of which you are lost".[1]

It is not the bread, it is not the Arab dishes, it is also not the holy Islamic site Abū-Mandūr and also not the Nile. It is not these images and impressions that constitute the "true Orient" for Gustave Flaubert as he goes for a walk in December of the year 1849 in Rosetta, near Cairo, on the Nile Delta – although such knowledge surrounding exotic details is quite well described, photographed, documented in the first half of the 19th century and very clearly determines the Oriental image, marks the Orient.[2] For Gustave Flaubert, however, the "true Orient" is a boat gliding on the water. The boat in movement is Orient because it expresses a certain mood, an existential being-exposed and promises an attractive disorientation. Already four days earlier, when Flaubert for the first time sets foot on "Egyptian soil" in the port of Alexandria, he feels ceremonial and full of unease.[3] The Orient: for Flaubert a threshold-experience, which challenges his realistic, dissecting description. For Flaubert naturally knows how to define his surroundings precisely, and he could undoubtedly travel like a learned tourist who *knows* what he is seeing, who *shows* what he sees. Yet while Flaubert is discovering the Orient in the Orient, he undergoes the experience of a boundary-removal. An experience that moves him to the contemplation of itinerancy. It translates his knowledge-saturated, precise observation into a reflexive, existential emotional state.

1
Flaubert, Gustave (1996): *Reise in den Orient*, Frankfurt am Main: Insel Verlag, p. 42f. Translated from the French here: https://fr.wikisource.org/wiki/Notes_de_voyages/%C3%89gypte: 100.

2
See on this: Said, Edward (2011): *Orientalismus*, Frankfurt am Main: Fischer Verlag, p. 235.

3
Flaubert (1996): p. 37.

Yet where does this experience come from? Why does he suspend his realistic description? It does not simply come over him because he is in the Orient. His desire was already present in France when Flaubert retains the actual grounds – the photographer Maxime Du Camp and Flaubert are underway on commission from the Ministry for Agriculture and Trade – for his Oriental voyage: He wants to get out of his own ego, to go "anywhere and everywhere".[4] Moreover, the switching of the narrative code in Flaubert also stands in an intertextual context. Approximately 30 years before Flaubert, the Orientalist Edward William Lane also describes the city of Rosetta.[5] Yet, differently than Flaubert's micrological depictions of the course of the Nile, Lane writes about the Nile city's diminished traffic in ships and goods and estimates its number of inhabitants.[6] He chooses an economic and macrological perspective. His account around the burial site Abū-Mandūr also departs decidedly from Flaubert's perspective. Lane lingers by the holy tomb of the Sheykh Abū-Mandūr and, on the basis of its "presumed" effective power, makes deliberations about the fatalism of the Muslims. According to Muslim belief, the grave protects the city from floods and is a site of "talismanic influence".[7] Lane's Orient in the Orient is not an existential, but more a cultural one, which differentiates between Orientals and Britons: the Oriental in Rosetta is, unlike the Briton, superstitious, very religious and at the end submissive to authority.[8] The Orient that Flaubert discovers in the Orient does not separate, however. Flaubert does not separate it from his surroundings, but rather incorporates it into the landscape. Where Lane interrupts his urban description, rich in facts, with religious categories and succumbs to speculations, Flaubert penetrates in the real and imaginary into the Orient: with the associations of the boat gliding in the water and even more with everything that surrounds him in the moment of narration. And in fact, after a several-month stay in Cairo and following a visit to the Pyramids in Giza, Flaubert and his companion Du Camp spend the most important part of their journey on a canja, traveling upriver from Bulaq/Cairo, via Asyut, Luxor, Esna, El Kab, Aswan, over the cataracts of the Nile, to Wadi Halfa.[9] Even if this section of their 16-month sojourn (from October 1849 to February 1851) only stretches from February to May 1850 and they afterwards tour Palestine, Syria and Lebanon, this journey on the Nile still forms the heart of their trip.

In the years 2005 and 2011 – that is, 160 years after Flaubert and Du Camp – the photographer Elger Esser toured the same sites on the Nile and the

4
Flaubert (1996): p. 15.

5
Flaubert was familiar with Lane's travel account *Description of Egypt*, which was among the most impactful and frequently read works in the 19th century on the Orient. See regarding this: Said, Edward (2011): *Orientalismus*, Frankfurt am Main: Fischer Verlag, p. 236.

6
Lane, Edward William (2000): *Description of Egypt*, Cairo/New York: The American University in Cairo Press, p. 49f.

7
Ibid., p. 50.

8
Lane, Edward William (2000): p. 51.

9
See on this Flaubert (1996): pp. 83–179.

same countries; and likewise recorded them photographically. His book *Morgenland* [tr. note: "morning land", i.e., "Orient"] shows photographs from Egypt, Palestine, Israel and Lebanon. And as in Flaubert's travel description, Esser's photographs of the Nile also appear to me to be the key to his Orient in the Orient. His relationship to the Orient is – as in Flaubert – not determined by the cultural touchstone-distinction of self and other, modern and non-modern, but rather by the differentiation between proximity and distance, belonging and not-belonging, morning and evening. But more on that later. For in order to be able to grasp more precisely what *Morgenland* the images of Elger Esser are showing, I want to attend very briefly to the emerging Orientalism of the 19th century, in the context of which Flaubert and Du Camp's Oriental voyage stands. Afterwards I would like to show in what respect Flaubert's descriptions of the Orient, occasionally also Du Camp's photographs, and Elger Esser's images of the Orient resemble each other and in what respect they differ.

It is important to stipulate that the most pronounced difference exists not between the Orient travellers of the 19th century (Flaubert and Du Camp) and the Orient traveller of today, Elger Esser. Rather, it is the descriptions of Flaubert and the photographs of Du Camp that stand in opposition to one another.[10] There where Flaubert describes the Nile, Egyptians, vegetation, boat moorings, temples and propylaea minutely and exhaustively, in close-up so to speak, and hence creates an extremely heterogeneous Oriental assemblage, in Du Camp's photographs the monuments of Egypt dominate. Pyramids, temples, mausoleums, mosques and Coptic churches are the motifs of the 220 photographs that Du Camp brings back to France in 1851. His exposures set the size and colossal quality of the monuments in the foreground or deliver complete views.[11] Frequently in the shots Flaubert can also be seen, who functions as a measure of scale next to the historic buildings. Flaubert additionally describes how cumbersome it was each time to find the appropriate elevation and site for Du Camp's tripod.[12] The well-known English photographic pioneer Francis Frith also takes identical points of view on his trips through Egypt and Palestine between 1856 and 1859. In their motifs, his pictures from Lower Egypt, from Thebes and of the Pyramids resemble the photographs of Du Camp;[13] Frith, too, incorporates people as a scale, and equally like Du Camp, he tries hard to find a suitable place for the camera in the "perfect chaos of the ruins".[14] The search for an all-encompassing, panoptic perspective is revealed impres-

10
Cf. Stoll, André (1996): "Die Entführung des Eremiten in die Wüste". In: Flaubert (1996), pp. 361–417, p. 391.

11
See on this the photographs in the publications: Flaubert (1996): "Bildteil". In: *Reise in den Orient*, by Gustave Flaubert, pp. I–XXXII.

12
Flaubert (1996): p. 55.

13
See on this: Stiegler, Bernd (2015): *Orientbilder. Fotografien 1850–1910*, Frankfurt am Main: Weissbooks, pp. 41–47.

14
From: Ibid., p. 40.

sively in the shot of the Isis Temple from 1862 by Francis Bedford, another British photographer.[15] Du Camp, Firth and Bedford document the size of the monuments, depict their representational power of culture and history. Almost one could think, the light from the East (the cultural guiding principle of the Romans) has triggered the shutter. Yet this light emanates solely from the French and British apparatuses that isolate in specific ways the Orient in the Orient. The Orientals themselves are rarely set in relation to the size, culture and history of their countries. They are arranged (especially in the photographs by Bedford) as a measurement unit and demoted – they come across as children who have accidentally assembled at these sites.[16] Yet also photographs that are devoted to the day-to-day life of the Orientals allot the native population neither a natural nor realistic place. They arise, as the photo book *Orientbilder. Fotografien 1850–1910* published by Bernd Stiegler documents, “in the studio of the big city”, in Cairo and Alexandria. For these photographs, either the studios were outfitted with props or a corresponding ambience was arranged in the open air. In the photo ateliers and rear courtyards, “a veritable Theatre of the Orient was brought on stage, in which the performers could take up various roles one after the other”; from dervish, to fez-wearer, to turban-bearer, from the veiled to the bared woman.[17] In doing so it was not about the representation of individuals, but of types who belonged to a general category and were timeless.[18] A special mark of the Orientalism of the 19th century is, according to Edward Said, that one not only perceived the native population less, but rather saw through them, practically ignored them.[19] It was thus rather an exotic playing around than an odd business when British and French had themselves photographed in Oriental clothing, as the photographs of the aforementioned photographers show. That an “Oriental” had himself photographed in Western clothing was photographically inconceivable. Concepts of a latent Orientalism, such as the “sensuality” of the Orientals, “their tendency towards despotism, their abnormality and their backwardness” became fixed over the course of the 19th century and created a conceptual system that, according to Said’s interpretation, legitimated the colonialism of the English and French at the end of the 19th and beginning of the 20th century. At the centre of this French and British Orientalism, suggests Said, stood the assumption that the Oriental will not be able to develop on his own power, that the West must undertake this modernisation process in order to occidentalise the Orient step by step. It is not the Oriental who relates to the old high cultures of the East, but

15
El Hage, Badr / Gordon, Sophie (2014): *Cities, Citadels, and Sights of the Near East*, Cairo/ New York: The American University in Cairo Press, p. 32

16
See on this: El Hage / Gordon (2014): pp. 53–55.

17
Stiegler (2015): p. 60. See the photographs in: Ibid., pp. 133–137; p. 149, 175 and 176.

18
See: Stiegler (2015): p. 61.

19
Said, Edward (2011): *Orientalismus*, Frankfurt am Main: Fischer Verlag, p. 237.

the Orientalists of the West. Such macrohistoric divides are only possible when observers take up a totalising perspective and claim it for themselves as self-evident. This is connected, as Flaubert's travel description shows, to high physical effort, a long search for the best site for the tripod, and the costly technical equipment. The photographs from the panorama perspective, however, conceal this effort, this search. For Said, connected to this perspective of the Orientalists is the goal of grasping "the whole panorama of the culture, religion, mentality history and society".[20] How long this perspective and this belief system endured is also shown by literary and Islamic-studies research on written sources from the Arab and Turkish regions. From the beginning to the end of the 20th century, the findings in many of these studies read that neither Arab nor Turkish authors and travellers composed "real" autobiographies and travel accounts. For the autobiography, an introspection is lacking; for the travel account, the ability to understand other cultures in their broad contexts. There were two reasons for this in the opinion of the researchers: Either their corporeality, sensuality and sexuality stood in the way for the Arab and Turkish authors; or it was Islam that hindered the development of the individual.[21] But already Flaubert's Orient in the Orient appears to contradict the Orientalist terms of East and West and of Edward Said. At some point the Egyptian temples get "terribly on his nerves", and he asks himself whether it would be just the same with "the churches in Bretagne, the waterfalls in the Pyrenees? O, necessity! To do what must be done; to be always according to the circumstances (and notwithstanding the repugnance of the moment turning you away from them) like a young man, like a traveller, like an artist, like a son, like a citizen, etc. has to be".[22] Flaubert's travel account is not determined by a being in history, but by a being in the given time. The narrative process which takes place in Flaubert's travel account resembles the perspective in the photographs by Elger Esser: both translate history into time and duration. Bearers of this process are, in both, varying observational positions that disclose them as persons involved in the landscape.

Flaubert describes the Orient from different perspectives, repeatedly takes up other positions, yet one narrative mode turns up again and again: It is a snapshot-like pictorial sequence, like that he chooses at the beginning of his journey when he glides on the canja past the Pyramids of Saqqara. "Sailor's dance. – Joseph at his ovens. – Boat canted over. – The Nile in the middle of the landscape. – We are in the centre. – The clumps of palms at the base of the Pyramids of Saqqara seem like nettles at the foot of tombs".[23]

20
Ibid., p. 274. Yet Said's oft-cited thesis has only a certain range – especially when one looks at Arab, Turkish travel accounts and scientific reflections from the 19th and 20th century in comparison to Western texts, which Said has omitted in his important study. For there are successful and failing constitutions of subject and culture in this period with different stamps in the Western as well as Near Eastern cultural space. See on this: Ezli, Özkan (2012): *Grenzen der Kultur. Autobiographien und Reisebeschreibungen zwischen Okzident und Orient*, Constance: Konstanz University Press.

21
See on this: Ezli, Özkan (2012): pp. 19–40.

22
Flaubert (1996): p. 126. https://fr.wikisource.org/wiki/Notes_de_voyages/%C3%89gypte: 185.

23
Ibid., p. 17. https://fr.wikisource.org/wiki/Notes_de_voyages/%C3%89gypte: 74.

As in our opening citation, Flaubert ties together different aspects, such as sensuality, eating, objects, historical monuments and fauna, into a landscape out of whose constellation no hierarchy arises. The only necessity is the gliding boat. His account comes off similarly "democratically" when they are in the canja shortly before Thebes.[24] "We will soon pass before Thebes. To the right, in front of us, behind the mountain is found the Valley of the Kings; to the left, in front of me, there is a small boat where there are some men fishing. The boat is touching a large shore of sand, at the end of which is a green line of palms. The wind just picked up, we are going faster".[25] Were we to imagine to ourselves a tourist from yesterday or today during this boat trip shortly before Thebes, the person's gaze would be directed only at the Valley of the Kings. Flaubert, however, ties together in one sentence the tombs of the kings with a fishing Egyptian. Who or what has priority here? Is there something that comes across as unbounded, monumental or timeless? Who is smaller and who therefore greater and who stands for what? Flaubert's break with colonialist representational politics is the result of his Orient in the Orient. On this temple visit in Koshtamna, he writes: "The colossi of the interior wear on the stomach, in place of the belt clasp, lions' heads. One is dazzled and stunned by the multitude of bats; they whirl and squeal; our Arab children shake their torches, one of them standing up on a table and raising the torch into the air. When the bats leave through the entry door, one sees the blue air through their thin grey wings. At the door a donkey was standing, cut out in the light; beyond, the sky and the Nile are completely blue; between the sky and the Nile, a yellow line, it's the sand".[26] Flaubert shows us not simply the Orient or what it stands for; instead, he lets us see it. His images are painterly, set our eyes in movement and allow a landscape to arise before them, because monument, bat, child, donkey, river and sand follow one another and produce a context. This realistic and simultaneously pictorialist sequence creates duration for the reader. A duration that evolves out of the perspective at eye level and thus enables a form of democratic seeing. As in Flaubert, the gliding boat is also a kind of "focus" in the photographs of Esser. The subject – the viewer likewise occupies this position – is part of the photographed surroundings. Whether it be the shots in the south or in the north of Lebanon, in En Naqora or the consecutive images of the saltworks in Enfeh – many of his shots Esser has presumably taken from a boat. His photographs show the water of the Nile in the lower third, then the boats follow to which are connected

24
On the connection between democracy and narrative, see: Koschorke, Albrecht (2011): *Wahrheit und Erfindung. Grundzüge einer Erzähltheorie*, Frankfurt am Main: Fischer Verlag, p. 38.

25
Flaubert (1996): p. 95. https://fr.wikisource.org/wiki/Notes_de_voyages/%C3%89gypte:153.

26
Flaubert (1996): p. 136. https://fr.wikisource.org/wiki/Notes_de_voyages/%C3%89gypte:196.

coasts and landscapes in the upper third of the image; boat moorings and river bends as in Flaubert. They are pictures that, at first glance, create distance to the opposing shores, and yet the photographer, the observer, is part of the photographed landscape; the gaze, the perspective, is part of the photographed landscape. The observer does not stand on the other side of the river; the observer does not belong *a priori* to another culture. Esser's photographs are not characterised by an identity-politics category of difference. His perspective is, rather, defined by a "hermeneutic distancing", as the literary scholar Andrea Polaschegg has mapped this out for German Orientalism of the 19th century. This does not separate the familiar from the strange, but rather brings both into a dynamic relation.[27] An approximating distance, which is also reflected in Esser's Lebanese diary from 2005, in which we likewise find the connecting logic of Flaubert. Buildings, objects, animals and people are brought into connection; the eye of the observer is set into motion.

In addition, the single-colouredness, the monochrome quality of Esser's photographs contributes to seeing the objects in conjunction and at the same time to leaving them in their places. How the picture arises in the picture is by all means comparable to the narrative method of Flaubert. Yet, despite all the similarity between Flaubert and Esser, a serious difference exists: corporeality and polychromaticity separate the two artists. Interestingly, it is precisely these aspects that prompted Said to identify Flaubert as an Orientalist.[28] Did Elger Esser exclude the body and colour in order to avoid the possible reproach of Orientalism?

Despite all similarities, Flaubert's approaches, like Esser's, are to be seen in historical-political contexts. Flaubert's travel account is a realistic, finely chiselled form of critique on Western civilisation and its colonialist endeavours. For Esser the political range of associations of the Orient and Occident is a different one, one that has been constituted global-politically only after Said's publication. For indeed one year after the appearance of his book *Orientalism*, a cultural revolution of Islamic stamp transpires in 1979 in Iran. Till the end of the 1990s, talk of Islamic fundamentalism spreads.[29] The Orientalist range of associations that Said still described with a systemisation of sensuality, despotism and laziness, begins to fundamentally change. With September 11th, with al-Qaeda and the emergence of the "Islamic State", the Orient factually and imaginatively either is understood in its own destruction; or it represents a strange and major

27
See on this: Polaschegg, Andrea (2005): *Der andere Orientalismus. Regeln deutsch-morgenländischer Imagination im 19. Jahrhundert*, Berlin/New York: Walter de Gruyter, p. 43.

28
Said's reading of Flaubert's travel account misinterprets the political dimension of corporeality in *Voyage in the Orient*. Through corporeality, Flaubert does not hierarchically distinguish the Western tourist from the native population, as Said interprets. Corporeality is not a category that differentiates him from the Oriental. Rather, he is similar to them in this.

29
For many instances: Heitmeyer, Wilhelm (1996): *Verlockender Fundamentalismus. Türkische Jugendliche in Deutschland*, Frankfurt am Main: Suhrkamp Verlag.

danger. In place of the underdeveloped, but hospitable, sensual, lazy Orientals, the dangerous ones have stepped in.[30] Any form of corporeality, the photographing of minarets or mosques, would be caught in Esser's photographs in this network of associations. A true seeing would be impossible. Yet precisely in this context his photographs break out from the – here only very briefly sketched – current discourse, become political in the Flaubertian sense. Sensuality and corporeality do not lie in Esser in the photographs themselves; rather, they trigger a corporeality in the viewer's own self. Esser's participatory photographs formally invite one to move into the scenes, to turn the head to the side in order to look at what may well lie there to the left of the boat. It is this physical mobility that Esser triggers with his images, which go beyond the expansion of perception. One wants to know what is situated behind or next to the massive stone walls of Akko in Israel (plate p. 56–59). One wants to walk into the ruins that Esser has photographed in Lebanon. And precisely in the triggering of these multiple body movements, Esser comes quite close to Flaubert's discovery of the Orient in the Orient, when the latter indeed mentions the mosque in Rosetta, but then passes it by and glances at the canja gliding in the water. Esser's perspective is to be thanked that the Orient is again attractive – a perspective that creates a suitable relationship between the observer and the motifs. And what could today be more political than to once more find an Orient in the Orient.

30 See on this: Ezli, Özkan (2010): "Der ortlose Muslim. Das Prekäre als Niemandsland. Ein kulturwissenschaftlicher Kommentar zu Thilo Sarrazins *Deutschland schafft sich ab*", https://www.exzellenzcluster.uni-konstanz.de/ortlose-muslim-sarrazin.html (1 March 2017).

Bibliography

El Hage, Badr / Gordon, Sophie (2014): *Cities, Citadels, and Sights of the Near East*, Cairo/New York: The American University in Cairo Press.

Ezli, Özkan (2012): *Grenzen der Kultur. Autobiographien und Reisebeschreibungen zwischen Okzident und Orient*, Constance: Konstanz University Press.

Ezli, Özkan (2010): "Der ortlose Muslim. Das Prekäre als Niemandsland. Ein kulturwissenschaftlicher Kommentar zu Thilo Sarrazins *Deutschland schafft sich ab*", https://www.exzellenzcluster.uni-konstanz.de/ortlose-muslim-sarrazin.html (1 March 2017).

Flaubert, Gustave (1996): *Reise in den Orient*, Frankfurt am Main: Insel Verlag.

Heitmeyer, Wilhelm (1996): *Verlockender Fundamentalismus. Türkische Jugendliche in Deutschland*, Frankfurt am Main: Suhrkamp Verlag.

Koschorke, Albrecht (2011): *Wahrheit und Erfindung. Grundzüge einer allgemeinen Erzähltheorie*, Frankfurt am Main: Fischer Verlag.

Lane, Edward William (2000): *Description of Egypt*, New York: The American University in Cairo Press.

Polaschegg, Andrea (2005): *Der andere Orientalismus. Regeln deutsch-morgenländischer Imagination im 19. Jahrhundert*, New York: Walter de Gruyter.

Said, Edward (2011): *Orientalismus*, Frankfurt am Main: Fischer Verlag.

Stiegler, Bernd (2015): *Orientbilder. Fotografien 1850–1910*, Frankfurt am Main: Weissbooks.

Lebanese Daybook

4—13 December 2004

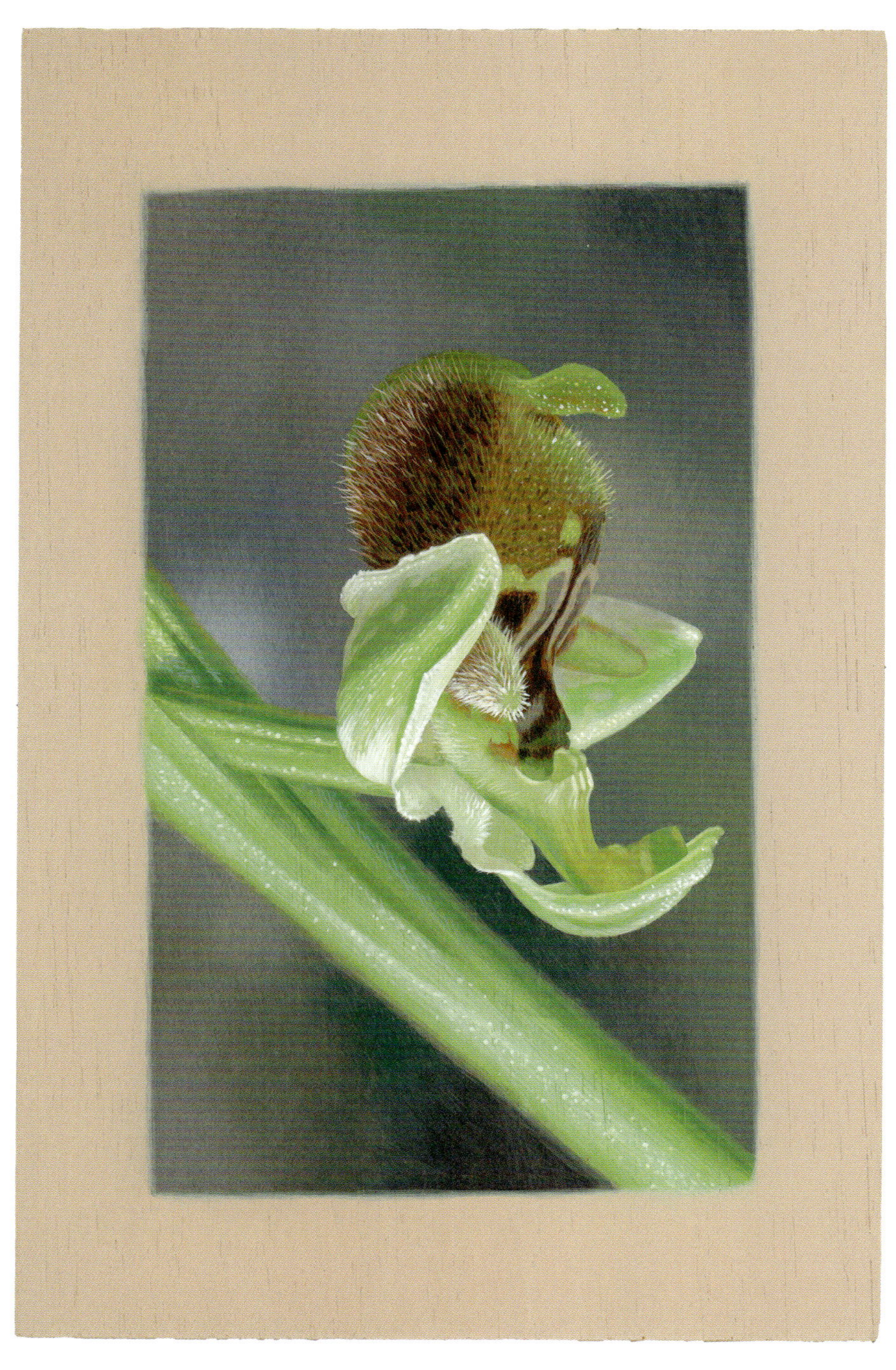

٤ ديسمبر ٢٠٠٤

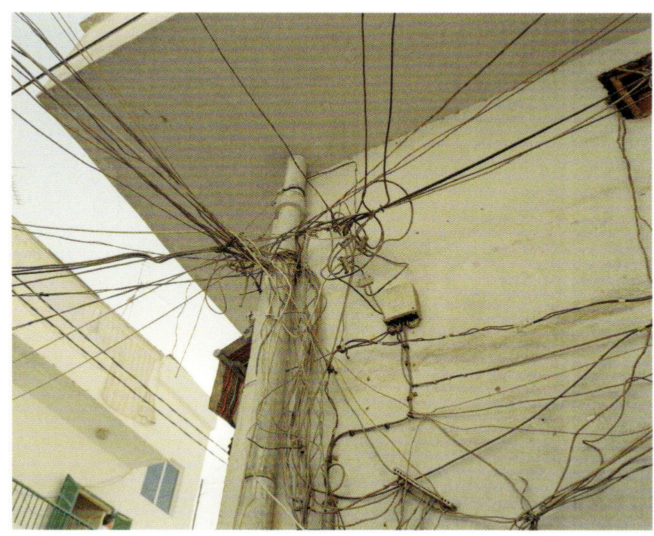

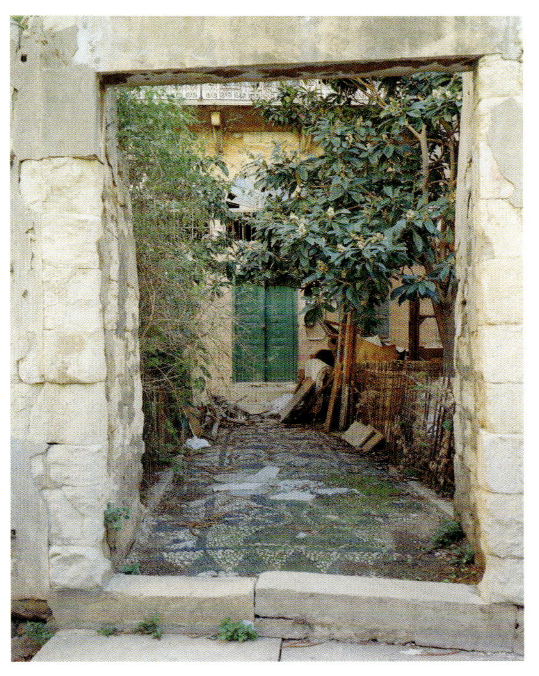

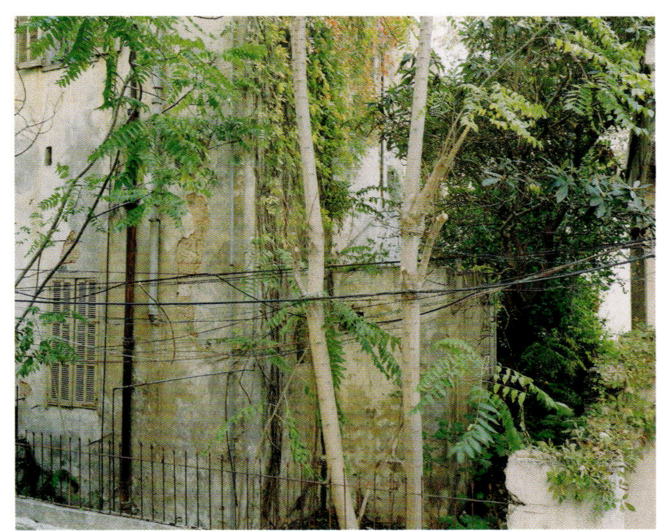

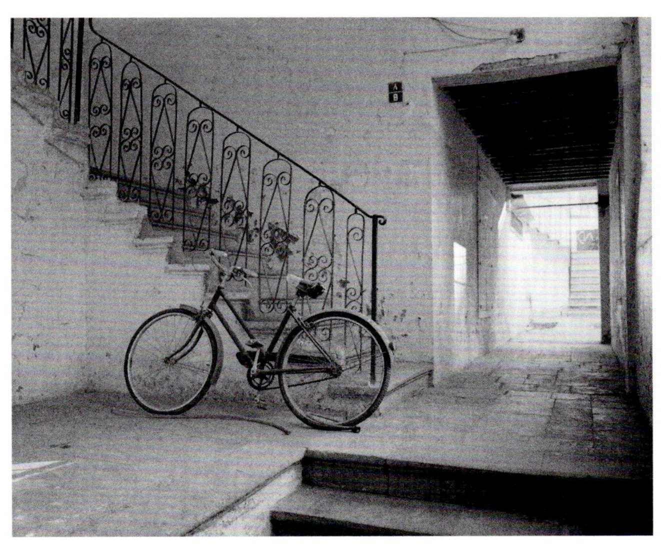

December, 4th

Beirut

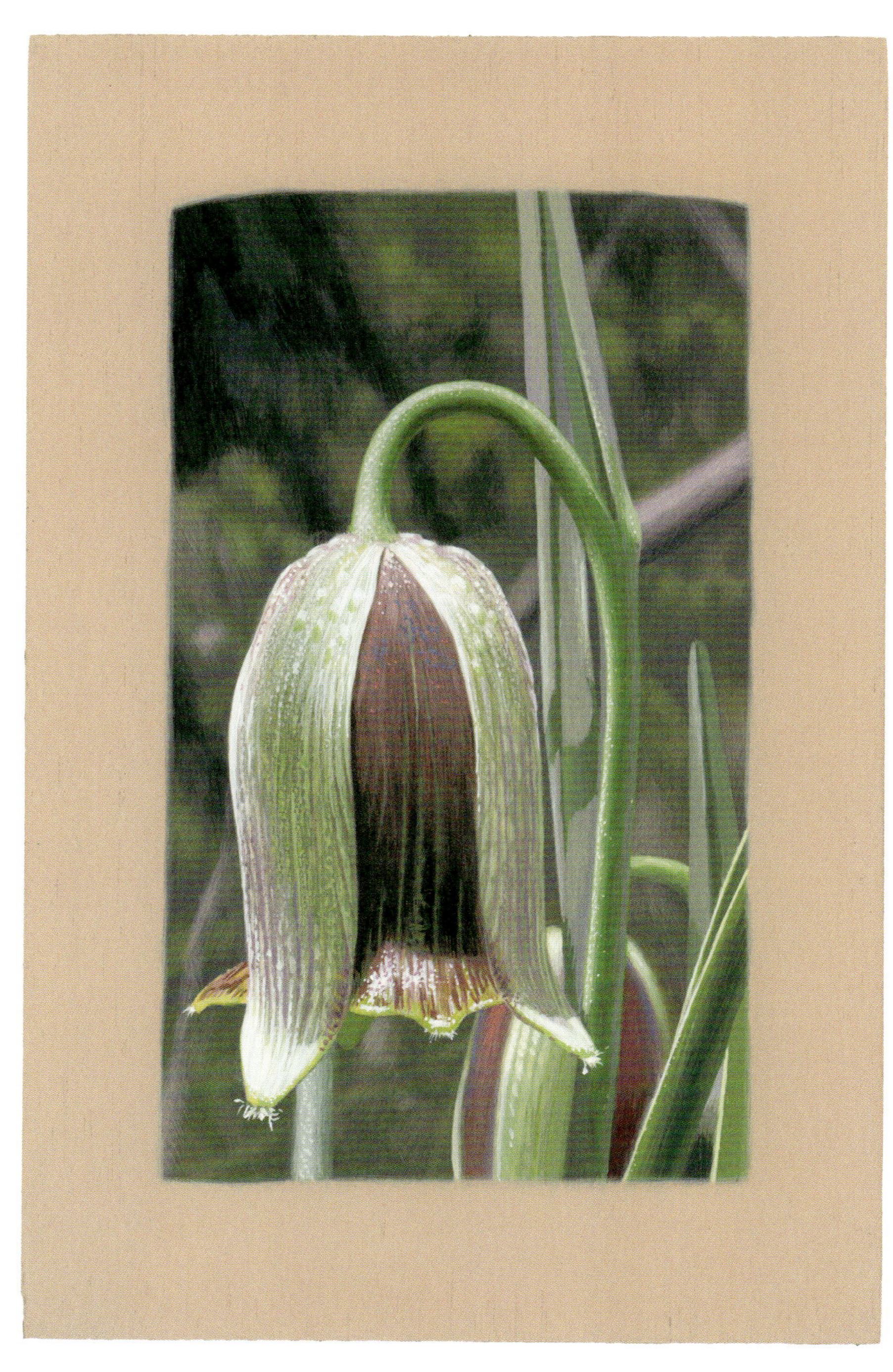

٥ ديسمبر ٢٠٠٤

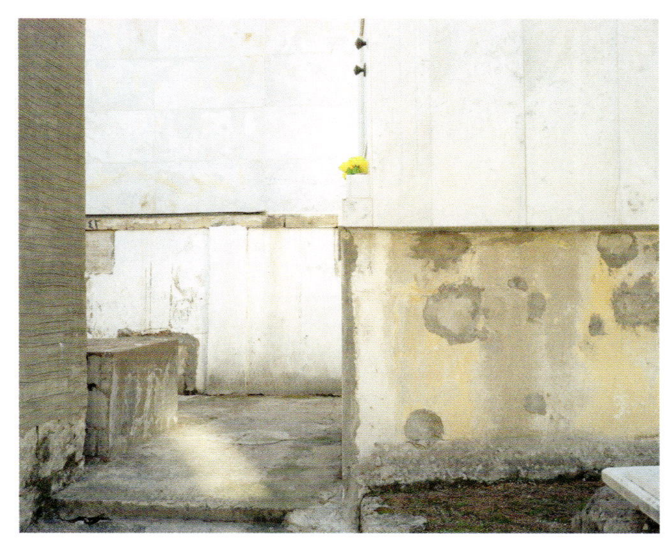

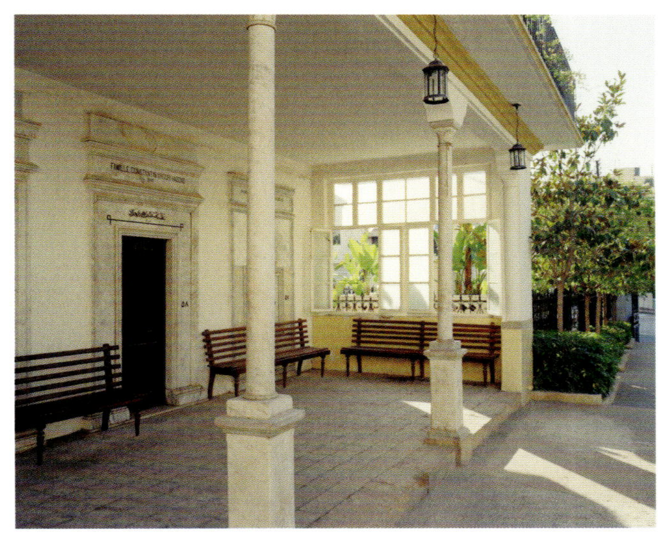

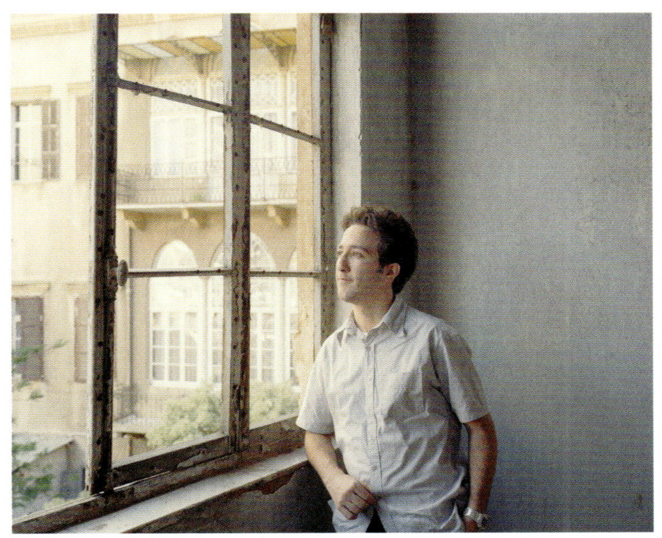

December, 5th

Beirut

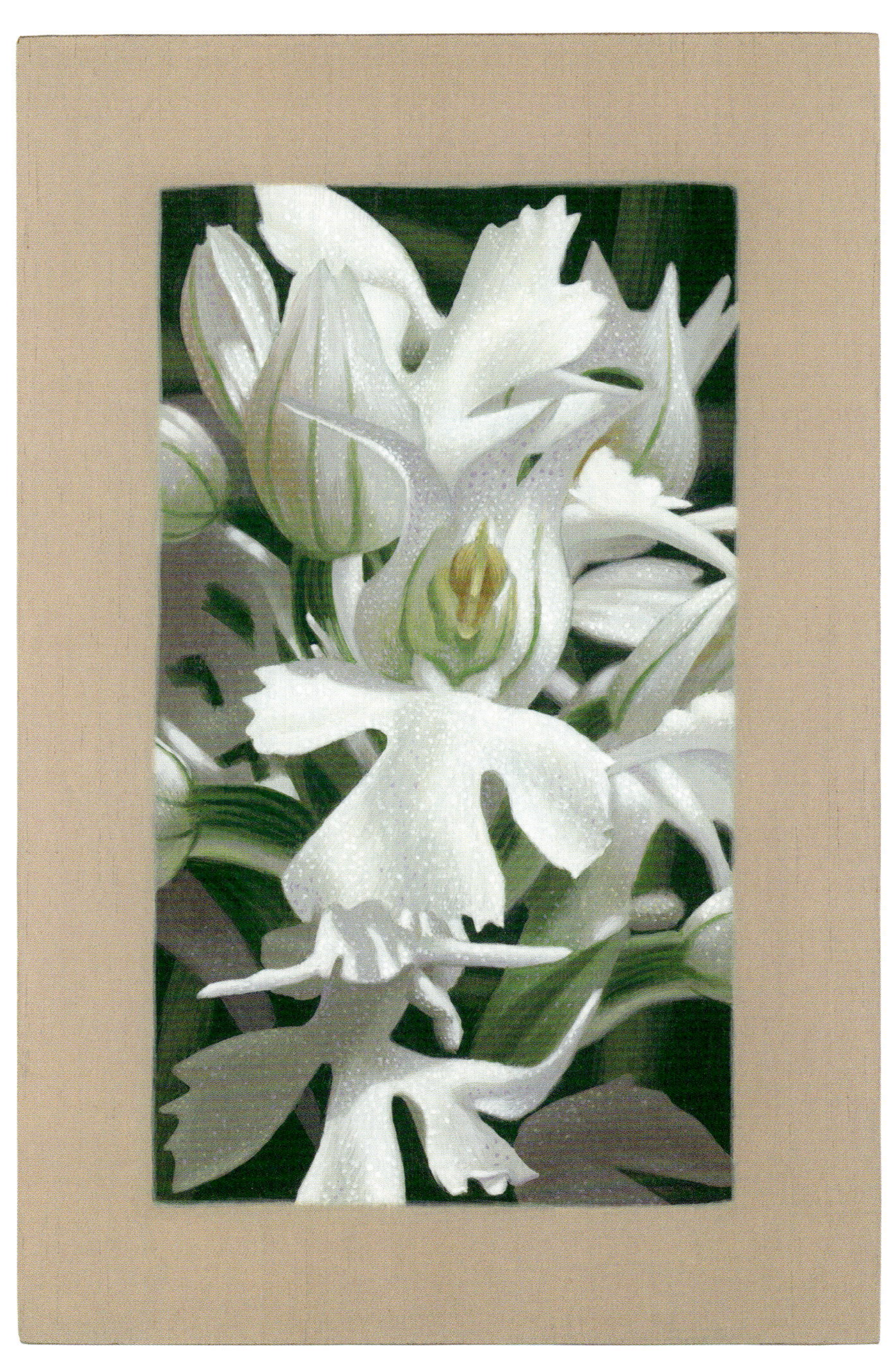

٦ ديسمبر ٢٠٠٤

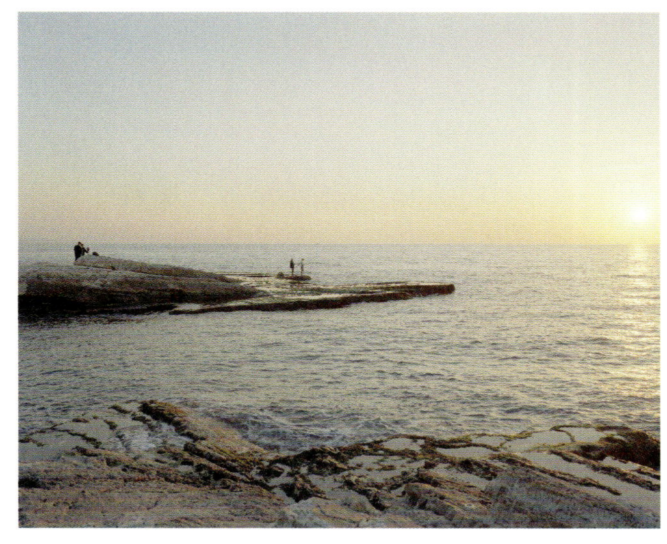

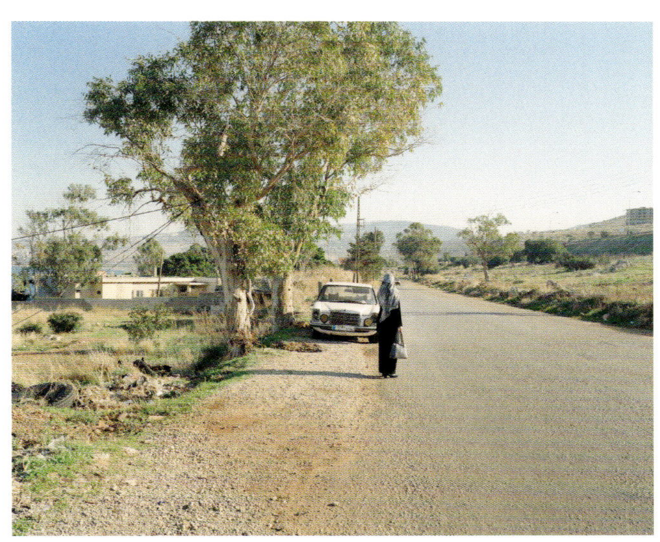

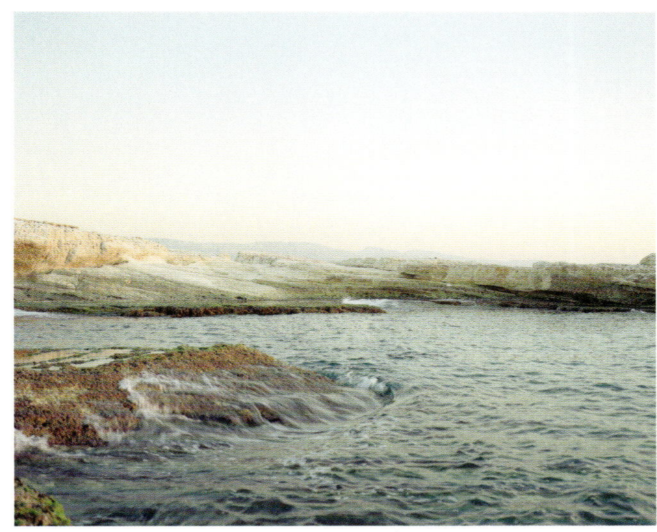

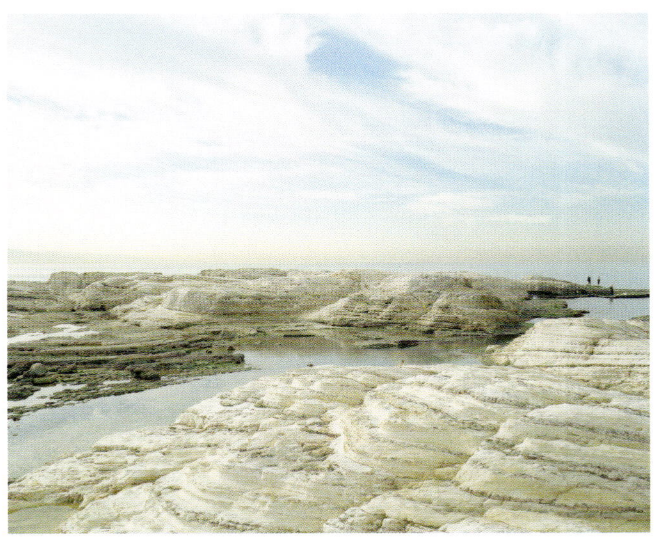

December, 6th

Damour, Raouché

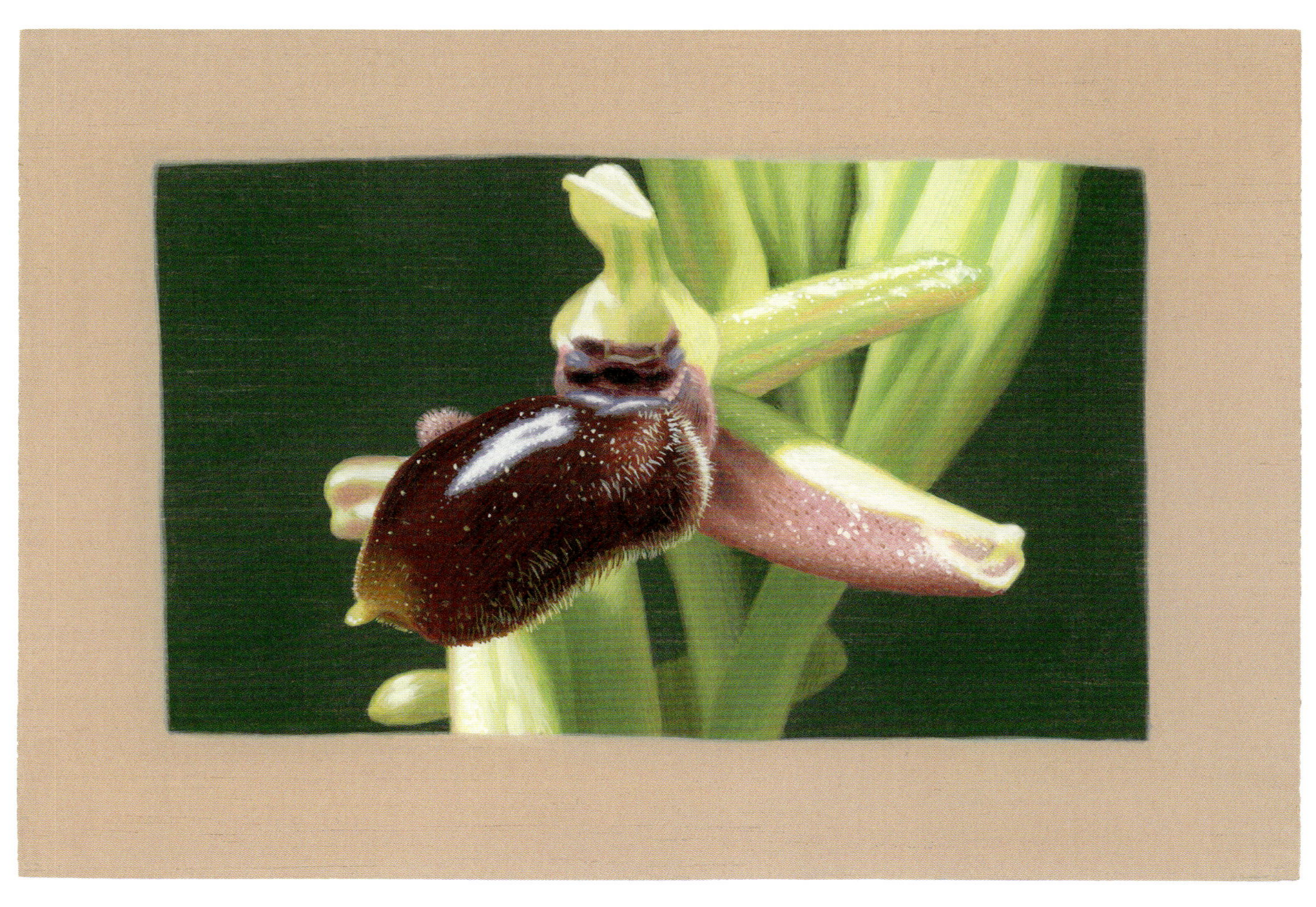

٧ ديسمبر ٢٠٠٤

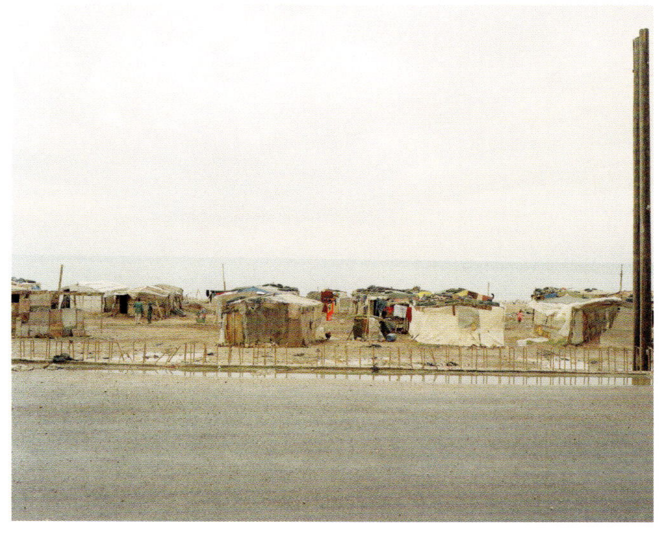

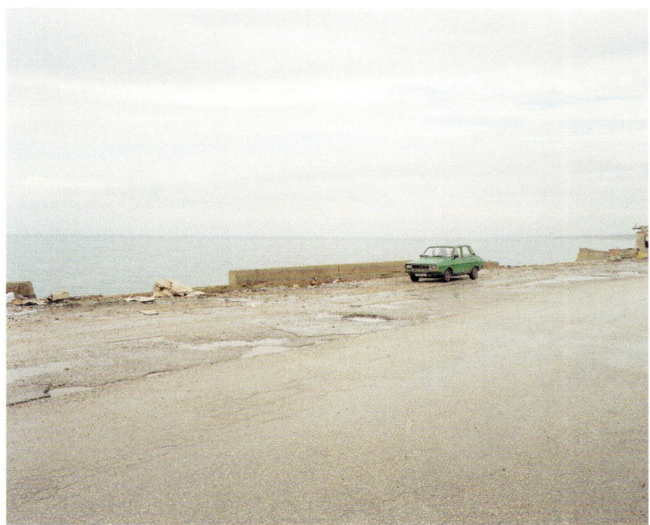

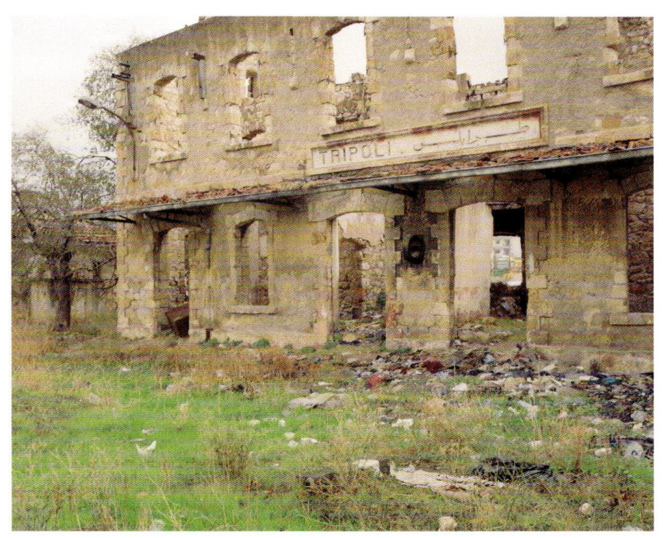

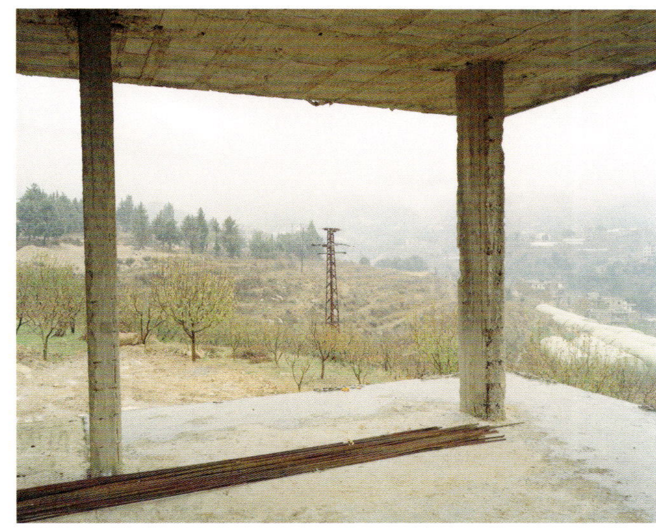

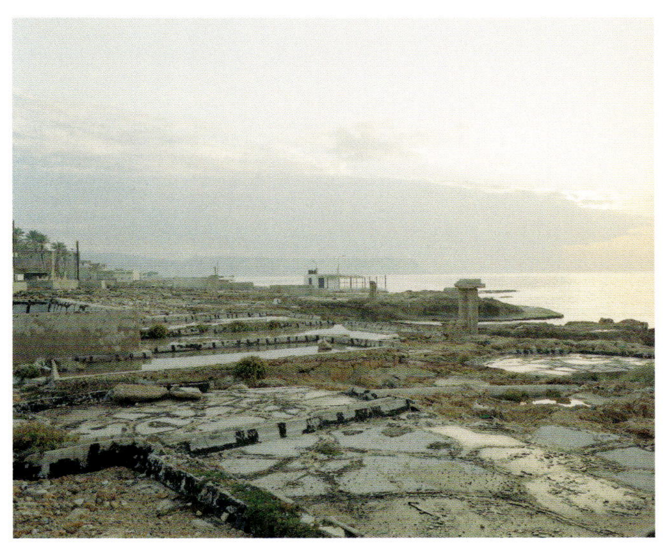

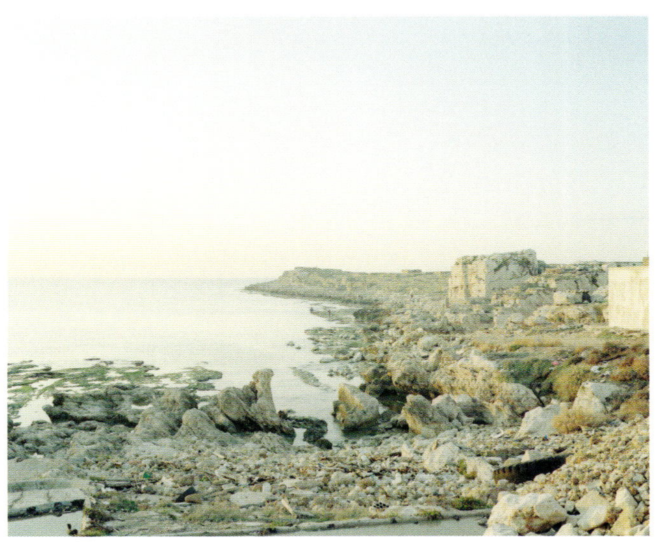

December, 7th

Byblos, Enfeh, Tripoli

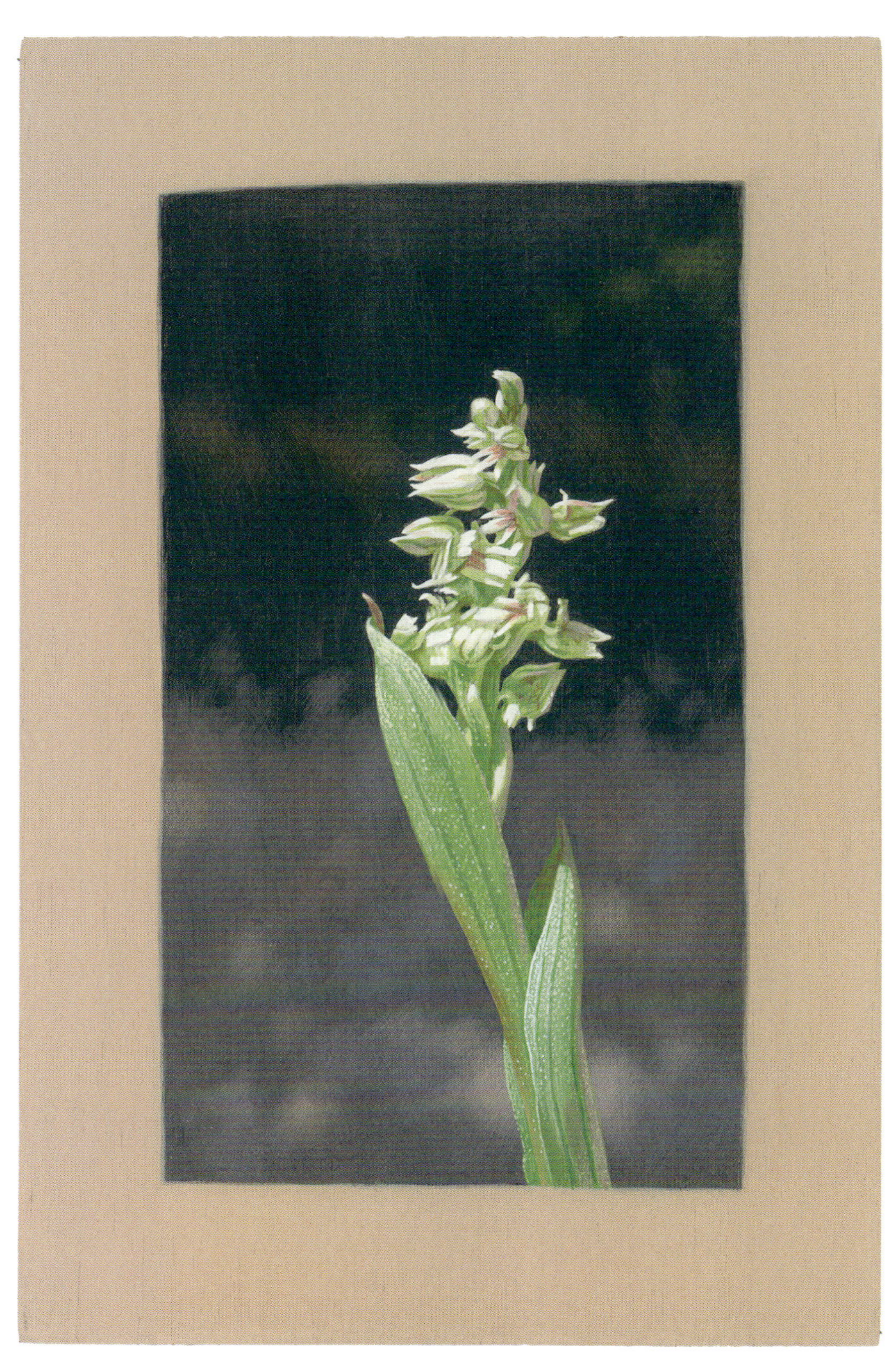

٨ ديسمبر ٢٠٠٤

SCHIRMER/MOSEL · SCHIRMER/MOSEL · SCHIRMER/MOSEL · SCHIRMER/MOSEL

PHOTOGRAPHIE UND KUNST AUS DÜSSELDORF

DIE LIEFERBAREN BÜCHER BEI SCHIRMER/MOSEL

BERND & HILLA BECHER

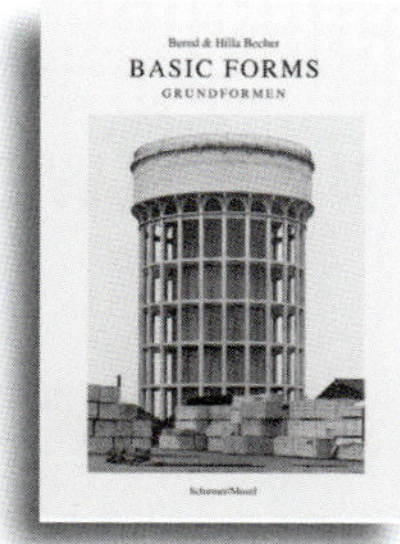

Bernd & Hilla Becher
Basic Forms / Grundformen
Dt./Engl.
ISBN 978-3-8296-0694-3
€ 29,80

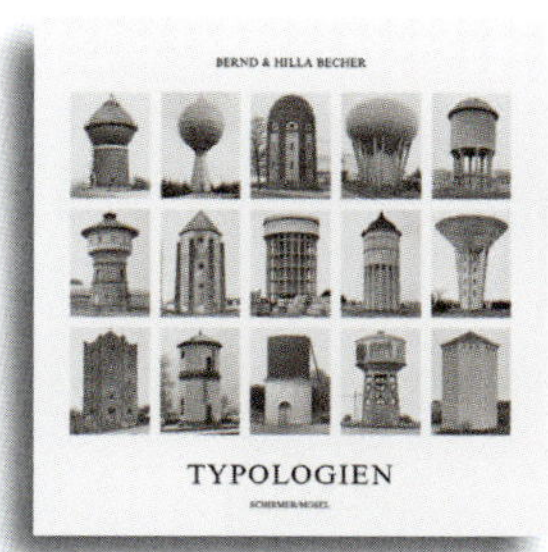

Bernd & Hilla Becher
Typologien
ISBN 978-3-8296-0092-7
€ 78,–

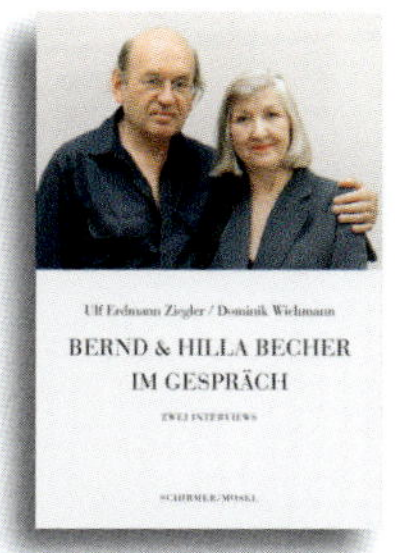

Bernd & Hilla Becher
Im Gespräch
ISBN 978-3-8296-0752-0
€ 24,–

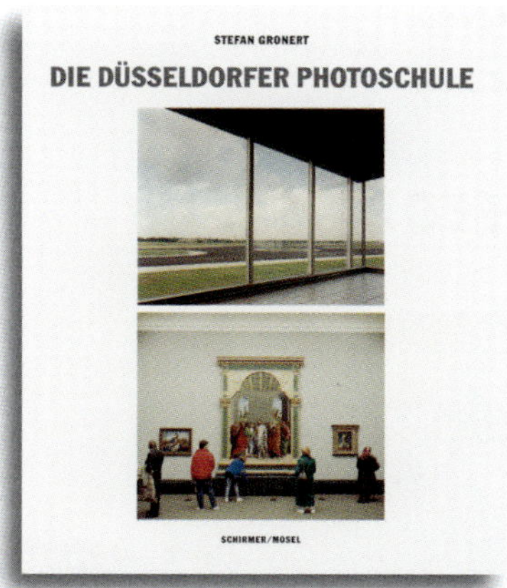

Stefan Gronert
Die Düsseldorfer Photoschule
ISBN 978-3-8296-0803-9
€ 68,–

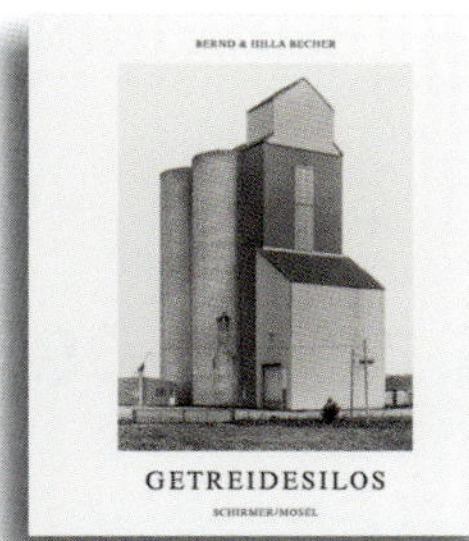

Bernd & Hilla Becher
Getreidesilos
ISBN 978-3-8296-0256-3
€ 68,–

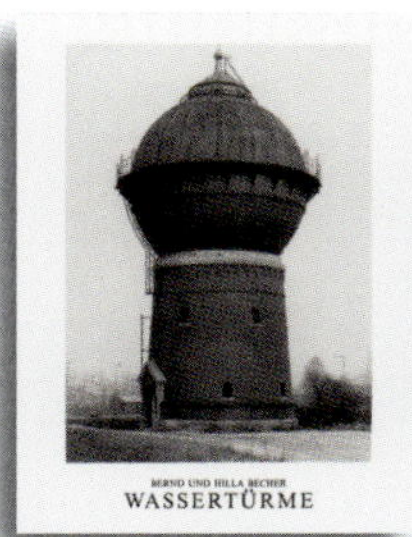

Bernd & Hilla Becher
Wassertürme
ISBN 978-3-88814-255-0
€ 78,–

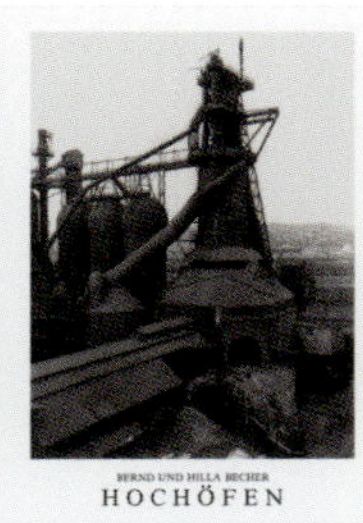

Bernd & Hilla Becher
Hochöfen
ISBN 978-3-88814-352-6
€ 78,–

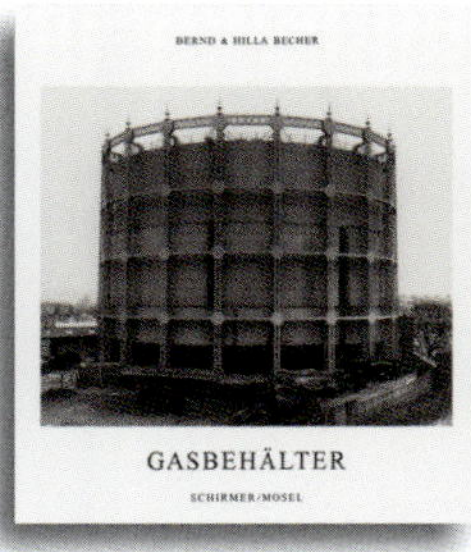

Bernd & Hilla Becher
Gasbehälter
ISBN 978-3-88814-493-6
€ 68,–

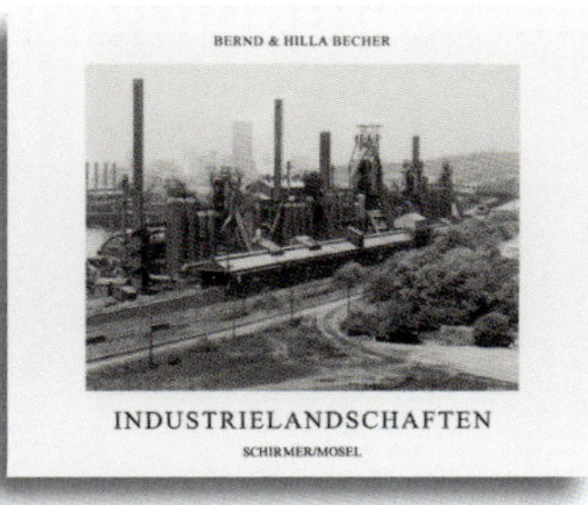

Bernd & Hilla Becher
Industrielandschaften
ISBN 978-3-8296-0003-3
€ 68,–

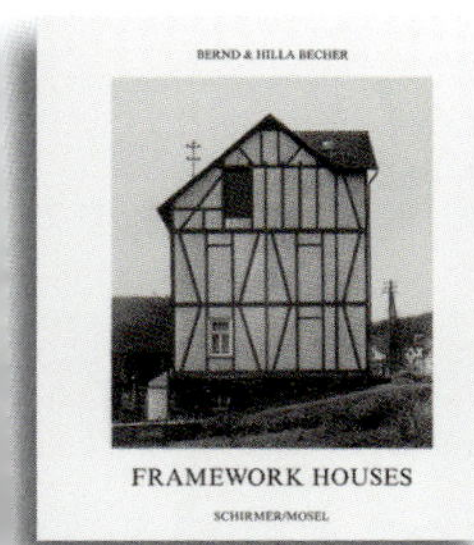

Bernd & Hilla Becher
Framework Houses
Engl. ISBN 978-3-88814-013-6
€ 68,–

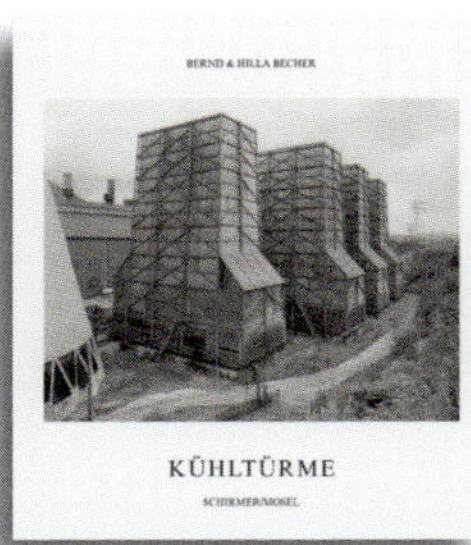

Bernd & Hilla Becher
Kühltürme
ISBN 978-3-8296-0192-4
€ 68,–

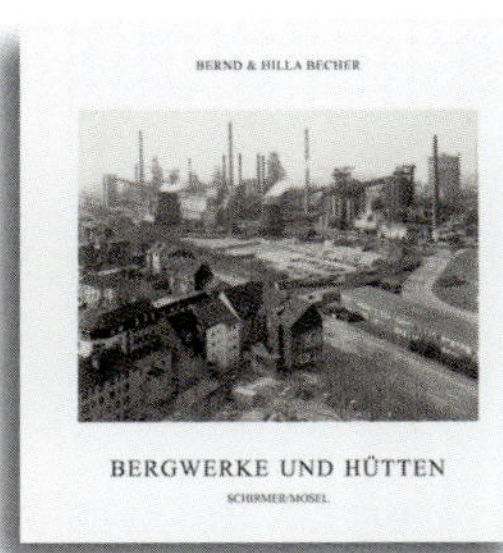

Bernd & Hilla Becher
Bergwerke und Hütten
Dt./Engl. ISBN 978-3-8296-0474-1
€ 58,–

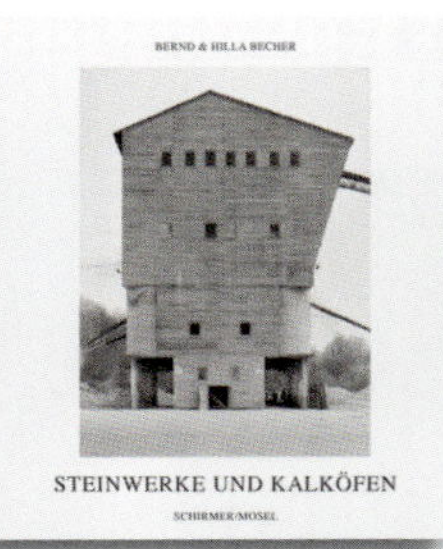

Bernd & Hilla Becher
Steinwerke und Kalköfen
ISBN 978-3-8296-0576-2
€ 68,–

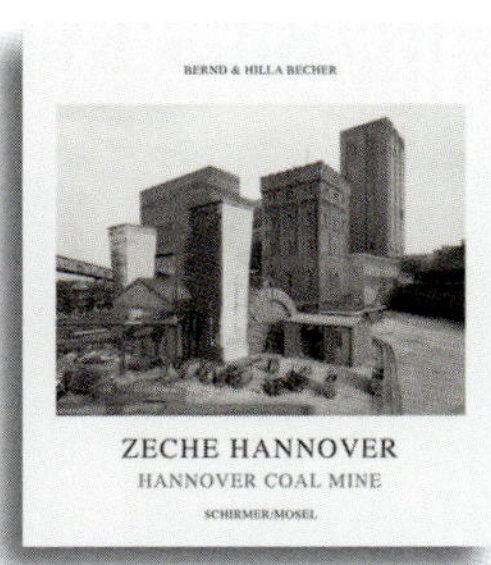

Bernd & Hilla Becher
Zeche Hannover
Dt./Engl.
ISBN 978-3-8296-0468-0
€ 68,–

www.schirmer-mosel.com · www.schirmer-mosel.com · www.schirmer-mosel.com

LAURENZ BERGES

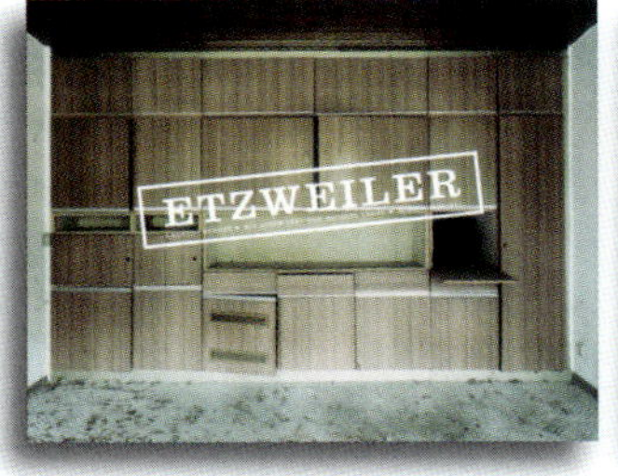

Laurenz Berges
Etzweiler
Dt./Engl. ISBN 978-3-8296-0176-4
€ 39,80

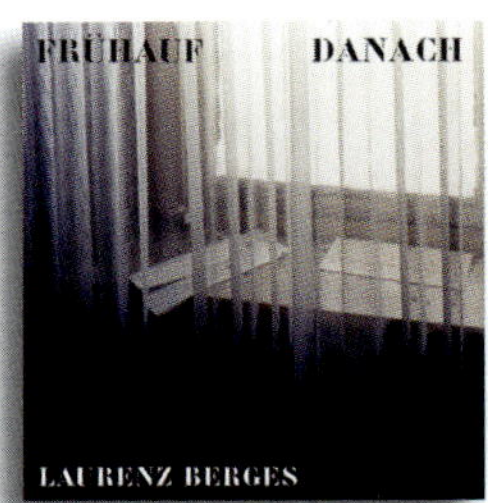

Laurenz Berges
Fotografien 1991–1995
ISBN 978-3-88814-931-3
€ 58,–

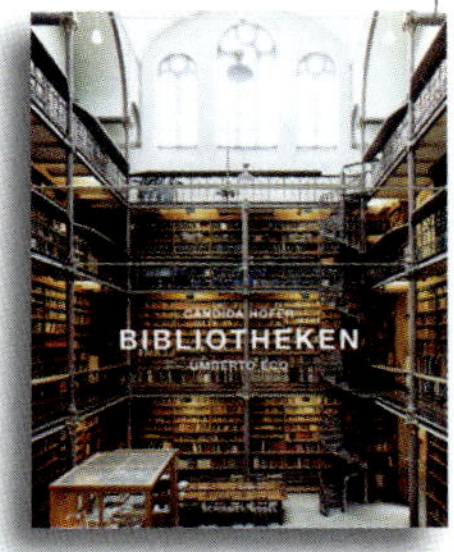

Laurenz Berges
Frühauf Danach
Dt./Engl.
ISBN 978-3-8296-0538-0
€ 49,80

CANDIDA HÖFER

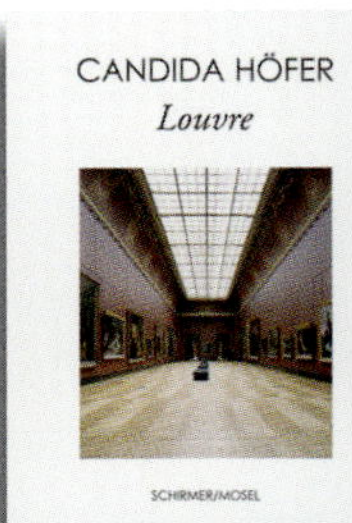

Candida Höfer / Umberto Eco
Bibliotheken
ISBN 978-3-8296-0178-8
€ 49,80
Engl. 0186-3 **€ 78,–**

Candida Höfer
Louvre
Dt./Engl./Frz.
ISBN 978-3-8296-0250
€ 39,80

ELGER ESSER

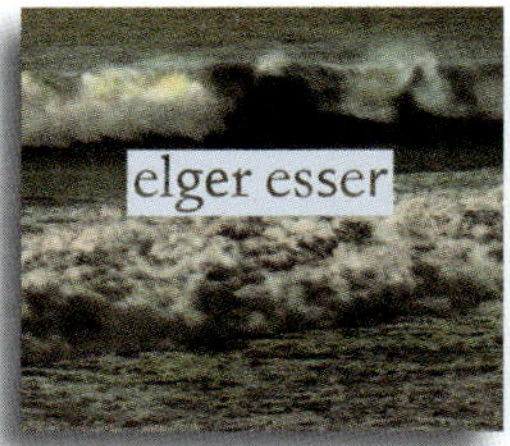

Elger Esser
Ansichten Views Vues
Dt./Engl./Frz.
ISBN 978-3-8296-0357-7
€ 49,80

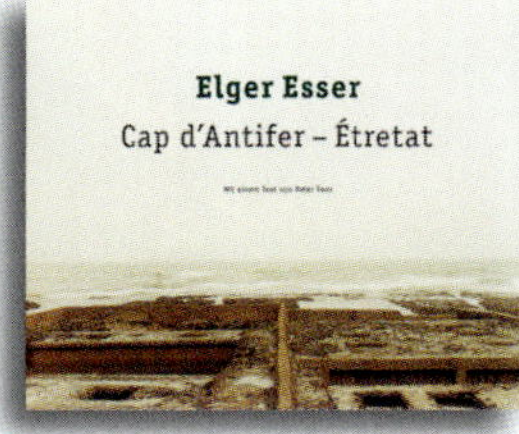

Elger Esser
Cap d'Antifer – Étretat
Dt./Engl./Frz.
ISBN 978-3-8296-0047-7
€ 39,80

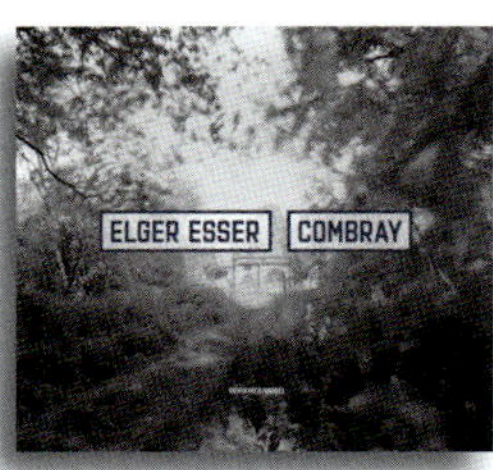

Elger Esser
Combray
Dt./Engl./Frz.
ISBN 978-3-8296-0751-3
€ 68,–

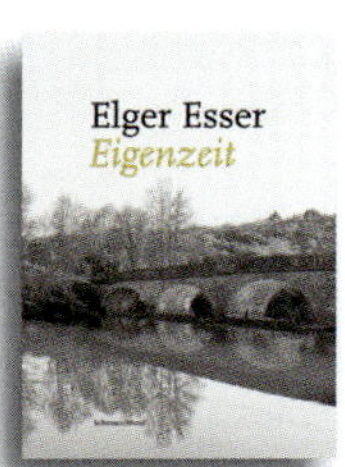

Elger Esser
Eigenzeit
Dt./Engl.
ISBN 978-3-8296-0418-5
€ 49,80

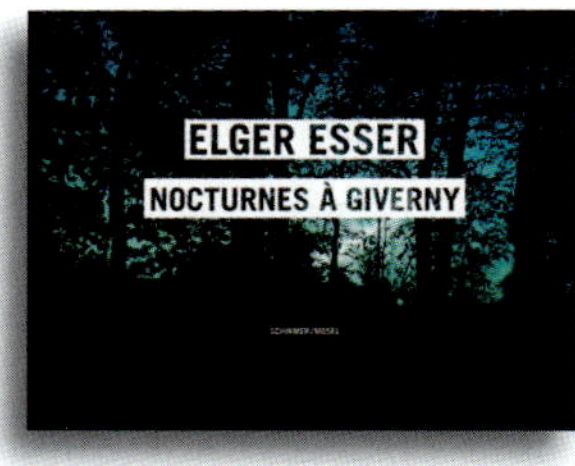

Elger Esser
Nocturnes à Giverny
Dt./Engl./Frz.
ISBN 978-3-8296-0578-6
€ 39,80

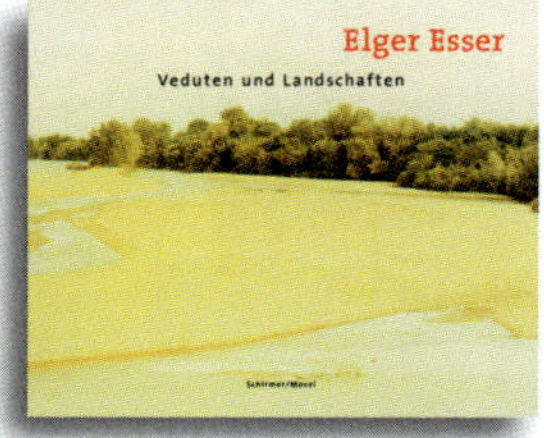

Elger Esser
Veduten und Landschaften
ISBN 978-3-88814-936-8,
Engl. 177-5
€ 68,–

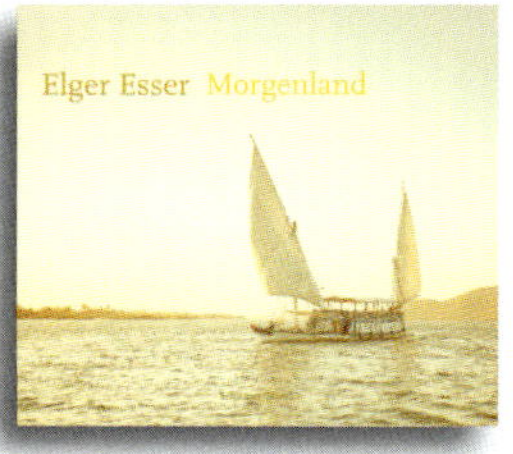

Elger Esser
Morgenland
Dt./Engl.
ISBN 978-3-8296-0797-1
€ 49,80

SIMONE NIEWEG

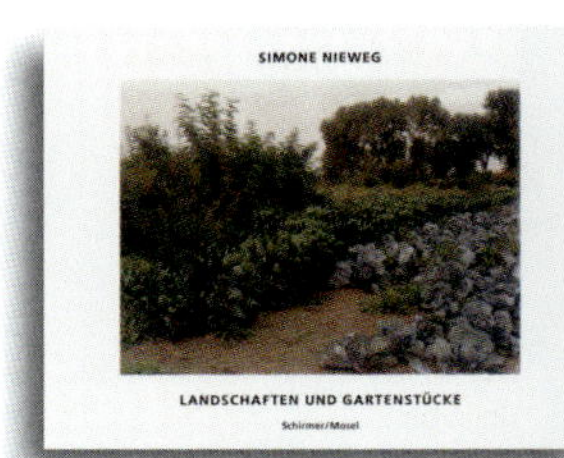

Simone Nieweg
Landschaften und Gartenstücke
Dt./Engl. ISBN 978-3-8296-0040-8
€ 49,80

MARTIN ROSSWOG

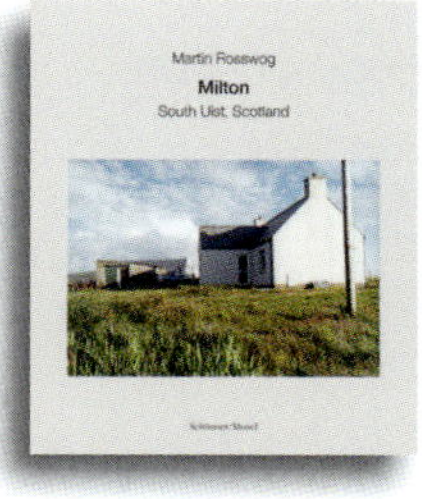

Martin Rosswog
Milton. South Uist, Scotland
Dt./Engl. ISBN 978-3-8296-0711-7
€ 34,–

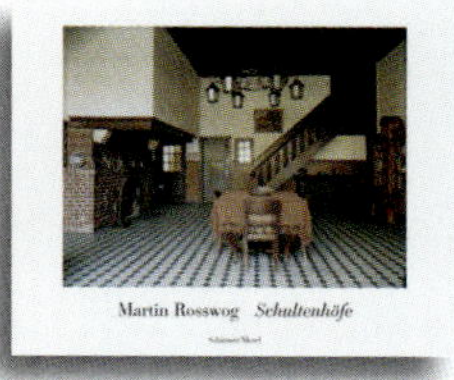

Martin Rosswog
Schultenhöfe
Dt./Engl. ISBN 978-3-8296-0206-8
€ 29,80

THOMAS STRUTH

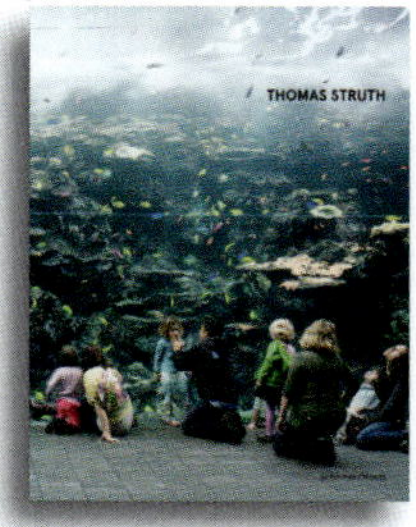

Thomas Struth
Retrospektive
Dt./Engl.
ISBN 978-3-8296-0798-8
€ 49,80

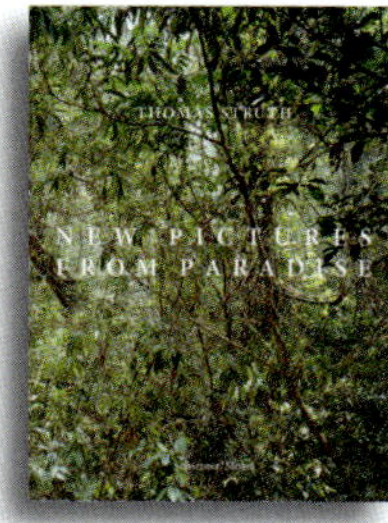

Thomas Struth
New Pictures from Paradise
Dt./Engl.
ISBN 978-3-8296-0759-9
€ 39,80

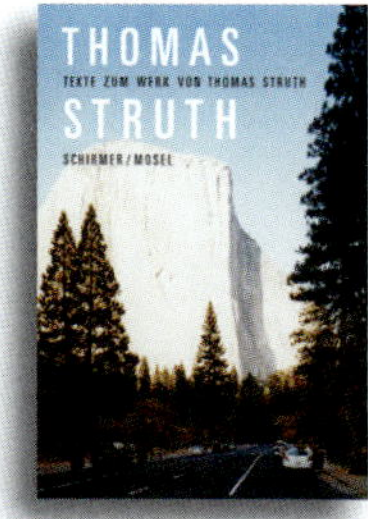

Texte zum Werk von
Thomas Struth
ISBN 978-3-8296-0386-7
€ 39,80

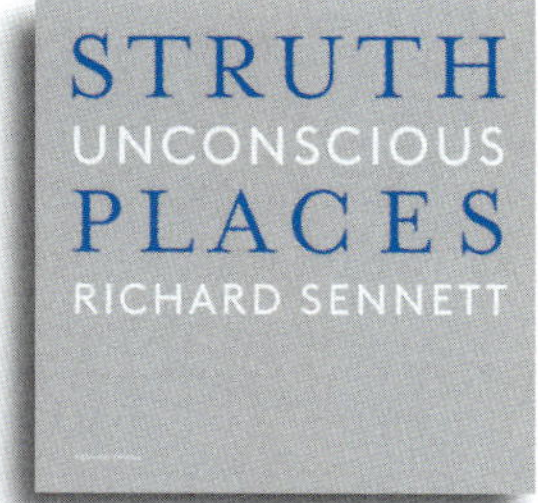

Thomas Struth
Unconscious Places
Dt./Engl. ISBN 978-3-8296-0618-9
€ 88,–

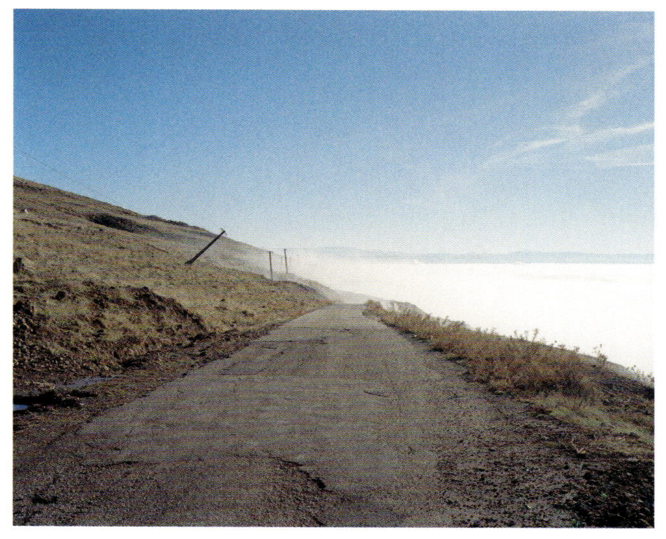

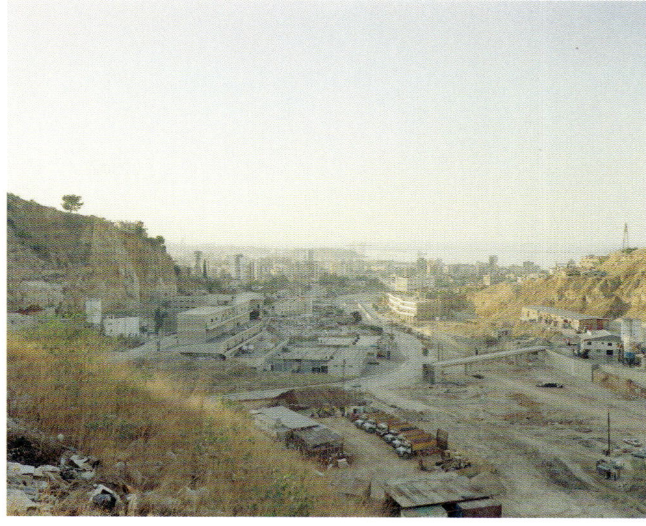

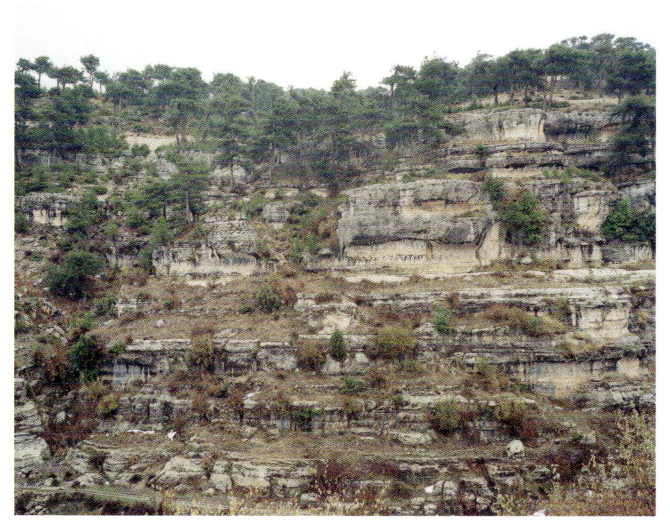

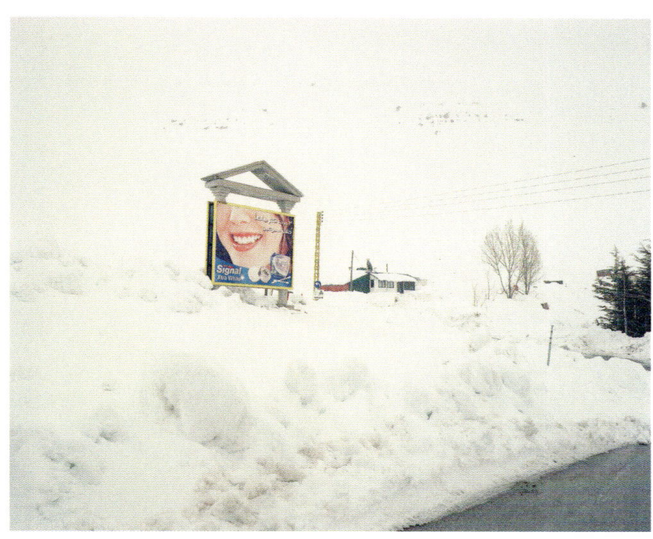

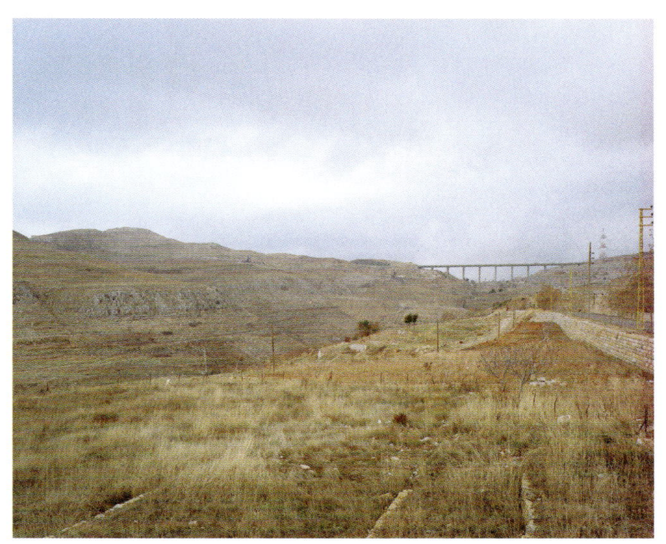

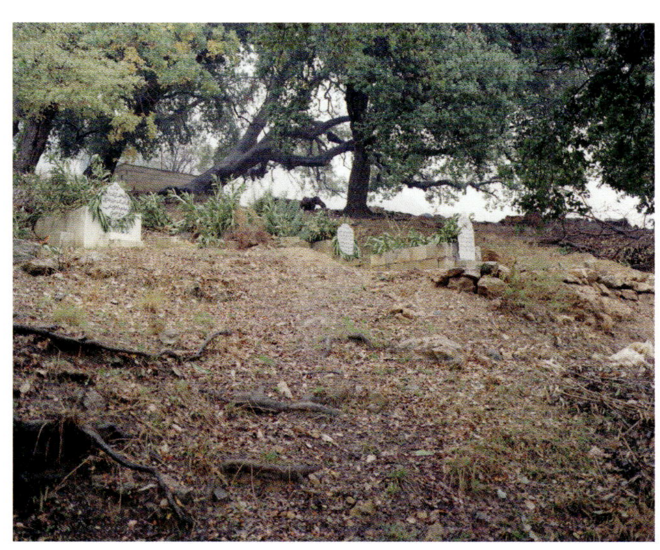

December, 8th

Hammana, Baskinta

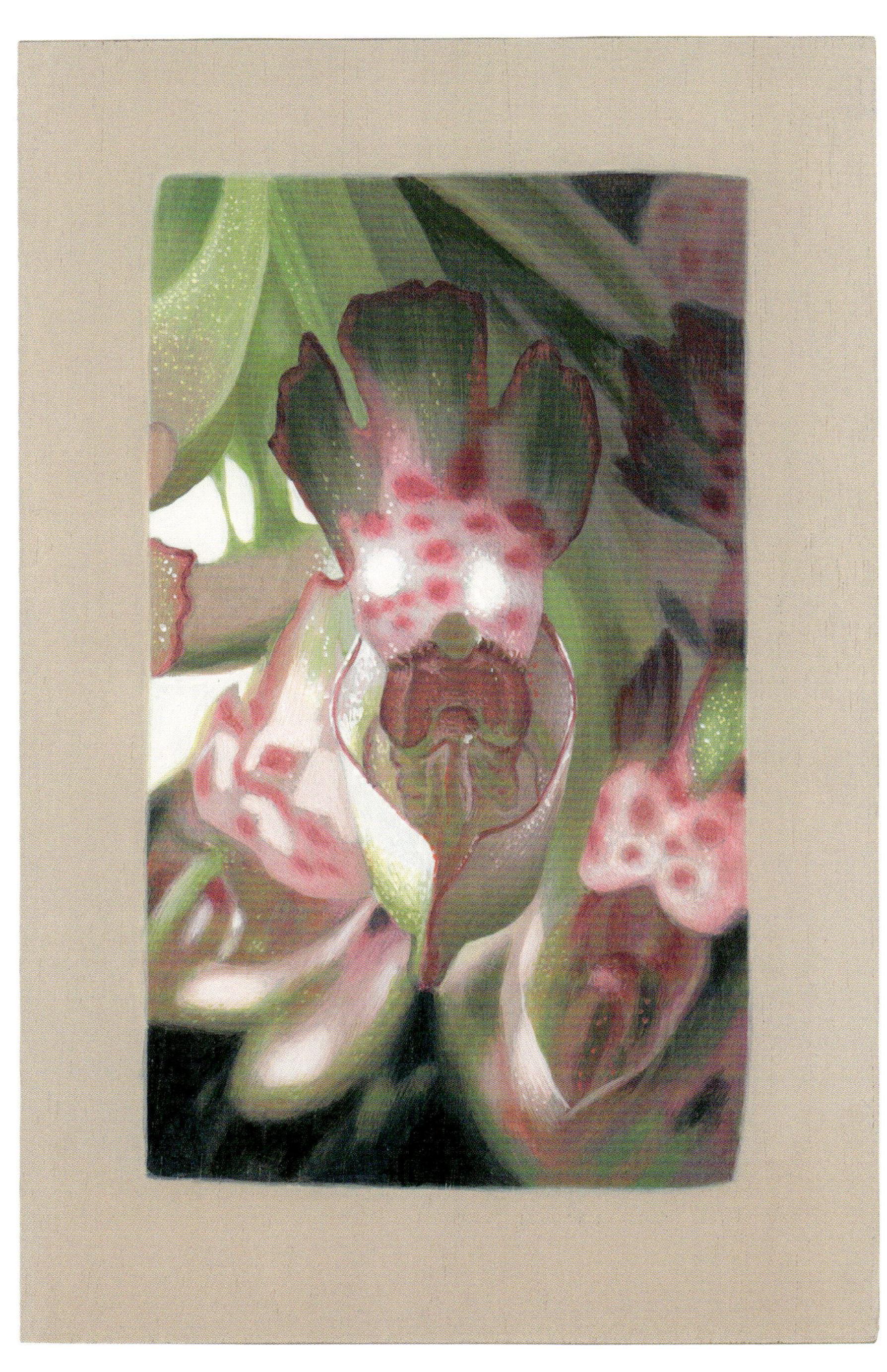

٩ ديسمبر ٢٠٠٤

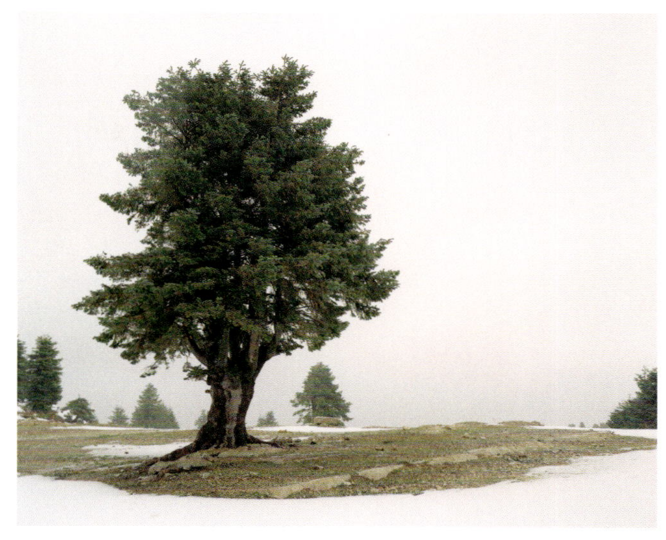

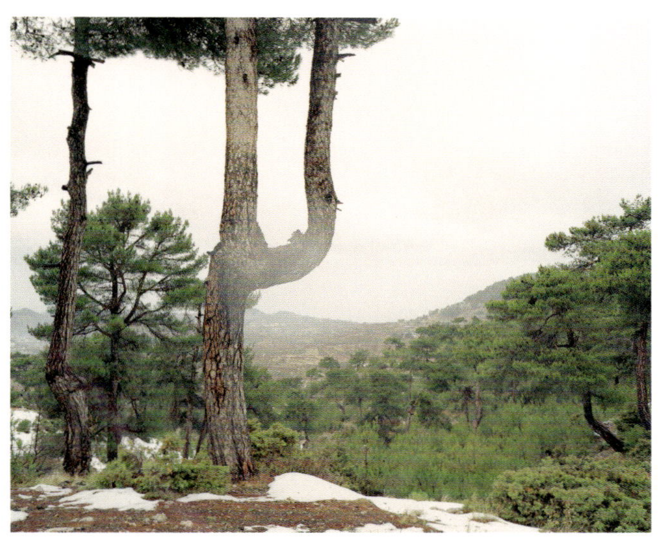

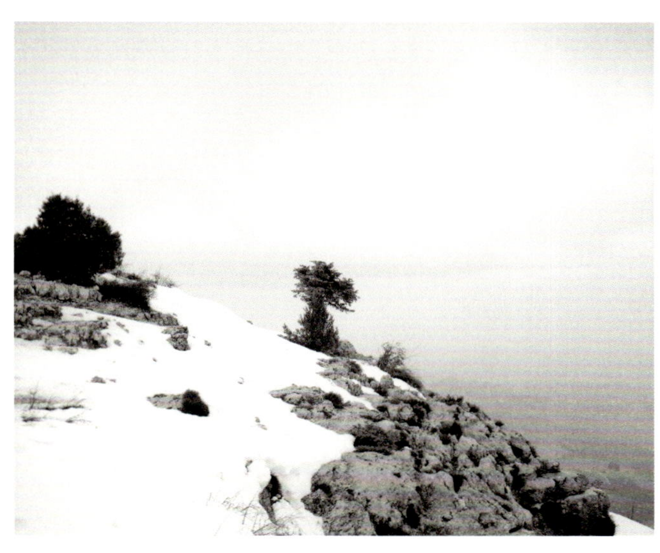

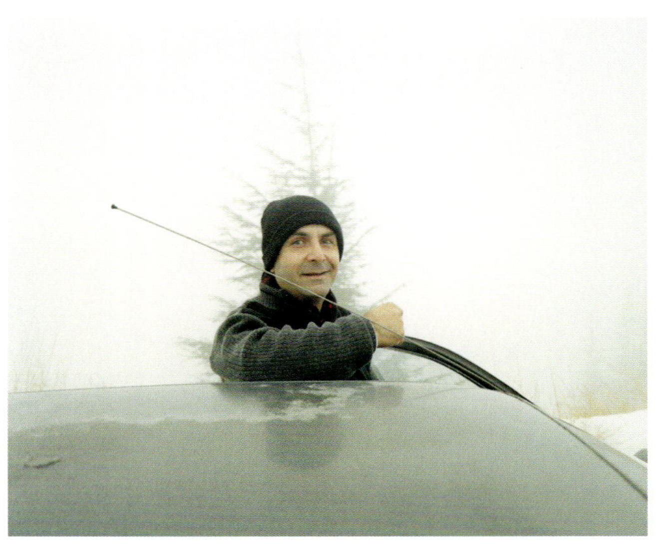

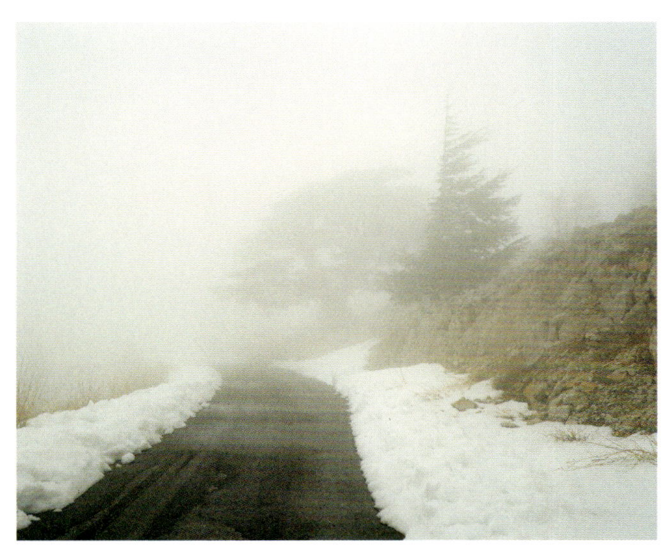

December, 9th

Bcharré, Qurnat as Sauda, Chouf

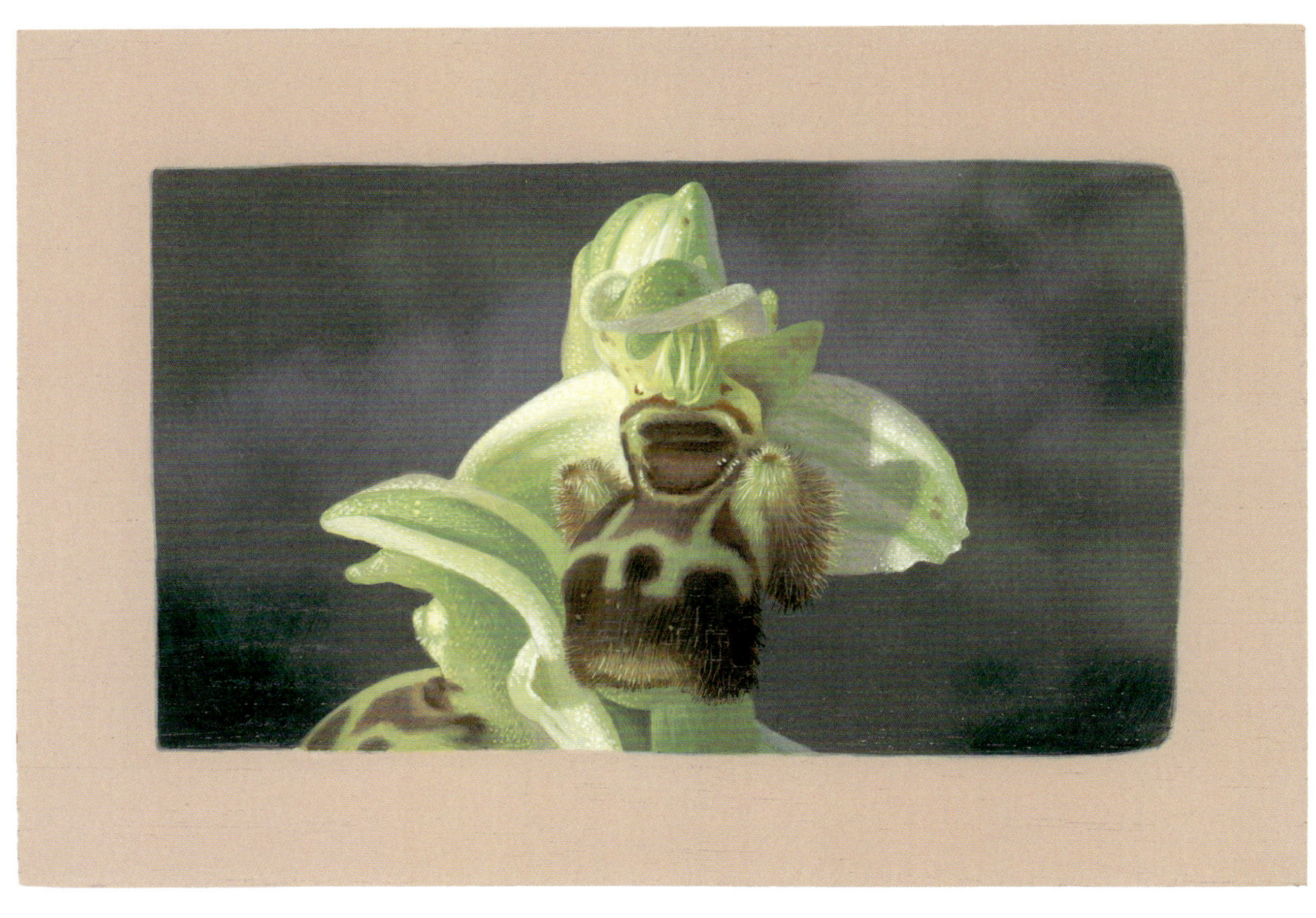

١٠ ديسمبر ٢٠٠٤

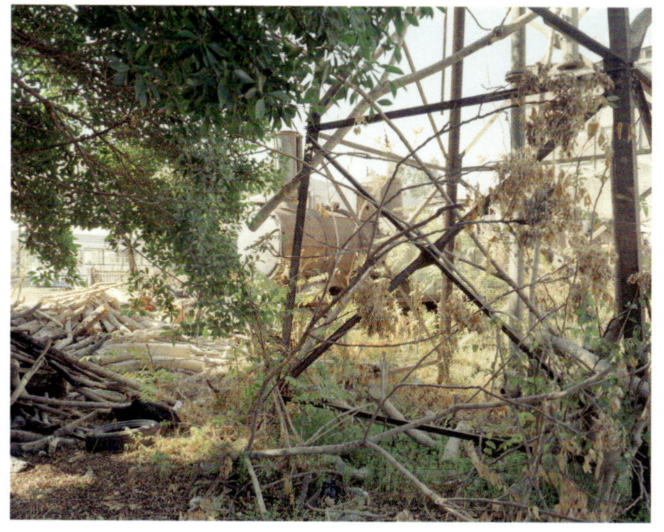
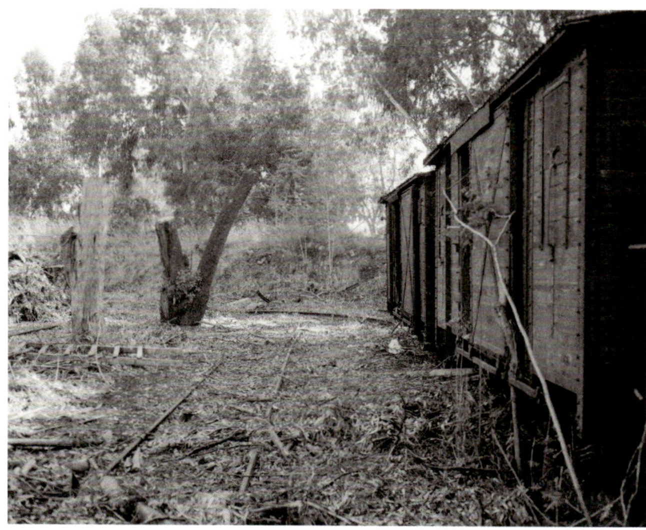
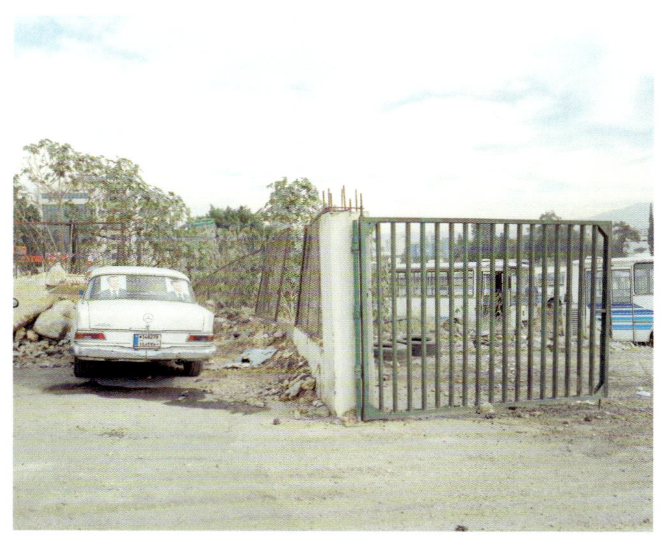
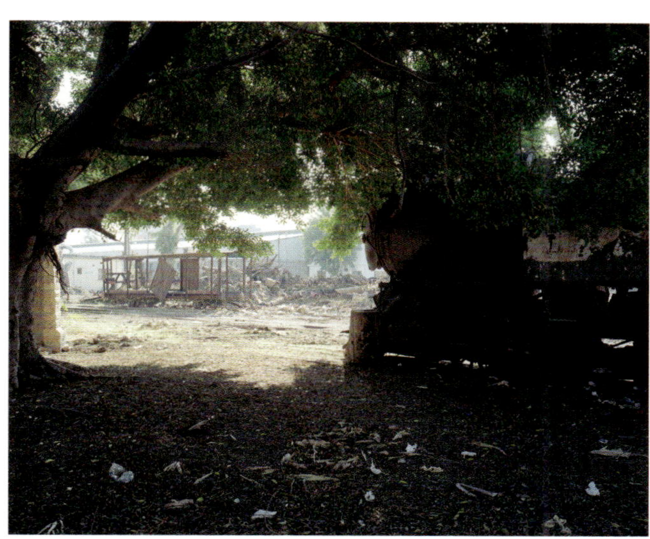
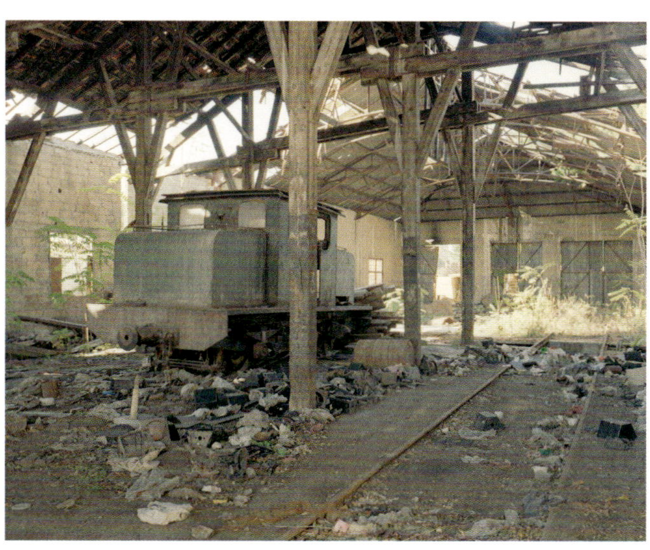

December, 10th
Beirut

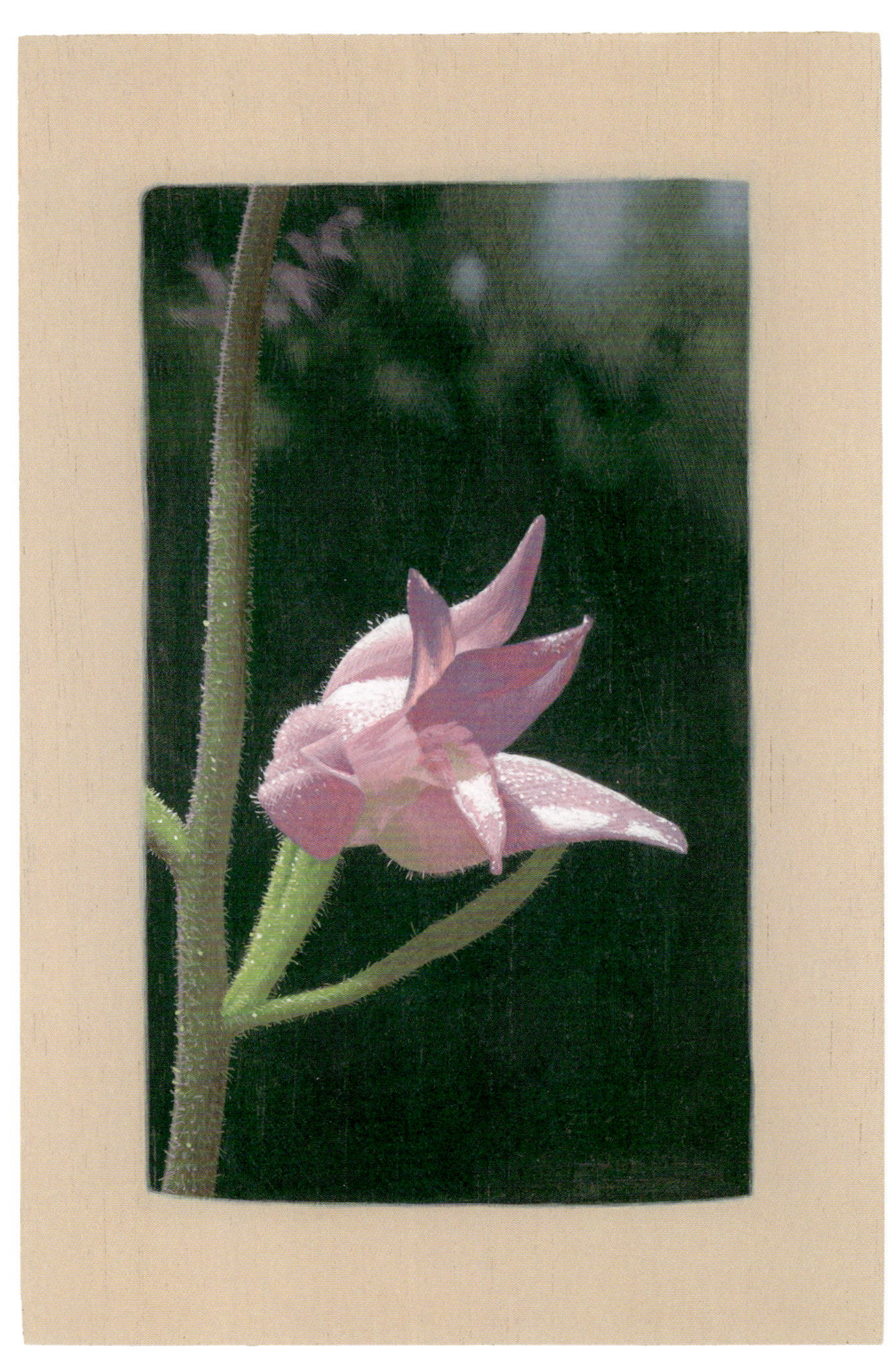

١١ ديسمبر ٢٠٠٤

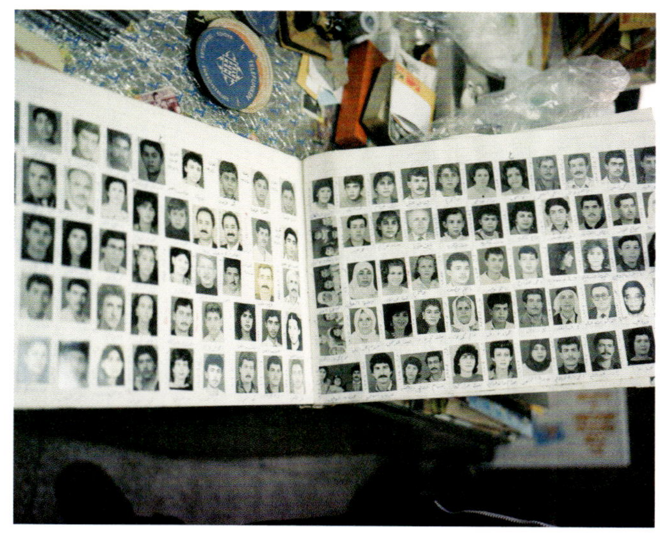

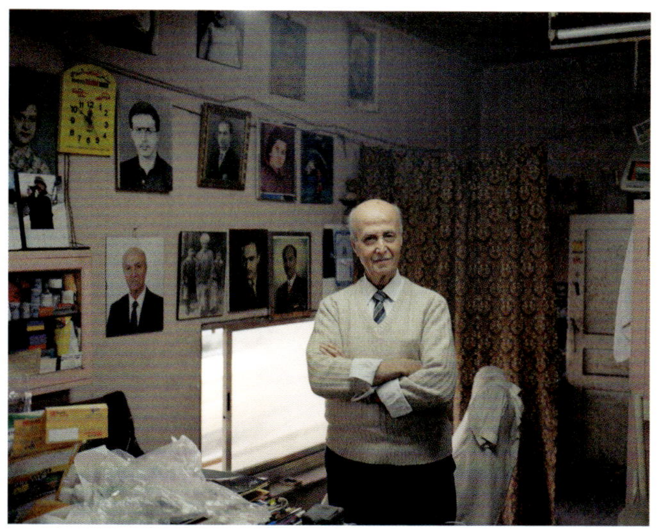

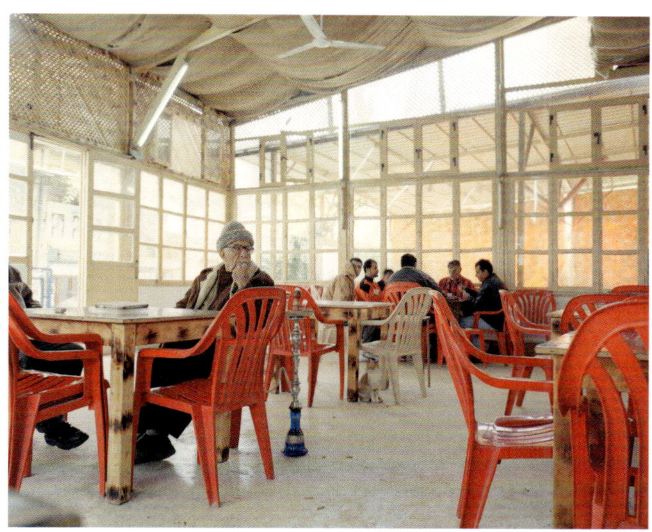

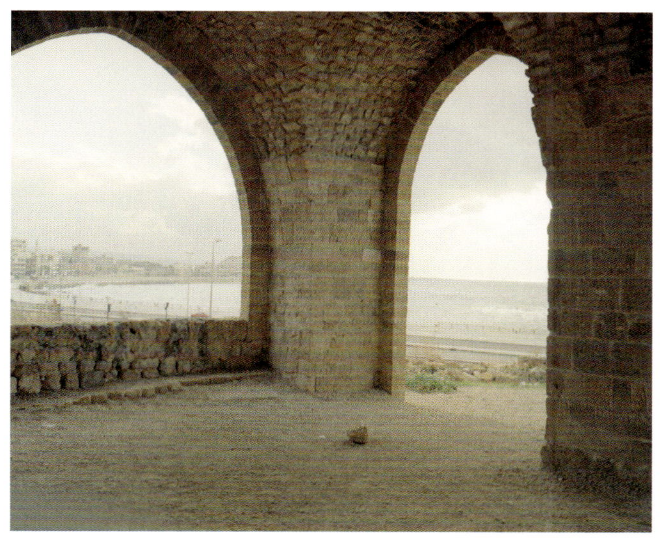

December, 11th
Saida

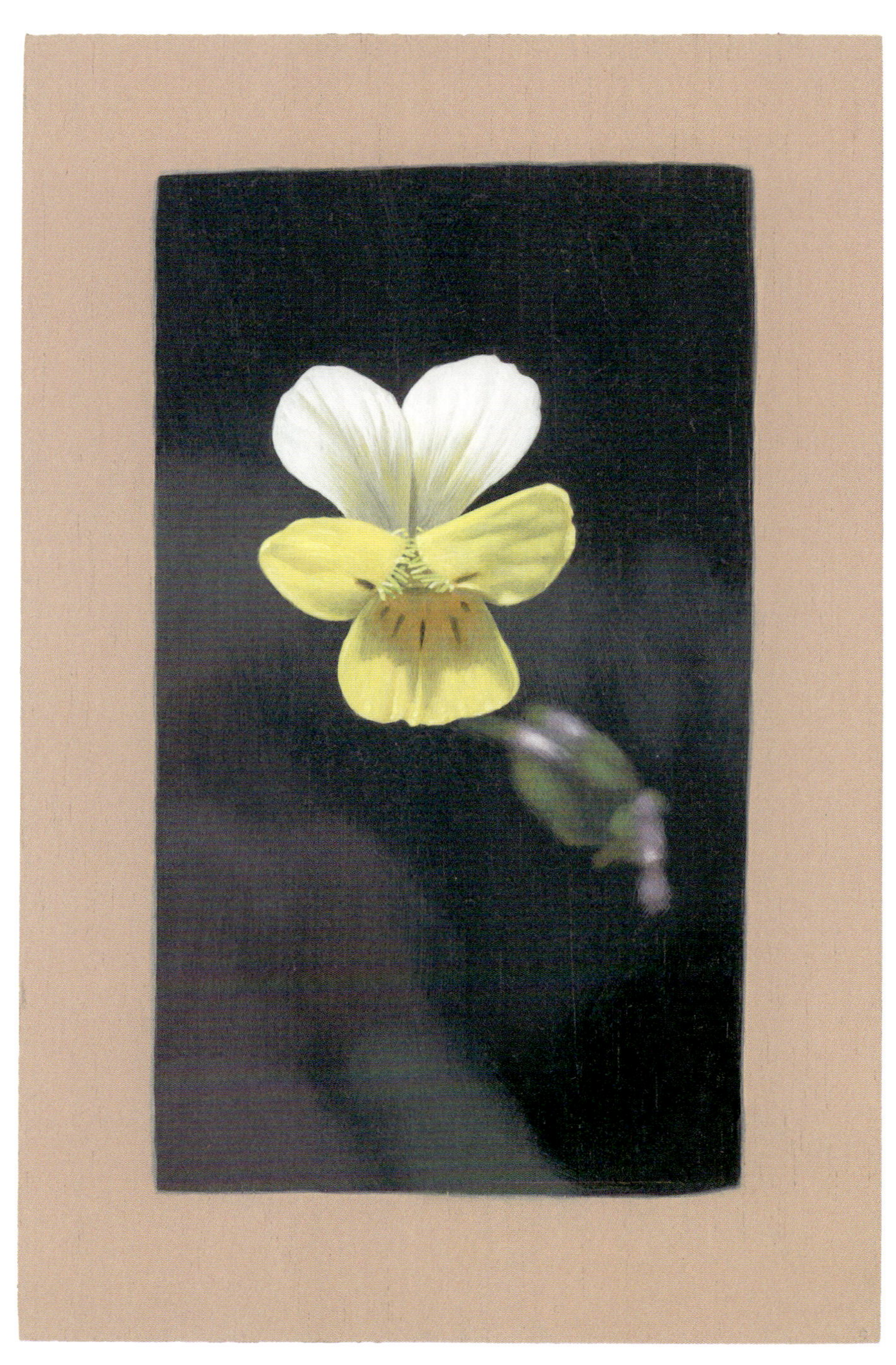

١٢ ديسمبر ٢٠٠٤

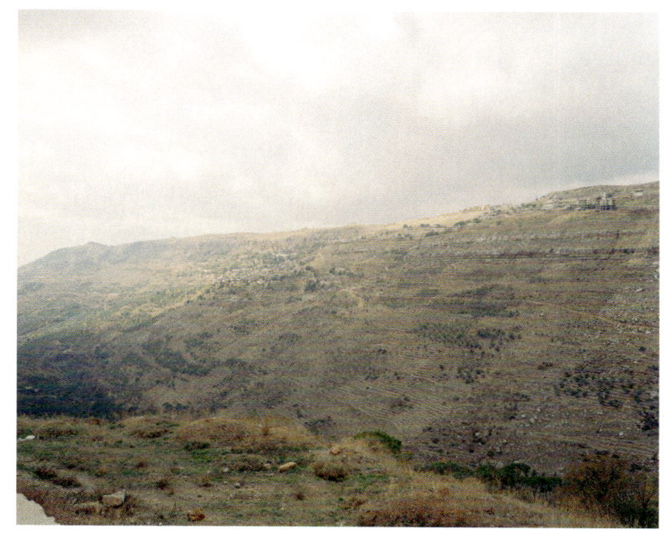

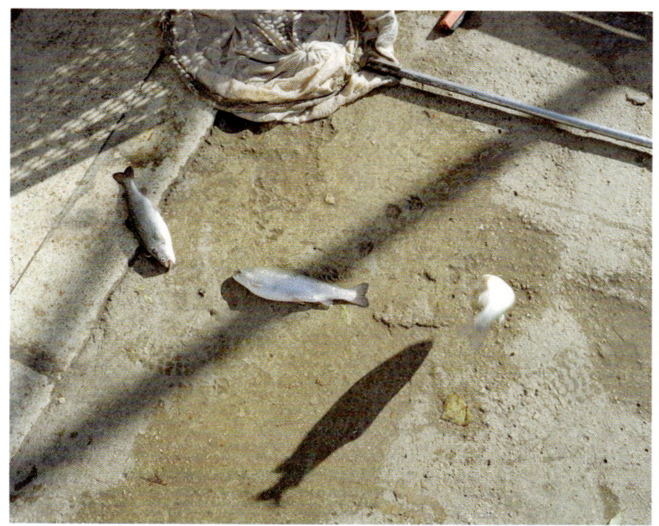

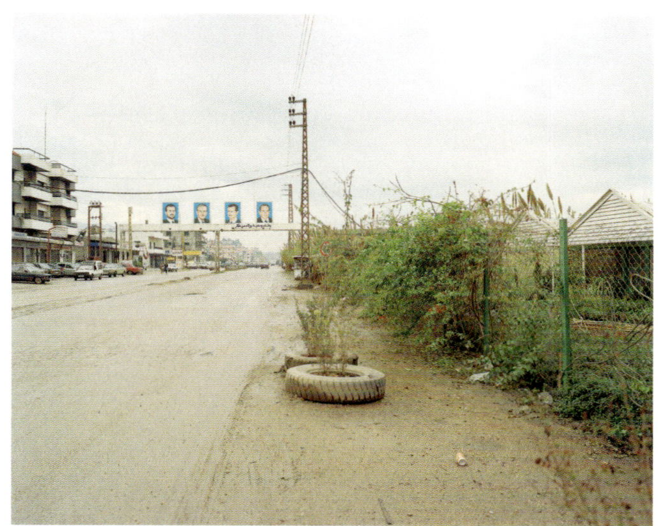

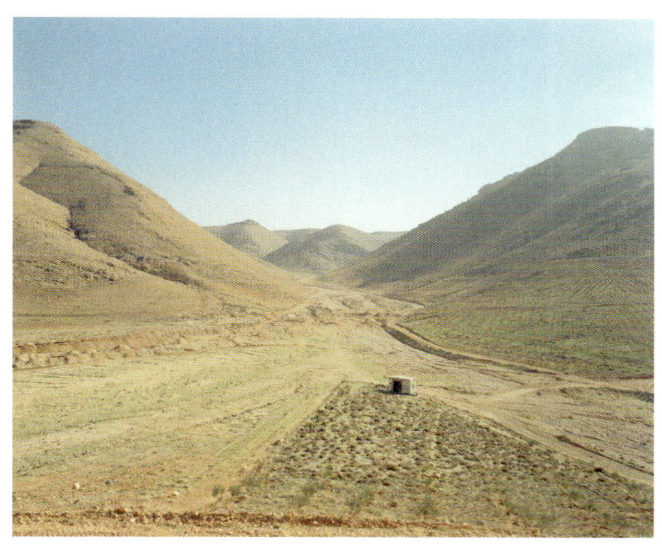

December, 12th
Bekaa

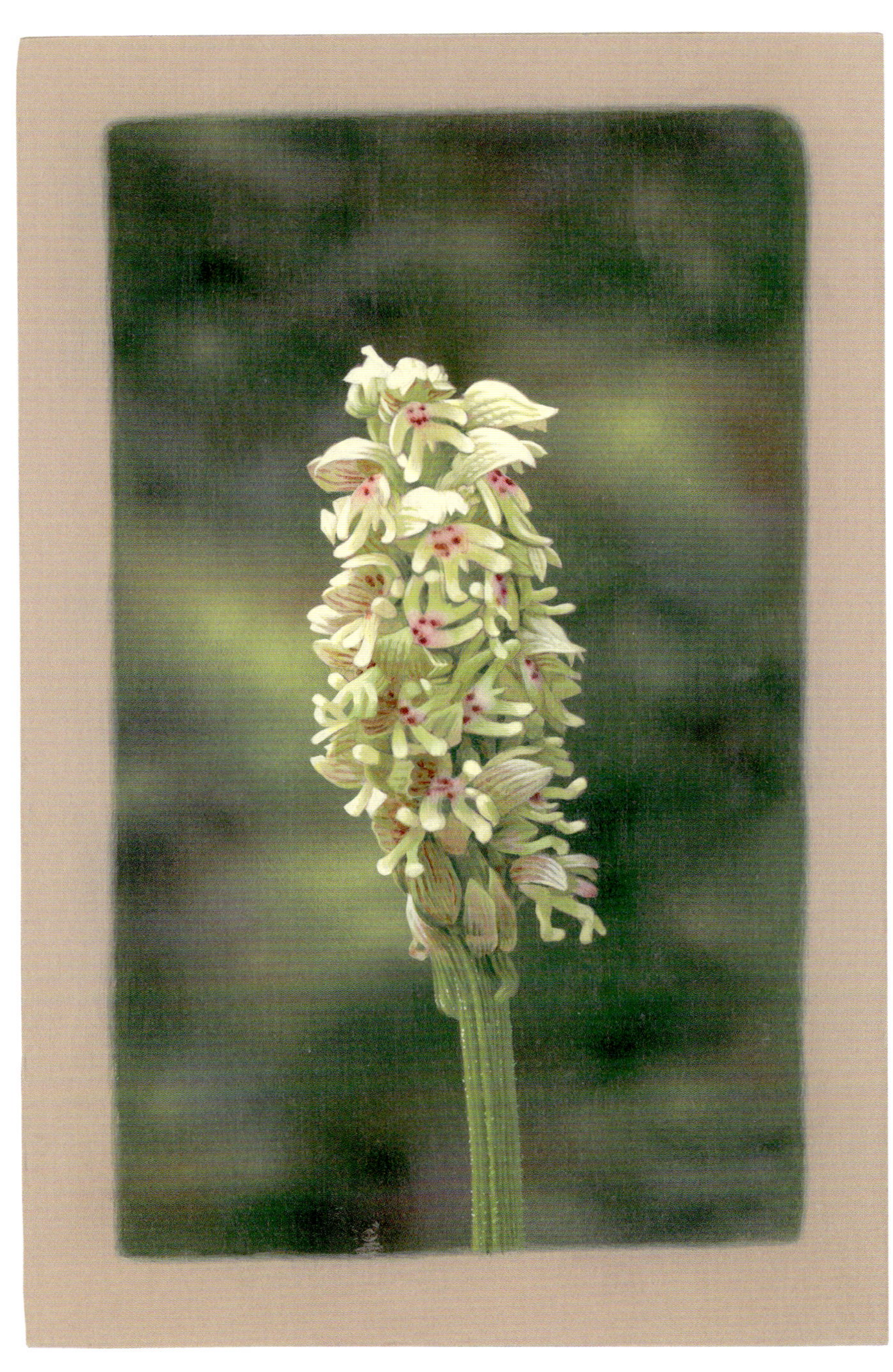

١٣ ديسمبر ٢٠٠٤

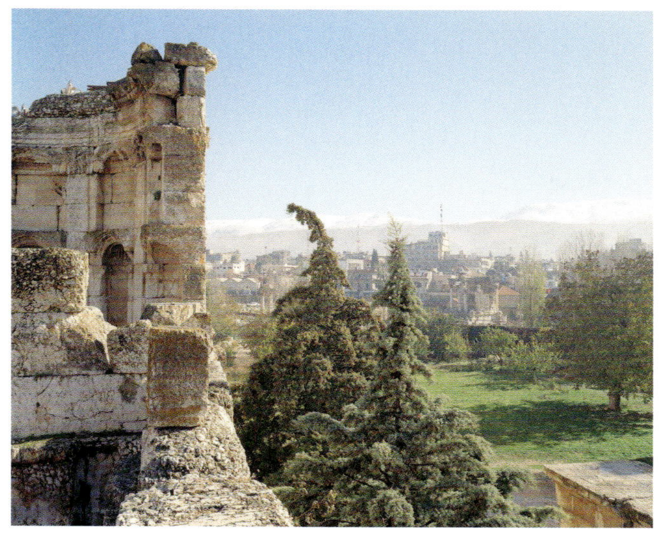
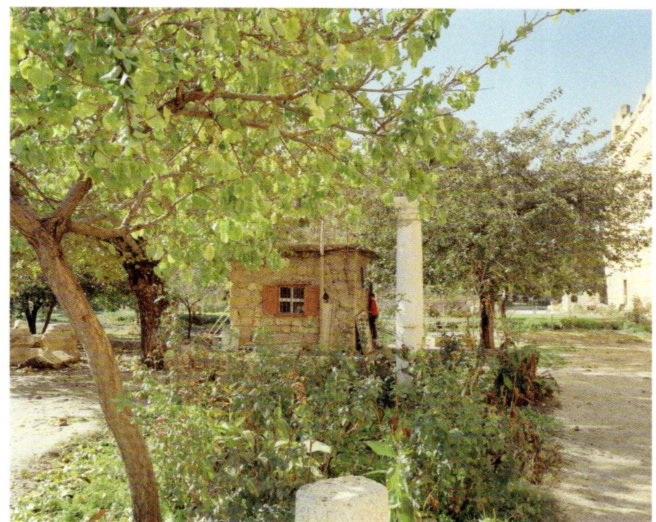
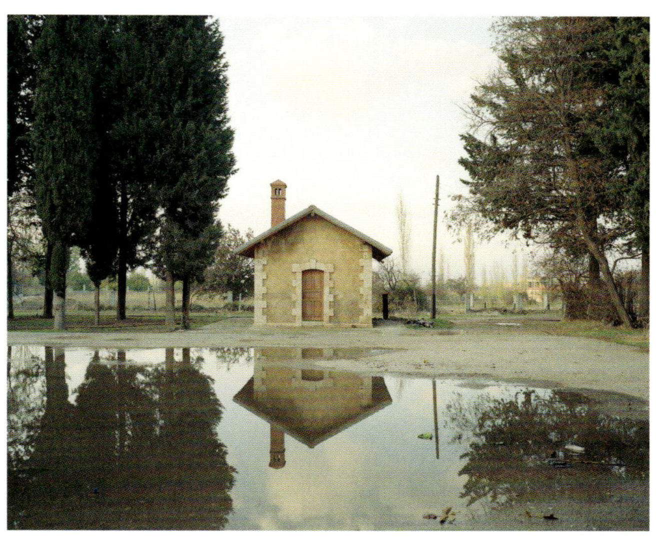
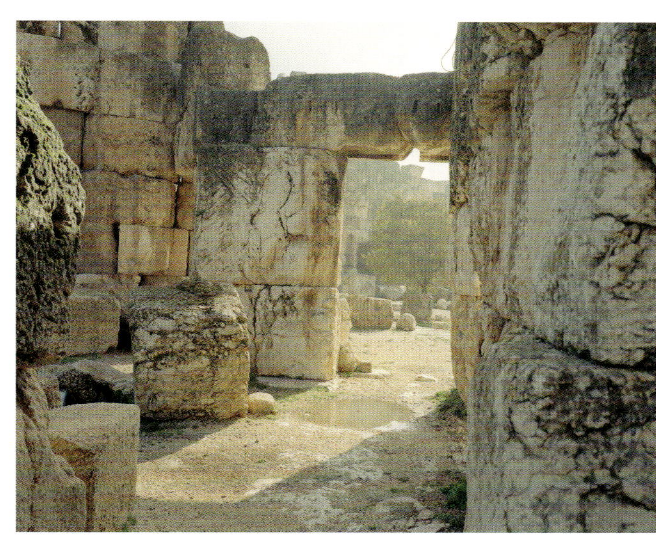
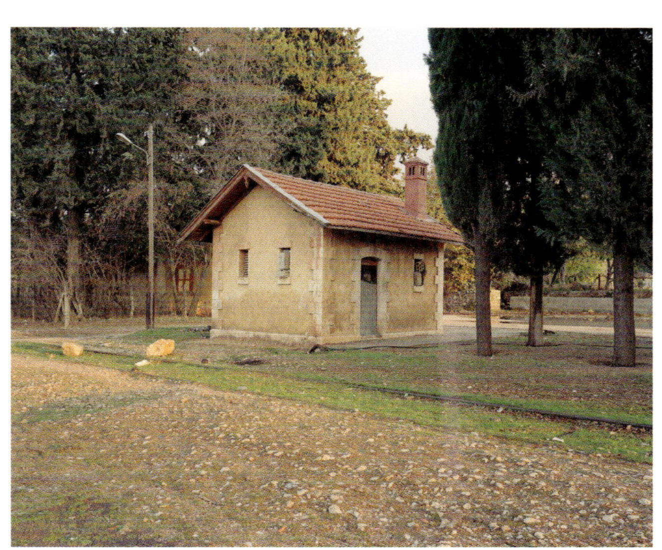
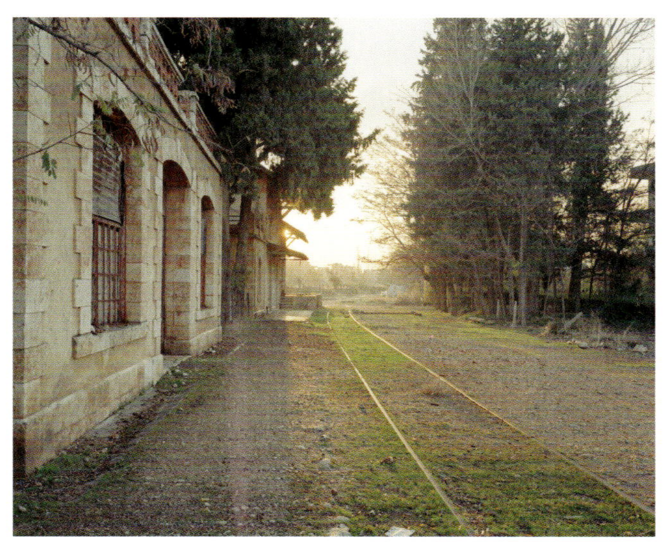

December, 13th

Baalbek

ישראל ISRAEL

2015—2016

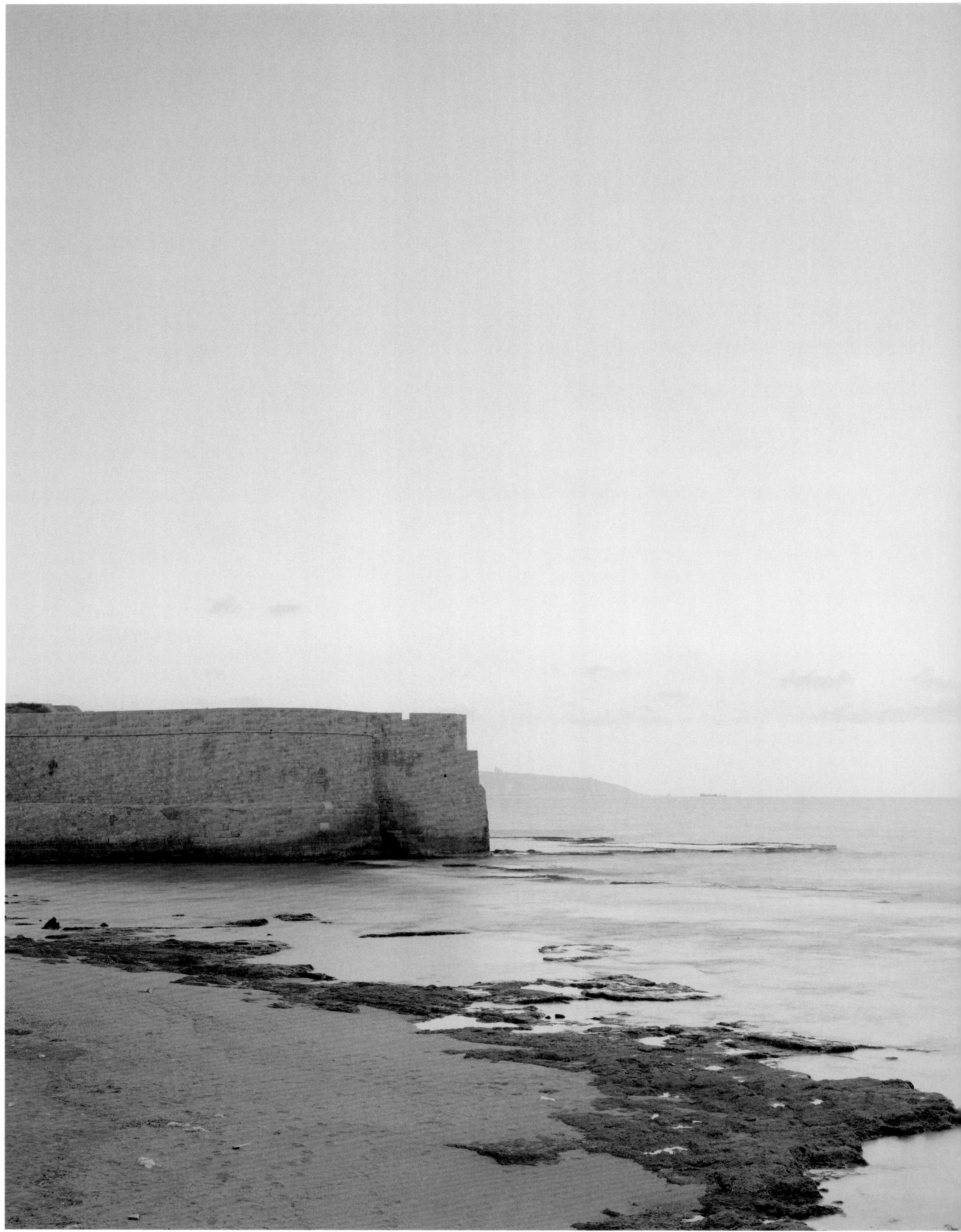

Akko IV 2015

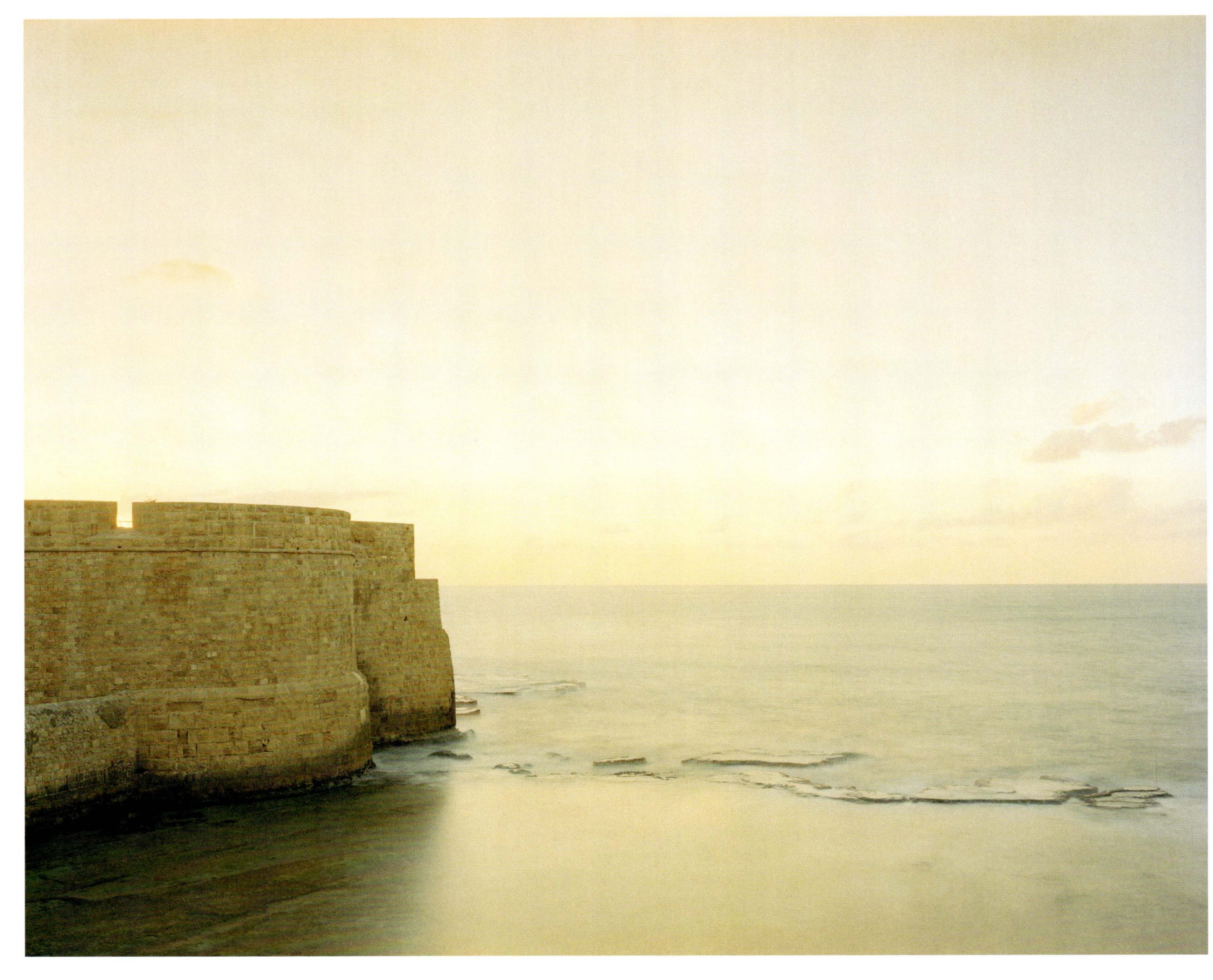

Akko III 2015

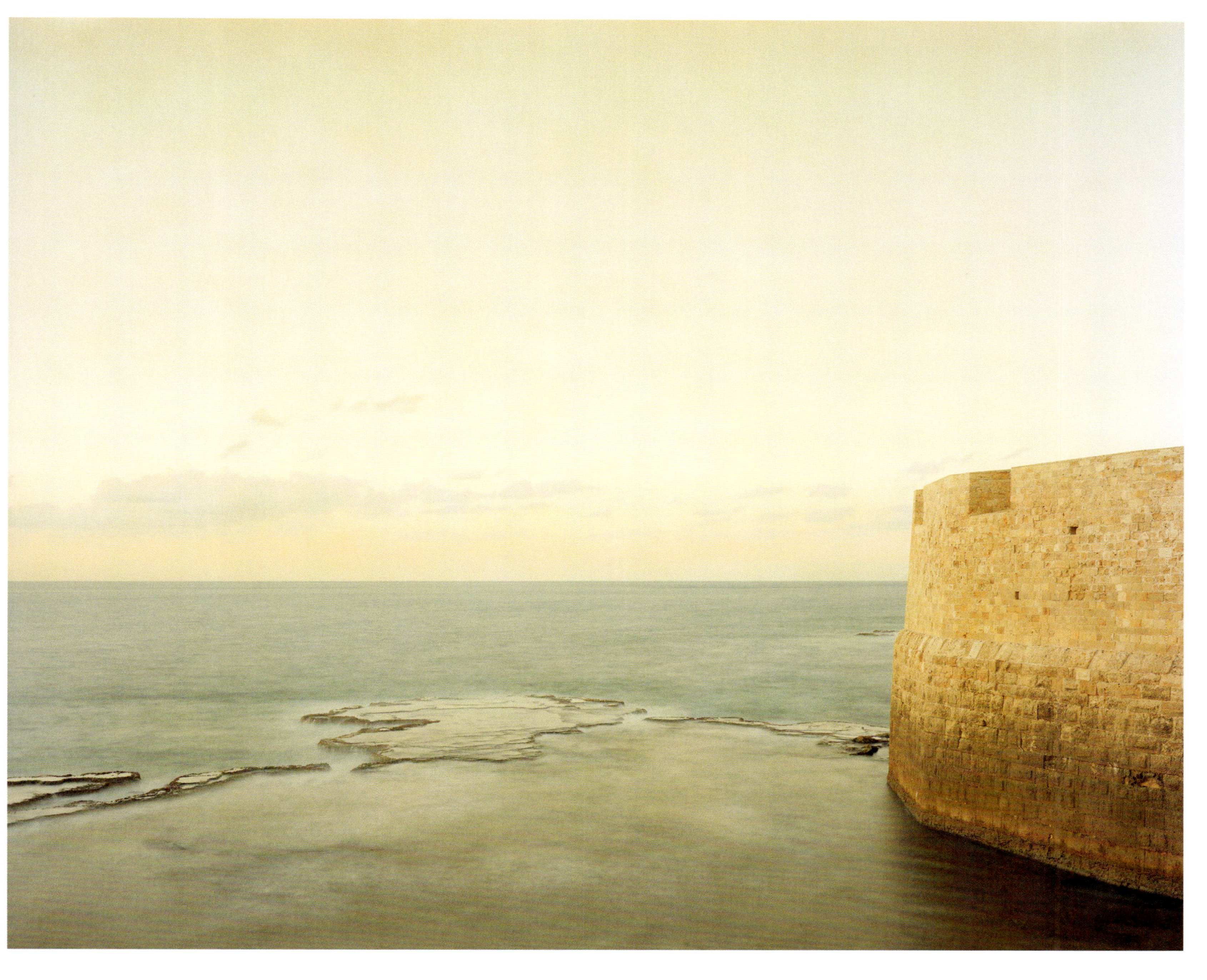

Akko II 2015

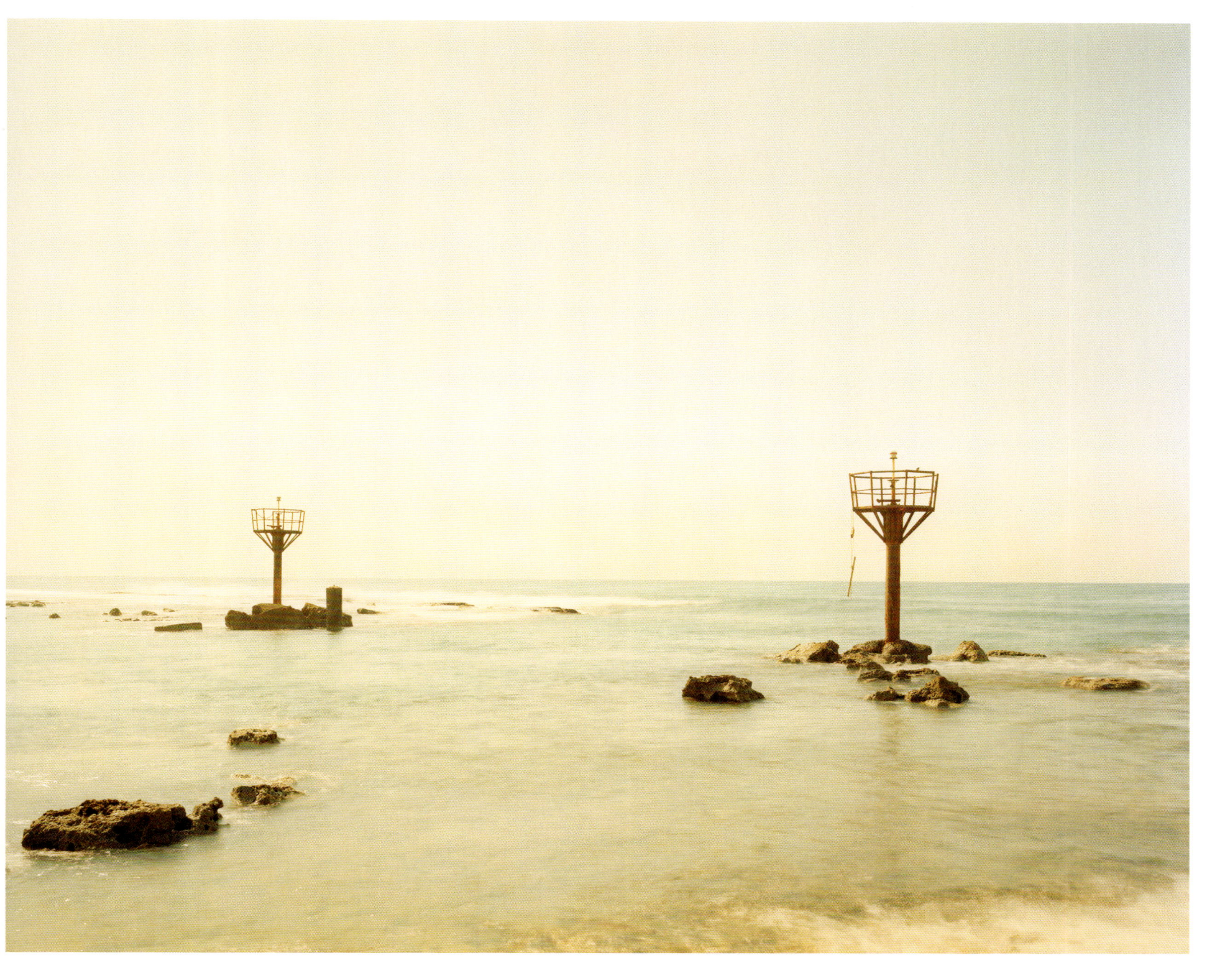

Jisr Az Zarqua 2015

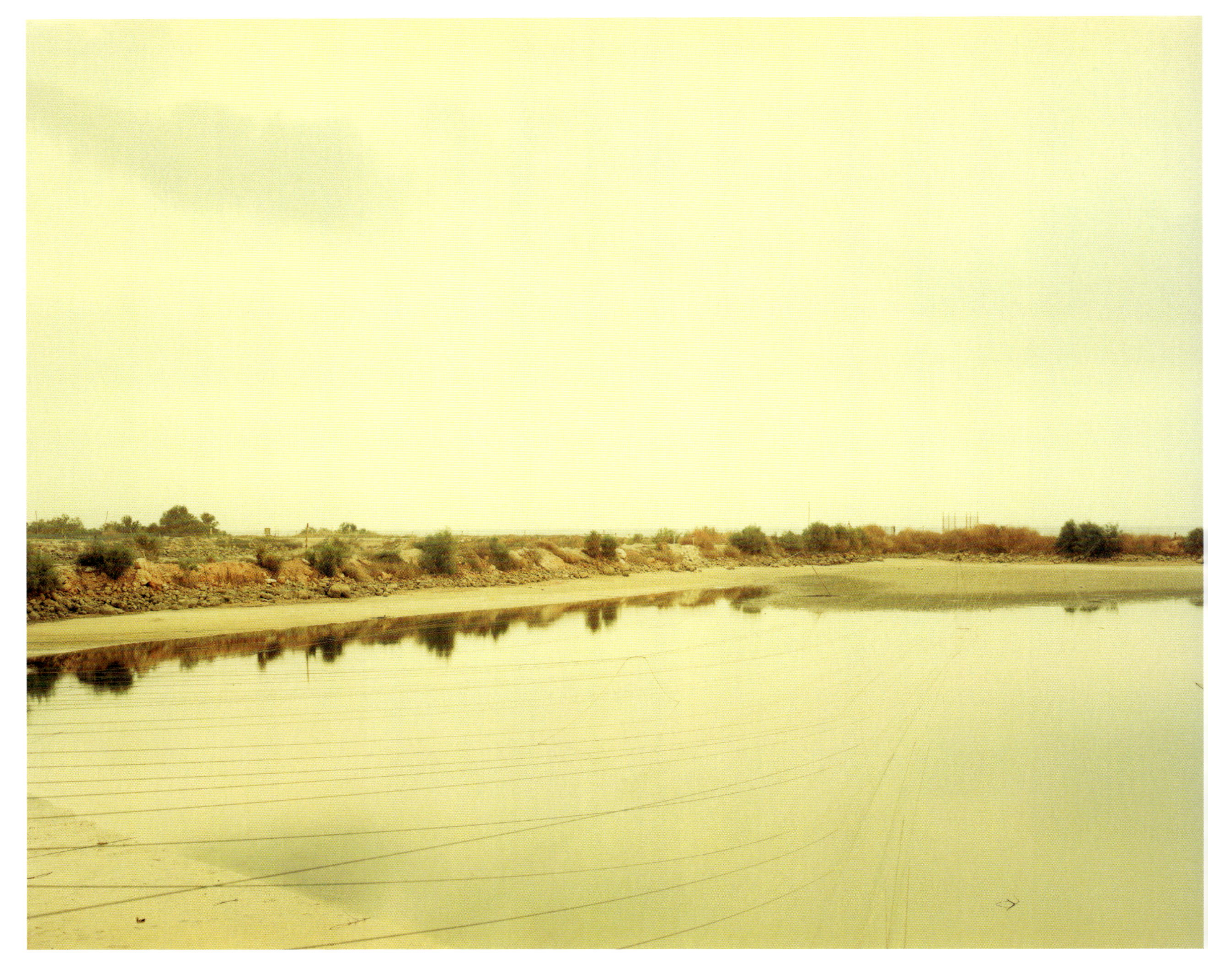

Ma’Agan Micha’el I 2015

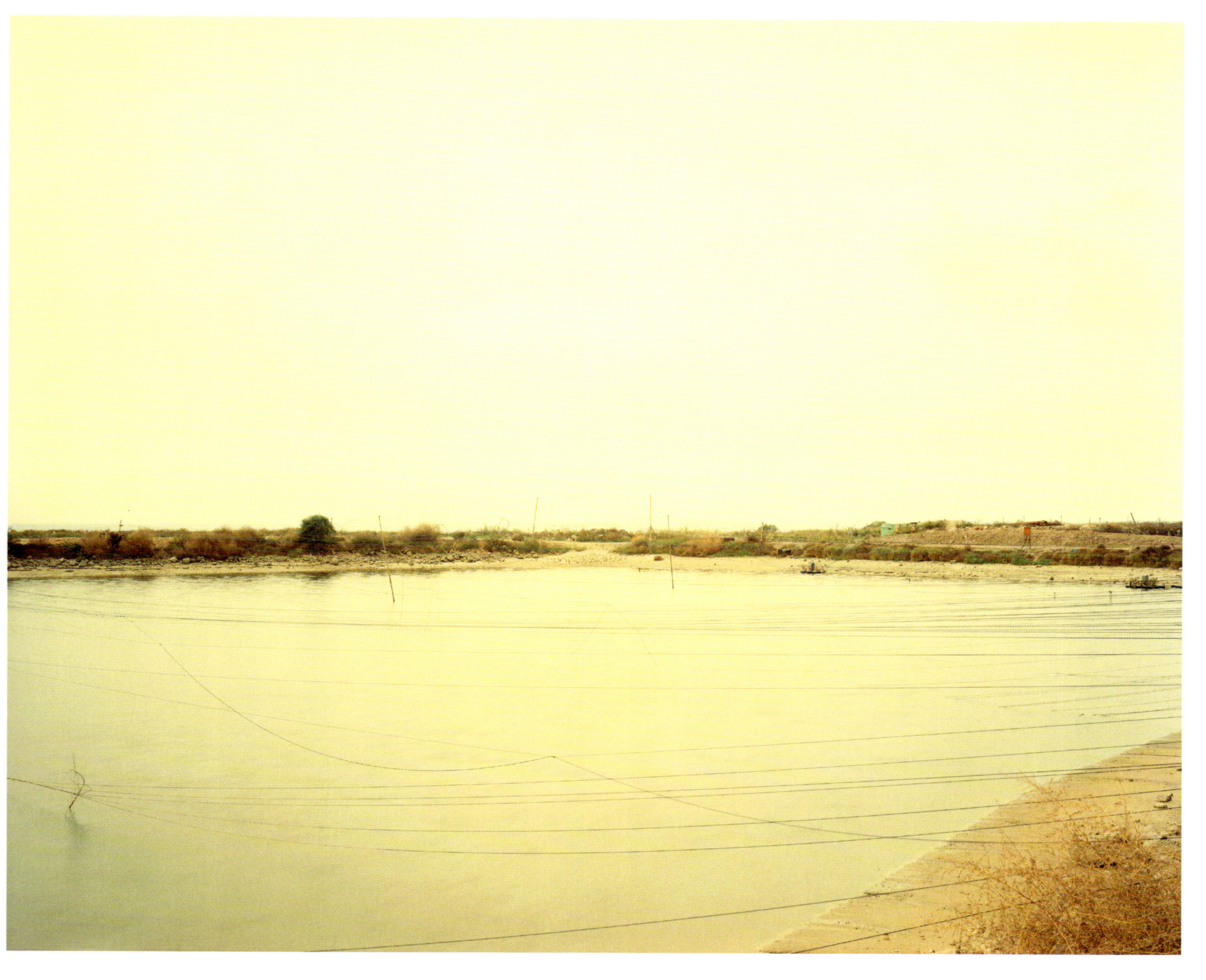

Ma’Agan Micha’el II 2015

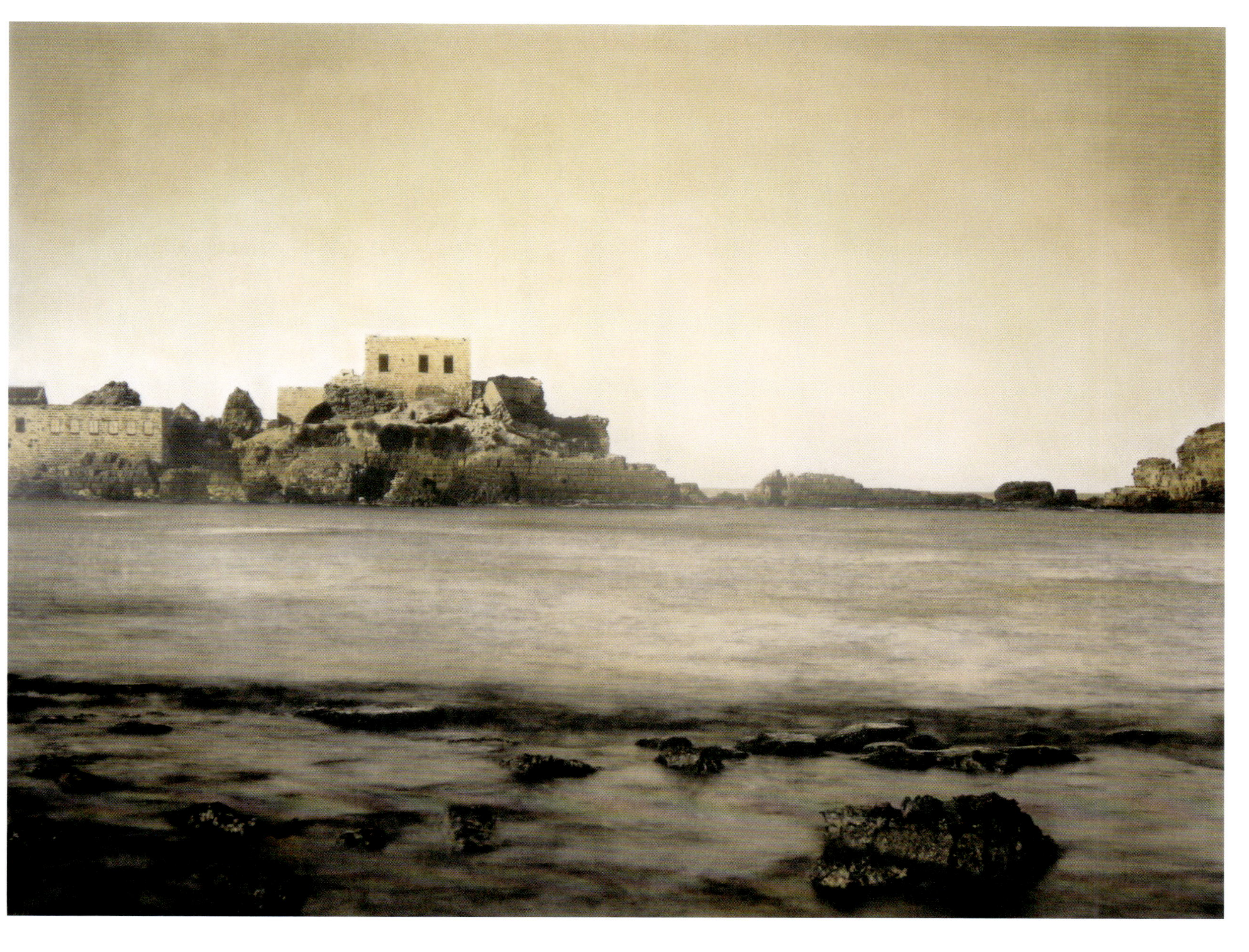

Môle de Césarée 2007

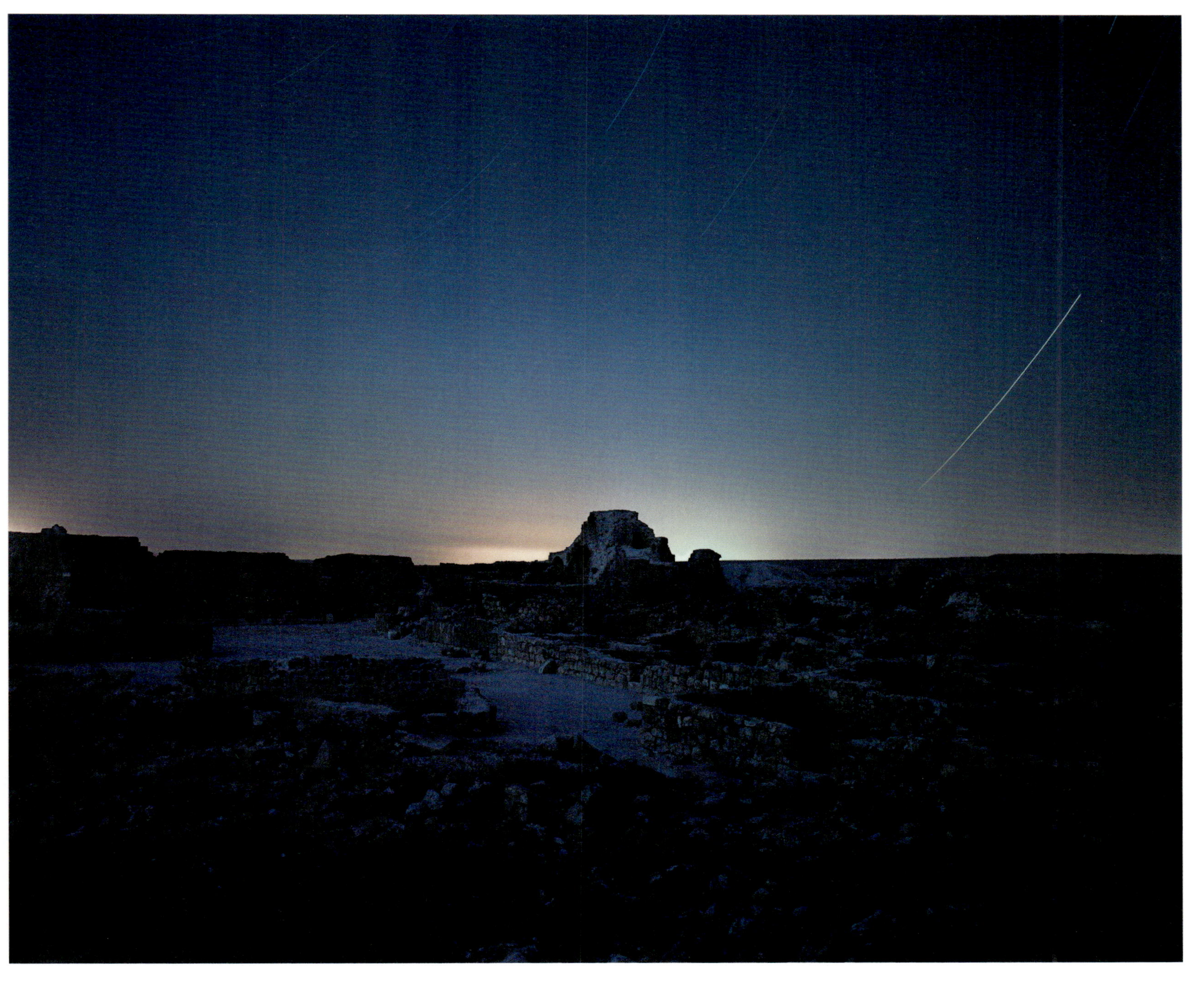

Shivta 2015

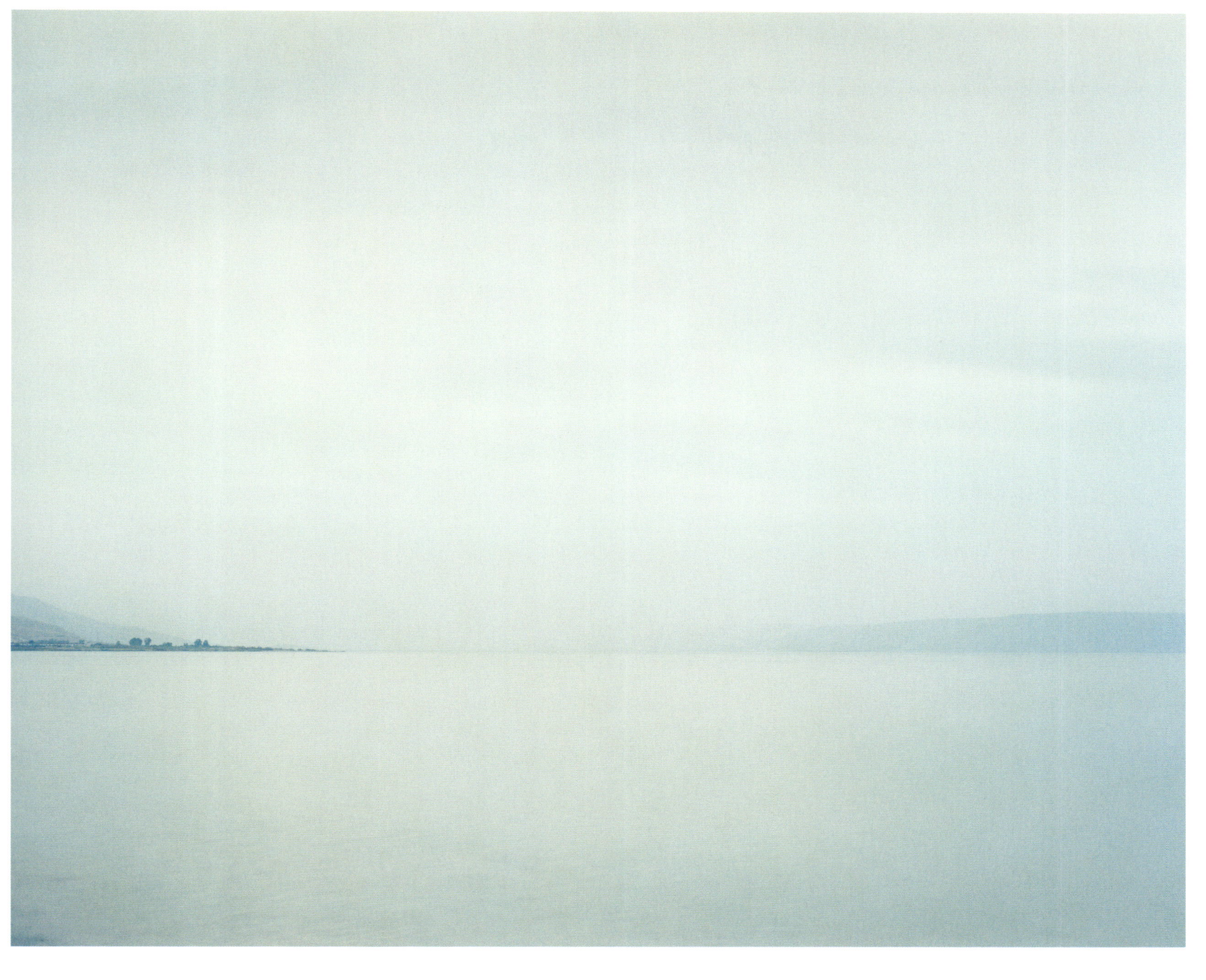

Sea of Galilee I 2015

Sea of Galilee II 2015

V.

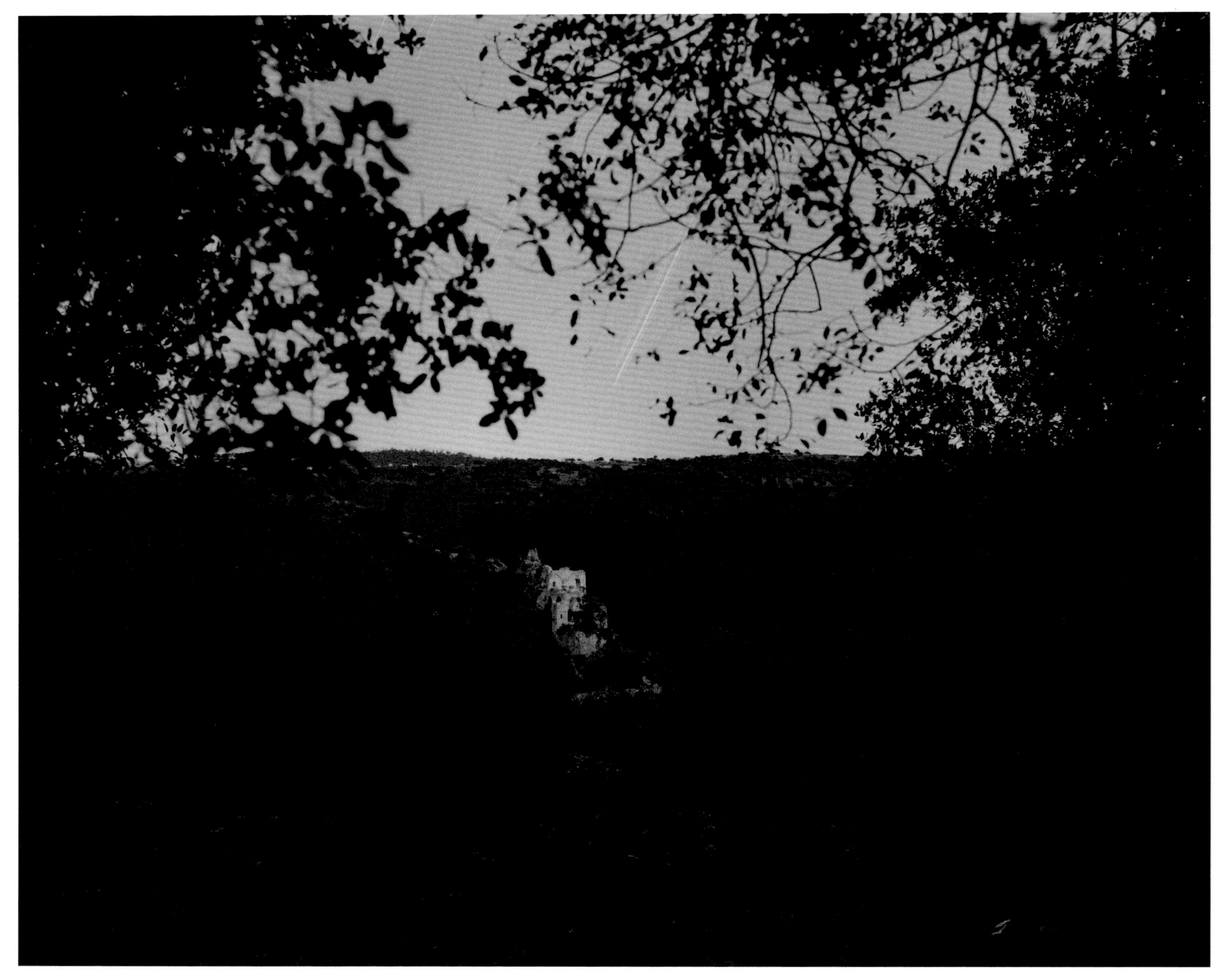

Montfort 2015

Uncomfortable Landscapes

OSNAT ZUKERMAN RECHTER

"Holy Landscape", W. J. T. Mitchell calls the landscape of Israel, which he prefers to call Israel/Palestine. Mitchell claims that the dominant visual-pictorial representation of landscape in the discourse of Western art history allows even the idealization of the scarred landscape of Israel, erasing any signs of violence from it.[1] The surface permits itself to be read through stereotypical patterns that contribute to the veiling of history and disrupt our ability to interpret it. Israel/Palestine, Mitchell claims, a territory sacred for the three major religions based on the Bible, can become an illusion of innocent nature, even though the surfaces of its landscape clearly display the signs of wars, power struggles and archaeological excavations. Its landscape, perceived as an escape from the figurative representation of graven images or likenesses prohibited by the Second Commandment, can paradoxically become an idol in its own right. Turned into an ideological representation, the holy, idolatrous landscape presents power relations as natural and as such, Mitchell argues, is subject to the false selectivity of memory.

The landscape photographs taken by Elger Esser during a three-week visit to Israel in autumn 2015 may foster in the viewer the illusion of innocent nature referred to by Mitchell. In his works, the landscape's surfaces are granted a pictorial/postcard-like visual representation, in line with the conventions of the Western tourist-pilgrim's picturesque gaze. The photographs suggest that Esser takes the possibility that the landscape is a holy idol as a point of reference. In all the photographs taken in Israel, and in most of his photographs in general, the photographed sites are empty of people and abstracted from the characteristics of their here and now. As a result, as Simone Schimpf has observed in an essay she wrote in one of Esser's previous books, we know where and when the photographs were taken, but we cannot determine the time to which we feel they belong.[2]

Esser's landscape photographs, and in particular his vedutas, represent themselves as a-temporal or timeless, while in fact engaging in the camouflaging of time and thus preventing the viewer from succumbing to

1

W. J. T. Mitchell, *Landscape and Power*, Chicago: University of Chicago Press, 1994, pp. 5–34.

2

Simone Schimpf, "In Combray and elsewhere", in *Elger Esser: Eigenzeit*, Munich: Schirmer/Mosel Kunstmuseum Stuttgart, pp. 146–149.

the illusion of innocence. The effort invested in them in cleansing the landscape of the characteristics of the here and now and in presenting it as idyllic creates estrangement and, as with the fragility of a landscape's reflection in still waters, exposes the fragility of the idolatrous illusion with which it could have been ascribed. Furthermore, in some of these photographs the single point of view is multiplied. They thus do not obey the panoptical model of one dominant point of view, an essentially overpowering and colonialist model typical of the tradition of Western-picturesque representation. These two technical decisions – camouflaging time in various ways and multiplying the points of view – create in this body of work a complex and ambiguous relationship to truth, authenticity, history and memory. Despite its complexity, however, this relationship remains faithful to the movements teeming on the surface and to photography as a medium for representing surfaces rather than representations or theories of depths (such as psychoanalysis, for example).
The body of work Esser made in Israel consists of three sections: a group of large-scale landscape photographs; the *Palestine 1948* photographs; and the series *One Sky*. In each of these sections, as well as in the relationships among them, concealment, visibility and flattening are engaged in a sophisticated role play.

I.

The large landscape photographs were shot with an analogue camera in various sites in Israel. The photographs of Acre, the Sea of Galilee and Jisr az-Zarka are dominated by water, a typical motif in many of Esser's photographs. For viewers informed about the history of these sites and what they represent politically and socially in Israel today, Esser's quasi-pastoral frames, in which time seems to stand still, harbor a quiet unease. The ancient and beautiful Acre has a mixed population and occasionally erupts due to social tensions. The Sea of Galilee, Israel's only lake, is a symbol of national anxiety over water shortages whose water level is measured and reported daily in the press. And Jisr az-Zarka, the most disadvantaged Arab community in Israel, is located near Caesarea, one of the richest towns in Israel. To this day, no Israeli artist dealing with Jisr az-Zarka, and there have been a few, has thought of turning their gaze from the poverty and violence that blight it to focus only on the sea. That is, to camouflage its deprivation through that single common denominator that connects it as an equal not only to its affluent neighbour, but also to the countries of the entire Mediterranean Basin, and, as an enriching point of reference, also to the Levant of this and former times.

The other works in this section are evening/night photographs of Montfort and Shivta, taken in long exposures of one and a half to two hours. An imaginary geographical line stretches in them between Montfort, an archaeological site in Northern Israel featuring the ruins of a medieval (13th-century) Crusader Castle, and Shivta, in Israel's southern desert, which consists of the ruins of a Nabatean city dated to the 1st–9th centuries. Along with the geographical-imaginary line, the photographs of these two sites also draw a cross-temporal line connecting two great past civilizations hundreds of years apart, and embodied by their archaeological remains. Choosing these two specific ancient sites in the north and in the south creates the affect of compressing historical time and physical space, among other things due to the long-exposure effect.

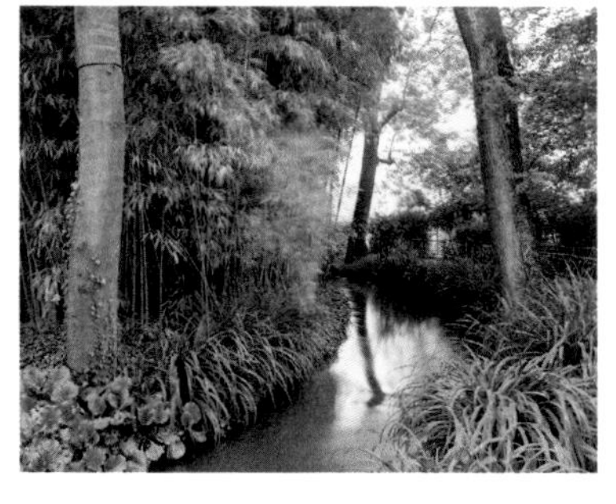

Elger Esser
Combray (Giverny I)
France (Haute-Normandie, 27 Eure) 2010

The photographs of Montfort and Shivta form a dialogue with the group of Nocturnals taken by Esser in Claude Monet's estate in Giverny (2010). In both groups of photographs, a technical decision was taken to open the shutter for long durations. In *Giverny*, the extended inscription of the light reflected from leaves and water as they lightly moved across the film plate emphasized the Nocturnals' painterly qualities. At the same time, these works highlighted the differences between the experience of a-temporality generated by Esser's photographs and the impressionist painterly motivation, which focused on pre-visual human perception and the experience of the moment/now, one of whose expressions is the water lilies Monet painted in the quasi-natural garden he created. In the Montfort and Shivta photographs, the long exposure produces different meanings than those of Giverny. The long exposure inscribed the stretches of sky in these photographs with scratches of light, as if falling stars were awakening a static primeval landscape from its slumber, instilling it with movement. The ensemble of times and periods already enfolded in the photographs of these historical sites were thus further bound with the circular motion of the earth and the ancient cosmic constellation of which it is part.

II.

The group of works *Palestine 1948* comprises 16 relatively small photographs of various sites in Israel/Palestine: Lifta, Caesarea, Maale Sdom, Beit She' arim, Tel Dan, Hirbet Tzunam, Nimord, Shivta and Arab al-Aramshe. The photographs are scorched, stained and marked with different stamps, including a censor's one. The name of the photographed site is printed in Hebrew letters on the bottom left of each photograph. To the naïve viewer these photographs may look like archive photographs. In Esser's show at Loushy Art & Projects' exhibition space in Tel Aviv, where the works were exhibited for the first time, they carried the inscription *The secret archive of Livi Benjamin*, hinting at the presence of a secret and implying concealment and censorship.

The processed photographs, taken by Esser in different sites in Israel during 2015, masquerade as archival photographs from 1948, the year the State of Israel was founded. The use of conventions such as captions, staining and stamping disrupts our ability to read the photographs, as it camouflages the time but not the place in which they were taken. Should the truth be revealed and the secret come to light, our trust in this group of works as representing historical truth and as an authentic document would be broken. And with it also our trust in its maker – the landscape photographer who enabled us to immerse ourselves in a timeless landscape, to feel as one with the creator, and is all of a sudden revealed as a cunning and deceitful demiurge who uses ruses to mislead us.

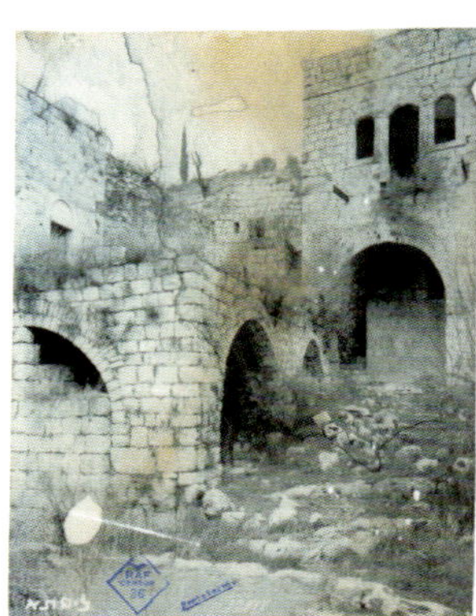

Elger Esser
The Secret Archive of Livi Benjamin, Palestine 1948,
Lifta III, 2016

The group of works *Palestine 1948* is an authentic, unique document, though not in the predictable and direct historical sense. It is a collection of photographs that Esser has printed and individually processed in his laboratory, and is therefore one of a kind, diverging from its status as a reproduced image. This collection claims for itself, in Walter Benjamin's terms, the aura of the original. Like the "deception" of cleansing the landscape of the characteristics of the here and now, the "deception" of the historical archive is a conceptual decision that in fact warns us against misconceiving what we see and blindly obeying patterns of thinking and looking. Tellingly, "exposure" and "bringing to light" are expressions whose moral meaning is related to the basic dependence of the mechanism of sight and of photography as a medium of light. Esser's fictive photographic archive does not suppress any historical or political secret; hence censorship is irrelevant to it. On the other hand, it is our historical patterns of thinking of and looking at Israel/Palestine 1948, exposed by the very use of the archive convention, which are able to surprise and shock us, and it is they, usually, who are also the reason for censorship. The identical format of the photographs, the uniform captions naming the sites and the direct and detailed treatment they each get give the photographed sites equal standing despite the great disparity in their historical, geographic and demographic status. The archive created by Esser is an act of democratization by means of a photography intended to camouflage and blur the prevailing reality in order to signal the existence of a different, more respectful and egalitarian possibility, if only for the gaze.

III.

The third part of this body of work, the series *One Sky*, features four metal plates silver printed with landscape photographs. Each plate carries two different photographs: 8 photos in total, one on each side. The technical decision to print on both sides forces the viewer to move between the two sides of the plate, which stands in the space like an obstacle, in order to perceive the two points of view that cannot be perceived together.

The photographs were taken simultaneously on both sides of the territorial border between Israel and Lebanon and in its proximity: one photograph in Israeli territory, facing north towards Lebanon, and the other in Lebanese territory, facing south towards Israel. Two digital cameras were operated simultaneously and aimed at a fixed and pre-agreed angle, diagonal to the landscape and pointing towards the sky. The conditions of two enemy states and a restive border imposed a total lack of communication between the photographers. The territorial border dictated restrictions of movement and communication that were translated into restrictions of body and gaze. In the course of the photographing processes, which took several days, the lack of communication meant a loss of control. If there was dialogue, it was imaginary and based on understandings and decisions taken ahead of time. In contrast to the panoptical point of view, Esser had to forgo control of the eyepiece, allowing another eye to decide some of the frames, and incorporating the point of view of the other into his work.

In *One Sky*, the landscape as a means for expressing meaning became an act of communication between people (and its absence), rather than merely an act of communication between the human and the non-human (the camera, nature).

Elger Esser's work deals with questions of camouflage. Camouflage, as Ayelet Zohar has remarked, does not mean not being seen, but rather not being interpreted.[3] Camouflage does not conceal something that does not exist, but flattens and assimilates visual information that does exist, making us interpret it incorrectly. Therefore camouflage is first and foremost a defence mechanism, like camouflage colours in nature, or the

3 Ayelet Zohar, "Strategies of Camouflage: Depersonalisation, Schizoanalysis and Contemporary Photography", ch. 8 in Ian Buchanan and Lorna Collins (eds.), *Deleuze and the Schizoanalysis of Visual Art*, London: Bloomsbury Books, 2014, pp. 173–201.

behavioural patterns of certain animals that freeze in the face of danger and pretend to be dead. Photography is a medium that from its inception was marked with a dimension of pretend reality and of freezing and deadening. Esser's landscape photographs do not deal with what we see because it exists, but rather with what we do not see even though it exists, like memory. And just as the visible elements of camouflage disrupt our perception and conceal that which exists, so the landscape revealed in the photographs camouflages what exists in it and what it is about – memory. This is how I understand Esser's tracing of Marcel Proust's remembrance of things past in his photographic series *Combray* (2007–2009).

In a lecture he gave to students in Israel, Esser recounted a childhood memory to do with Venice. When he was about 10 he fell on his head while building a tree house in the courtyard. His resulting concussion disrupted the family's holiday in Italy and prevented them from getting to Venice. This memory, later joined by the memories of his mother's frequent trips to Venice for work, during which he was left behind in their home in Rome, and the little presents his mother brought him from there, caused Esser to identify Venice with a sense of absence. Thus, despite the many times he has visited Venice as an adult, it has remained, as he says, unattainable for him. "Venice is pure reflection, in the water as in the sky", Esser said, and every visit to the city is like the first time. "Venice is everywhere and even most within ourselves. She is our portrait turned to stone. Stronger than Rome, than the Levant, than Constantinople, and of course than the new world".[4] Esser's landscapes and vedutas are portraits of the human. Not of one person or one city, but of humans and their endeavours on earth, as they are reflected through the lens of memory in the water and the sky.

In his series of photographs of the Levant *(Morgenland)*, Esser turns his gaze to the east of Venice – to Lebanon, Egypt and Israel, to the region whose name derives from the rise of the sun and is the focal point of constant tension and of crises that in recent years have threatened to change the face of Europe.[5] The "Levant" is a geographical-cultural organizing category whose boundaries have changed in the course of history and which defines the gaze directed from there, from Europe, towards here. Looking at Esser's photographs of Lebanon and Egypt, countries which to my deep regret I have never visited, and which alongside Israel form part of his Levant trilogy, provoked in me – a native of Israel, a Jew of Eastern-European descent – mainly feelings of in-betweenness. These feelings were ably ex-

4
Elger Esser in Shenkar College of Engineering, Design and Art, November 16, 2016. Lecture title: "It is always the first time."

5
Venice, which built its power as a maritime empire on its trade relations with the countries of the Mediterranean Basin, constituted a significant cultural and commercial reference point in relation to the Levant for hundreds of years.

pressed by Jacquelin Kahanoff, an Israeli writer who was born and raised in Egypt and wrote in English:

In truth, there was a third, acutely uncomfortable category of people between the pink and the brown, people like ourselves, Jews, Greeks, Syrian, Christians, Armenians who were natives in some ways, Europeans in others, people that were called Levantines, and Jews seemed to be the worst of the lot, according to some nannies, although they were all two-faced people who never told the truth. For those in-between people, like us, how difficult it was to know what to choose, who to be like, or for, the British or the natives! [6]

These in-between people, whose split identity, mutated culture and lives between worlds Kahanoff describes, seem to share the same sea, the one sky and the same irritatingly uncomfortable landscapes that Esser's Proustian photographs reflect.

6

Jacquelin Kahanoff, "The Blue Veil of Progress", 11.6.1967. Quoted with the consent of Laura d'Amade, and the assistance of the Hebrew Literature Archives at the Heksherim Research Institute at Ben-Gurion University of the Negev – Prof. Yigal Schwartz and Ilan Bar-David.

The Secret Archive of Livi Benjamin, Palestine 1948

2016

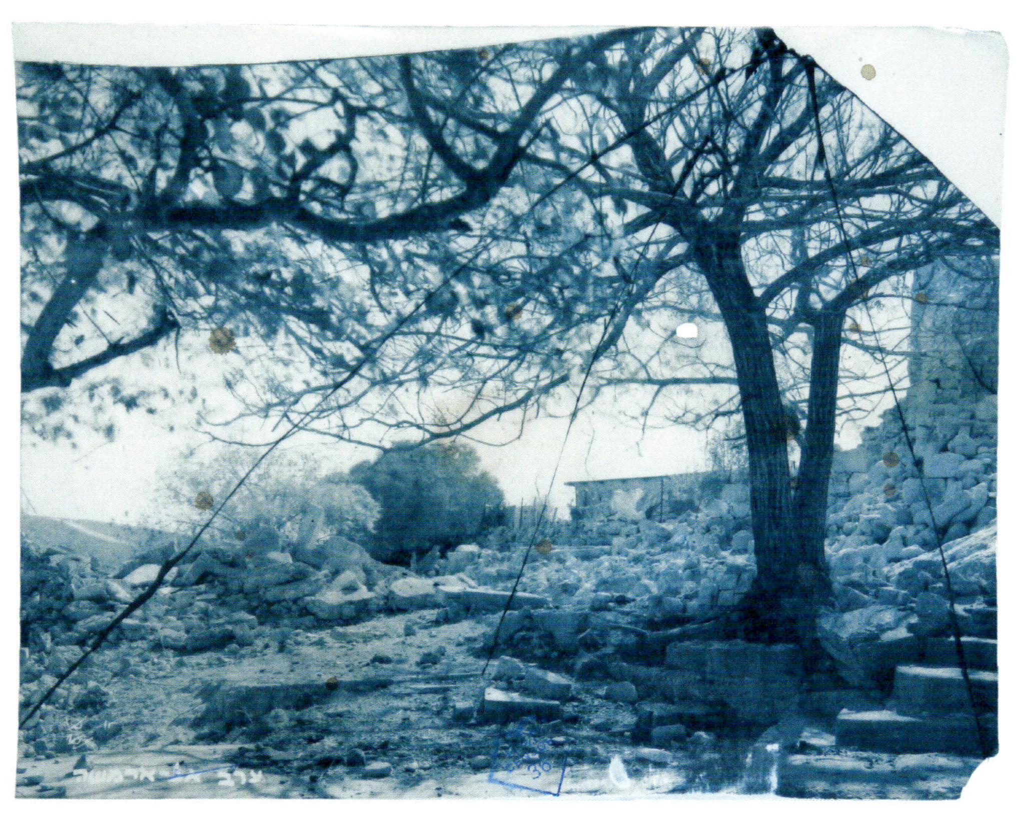

Arab Al Aramshe I Palestine 1948 / 2016

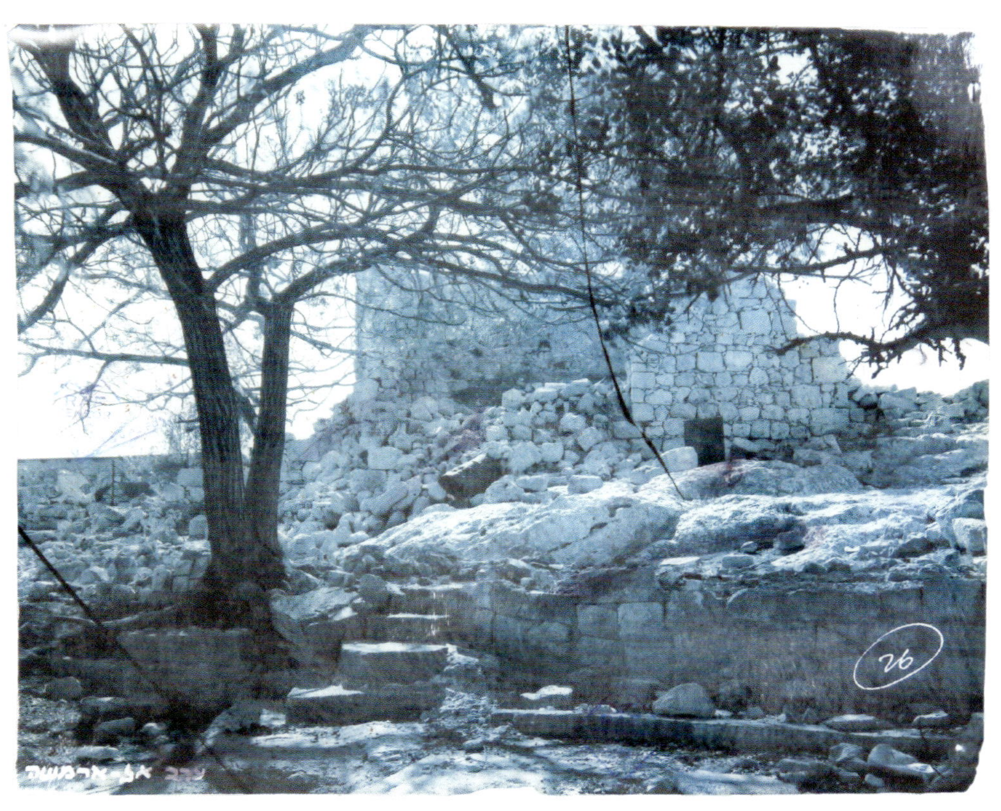

Arab Al Aramshe II Palestine 1948 / 2016
Front and back

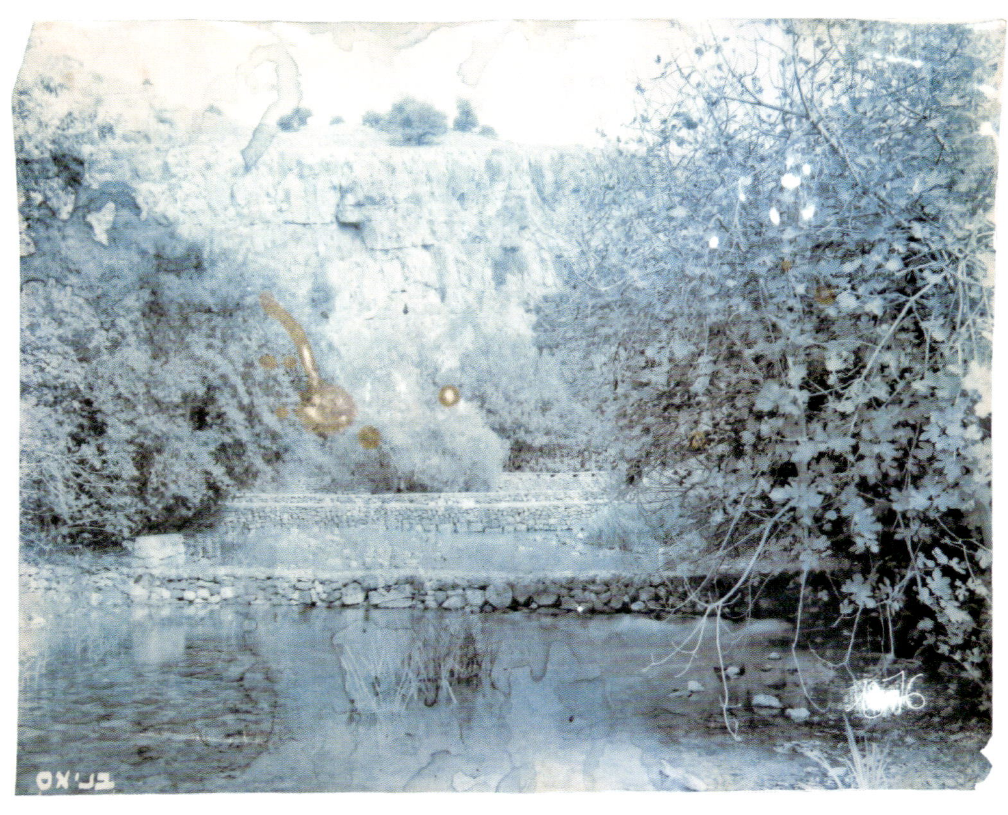

Banias Palestine 1948 / 2016

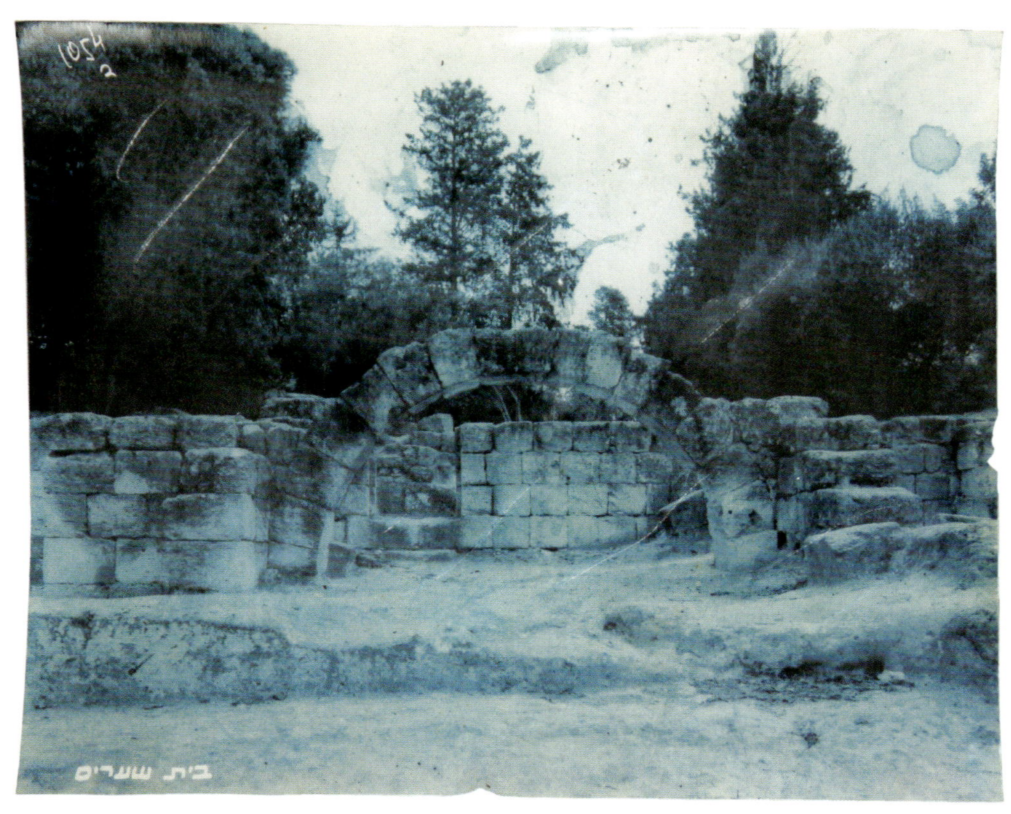

Bet She'arim Palestine 1948 / 2016
Front and back

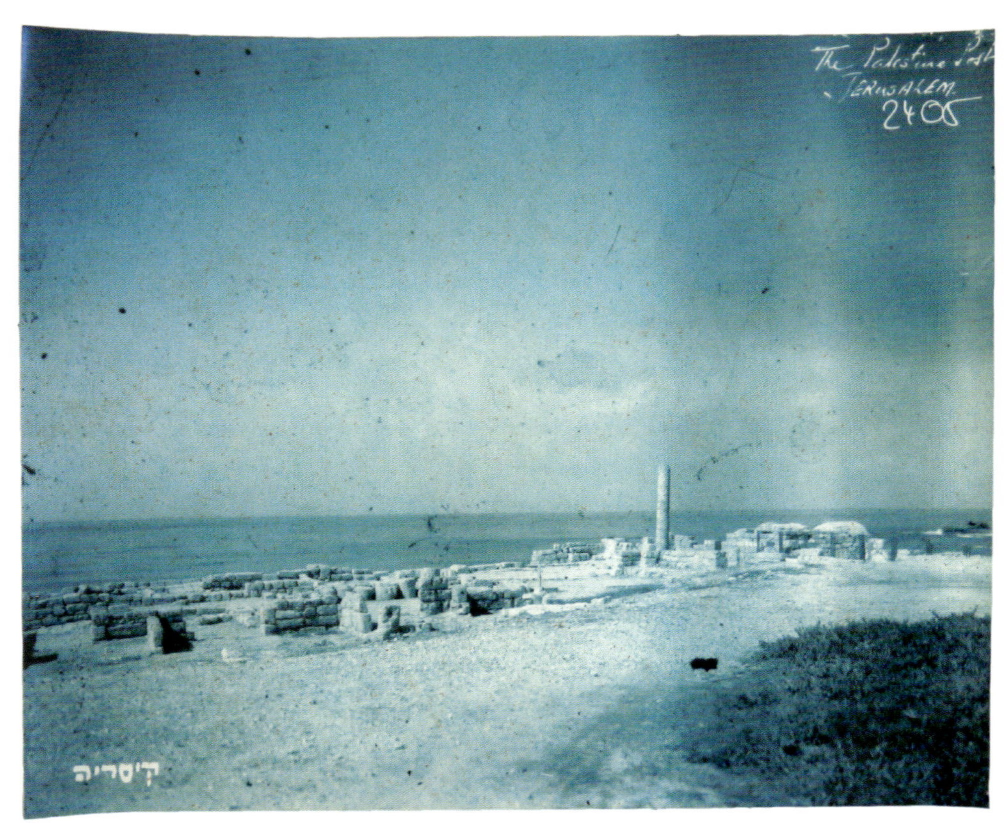

Caesarea I Palestine 1948 / 2016

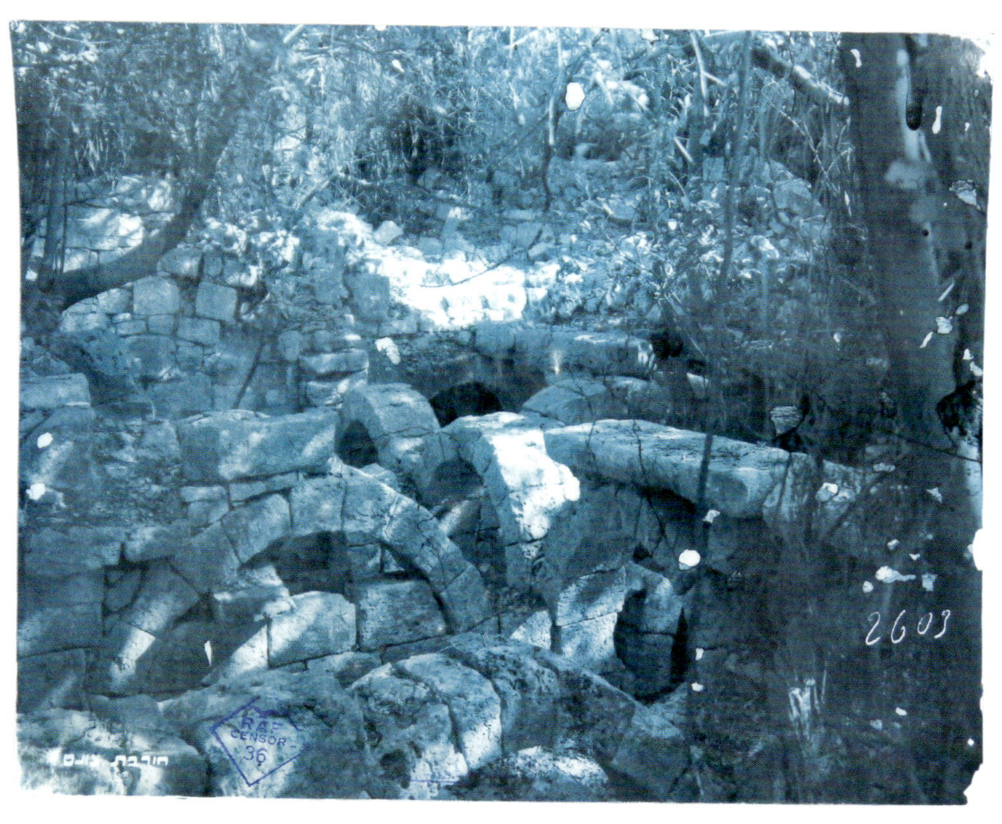

Hirbet Tzunam I Palestine 1948 / 2016

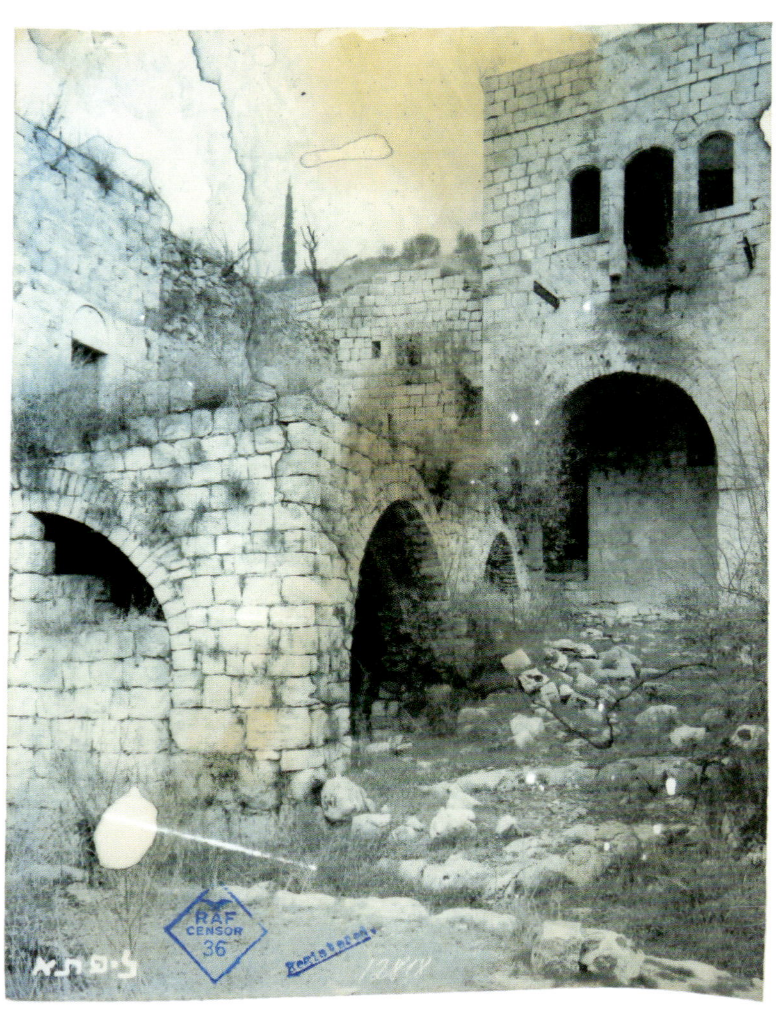

Lifta III Palestine 1948 / 2016

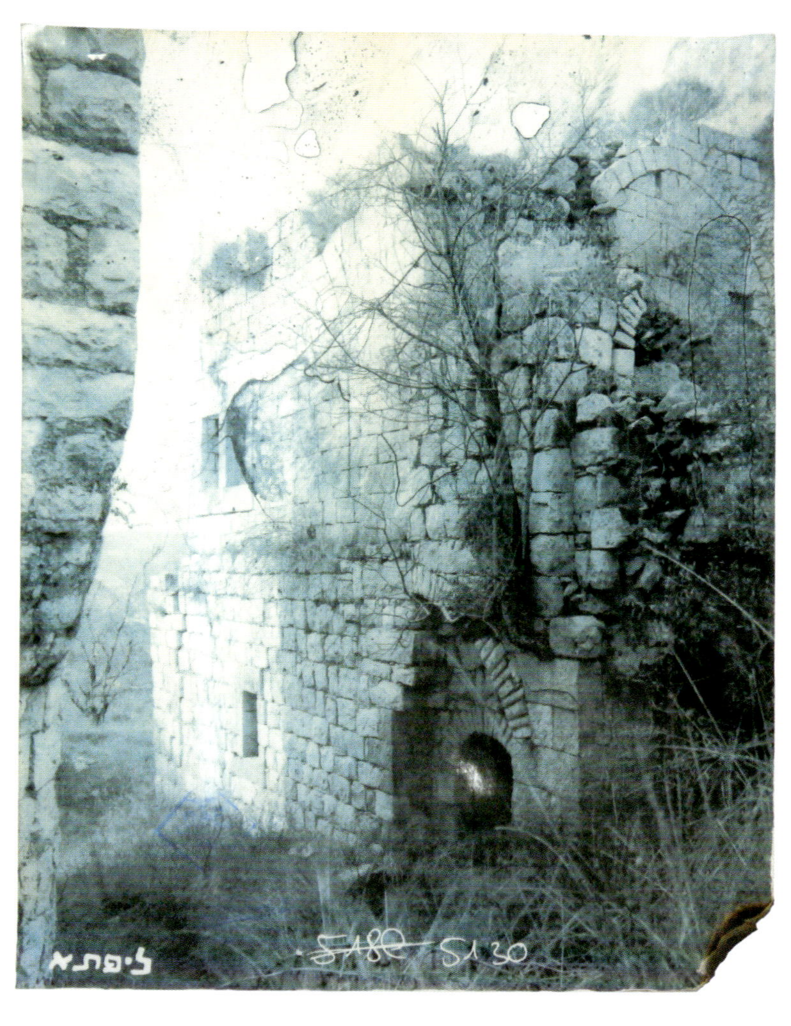

Lifta IV Palestine 1948 / 2016

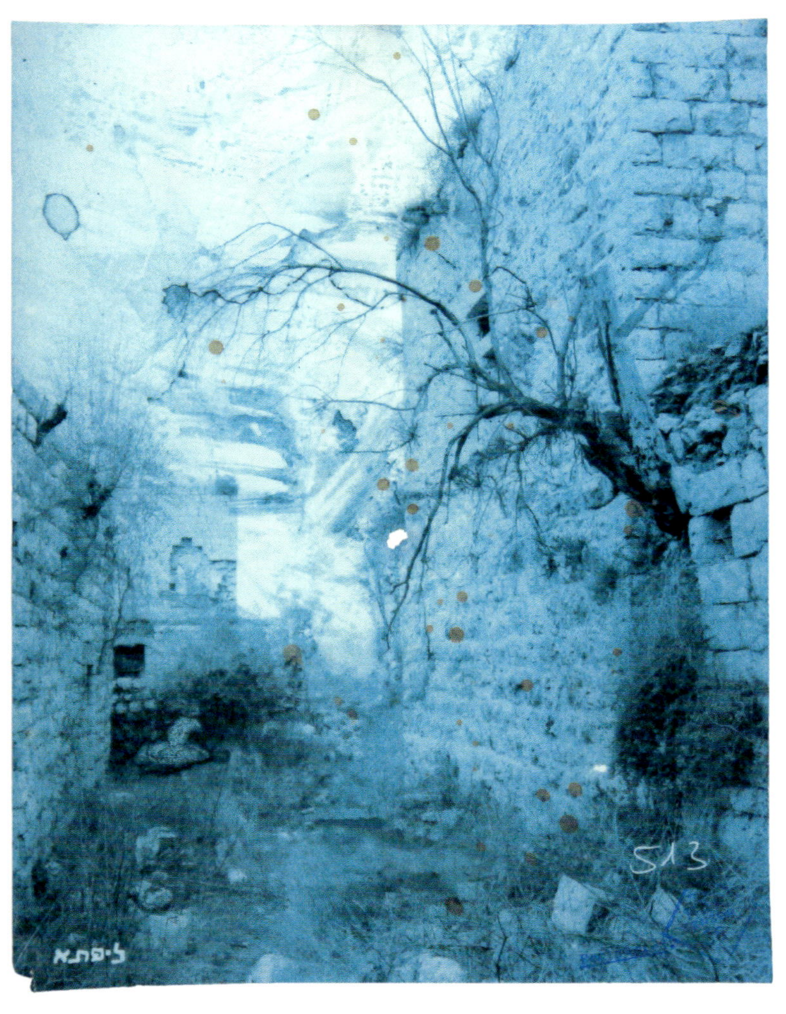

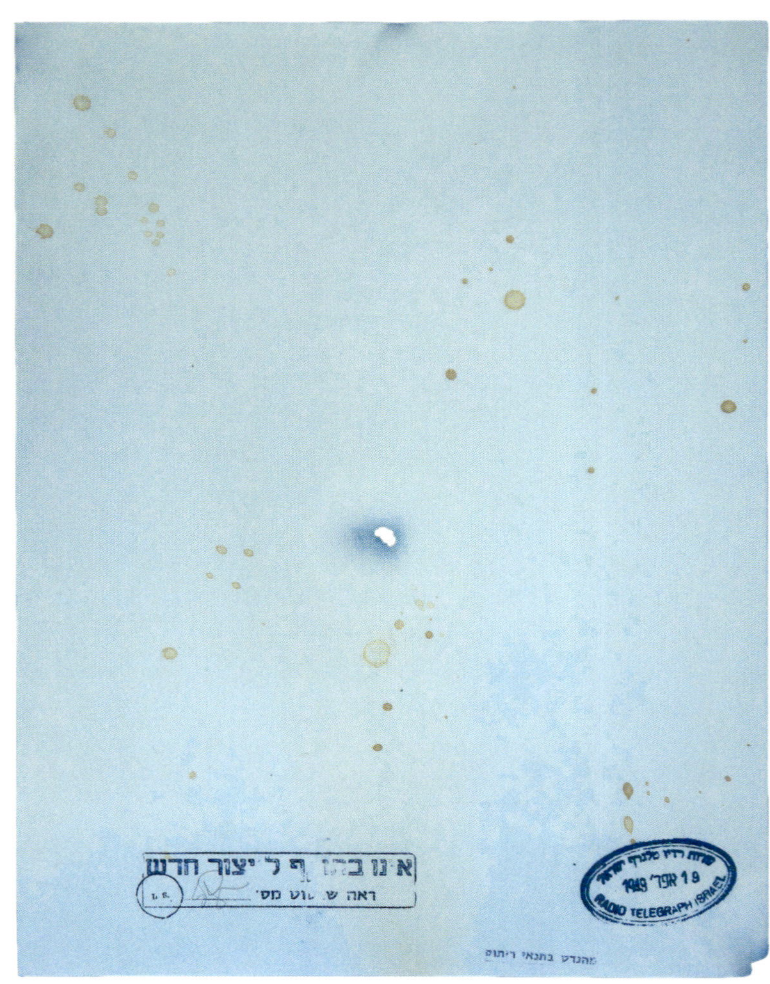

Lifta VII Palestine 1948 / 2016
Front and back

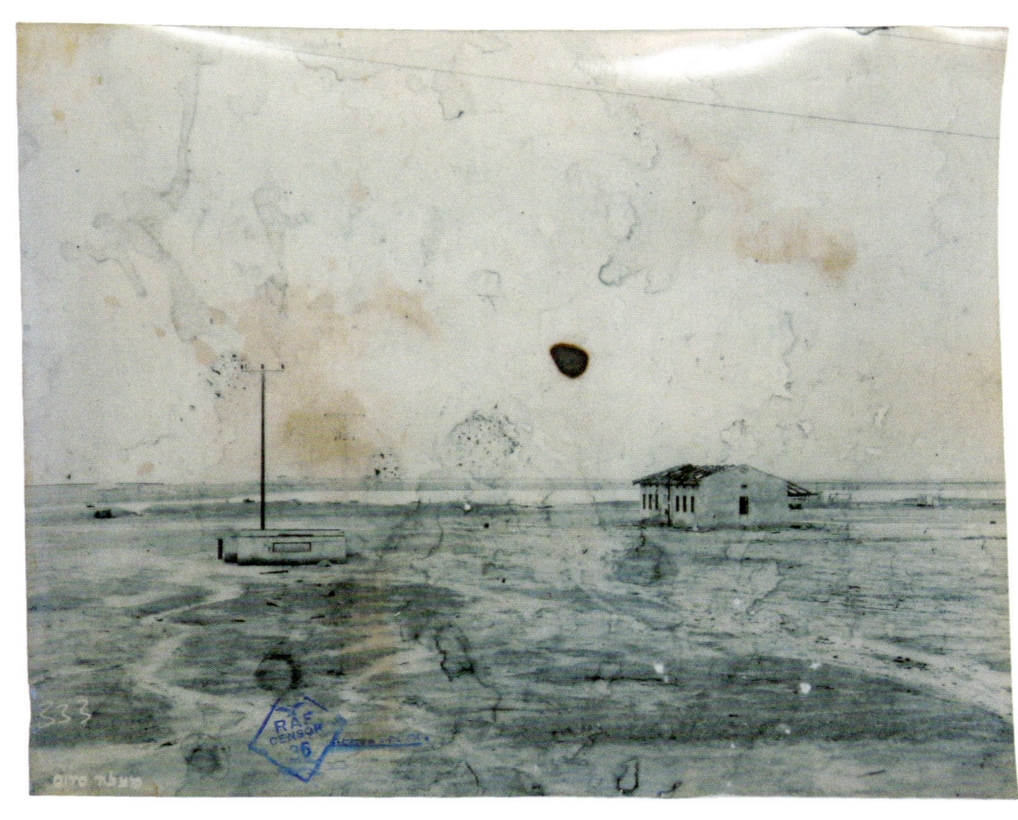

Maale Sdom Palestine 1948 / 2016

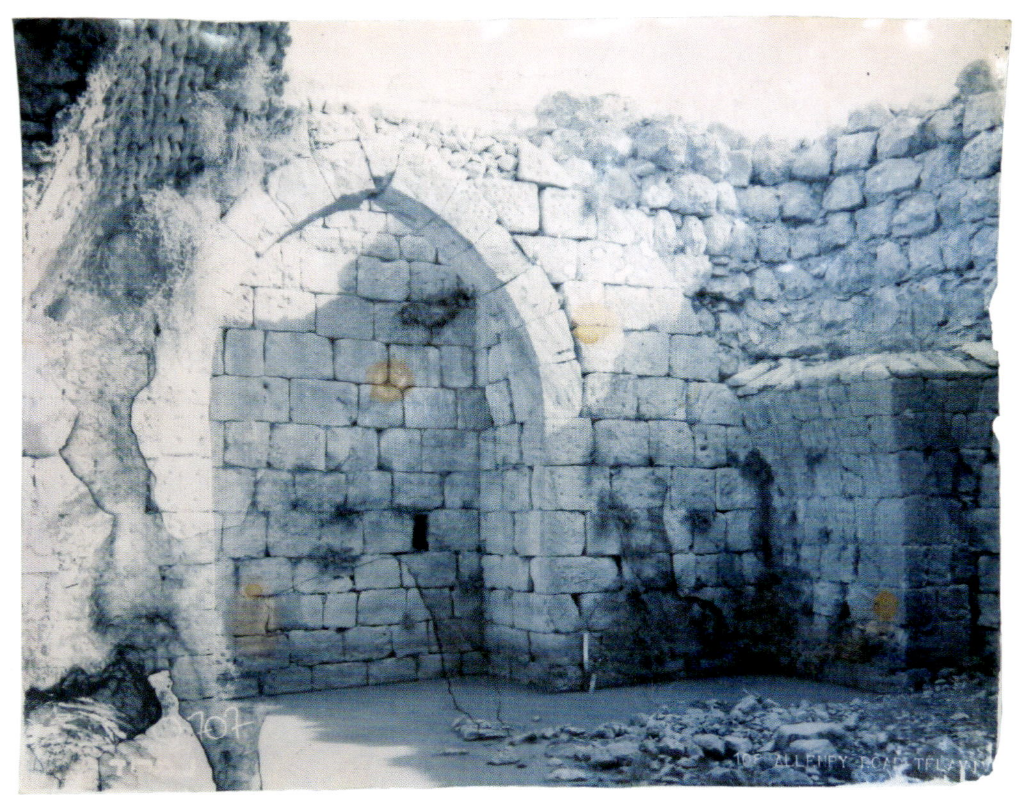

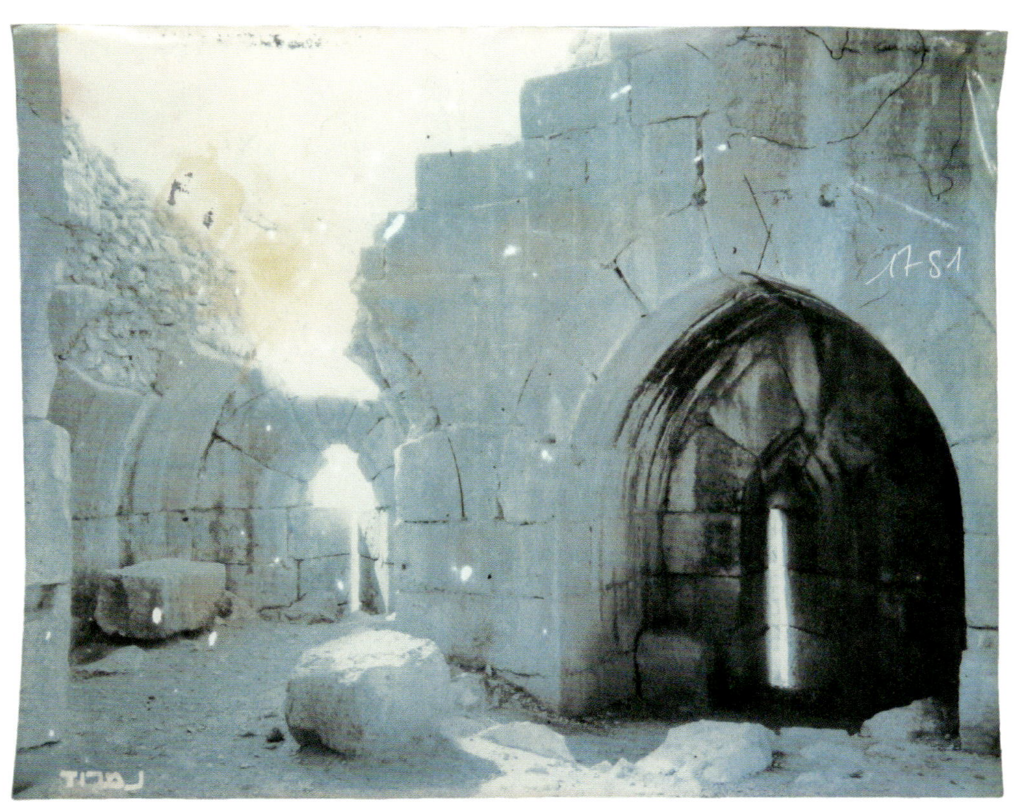

Nimrod II, III Palestine 1948 / 2016

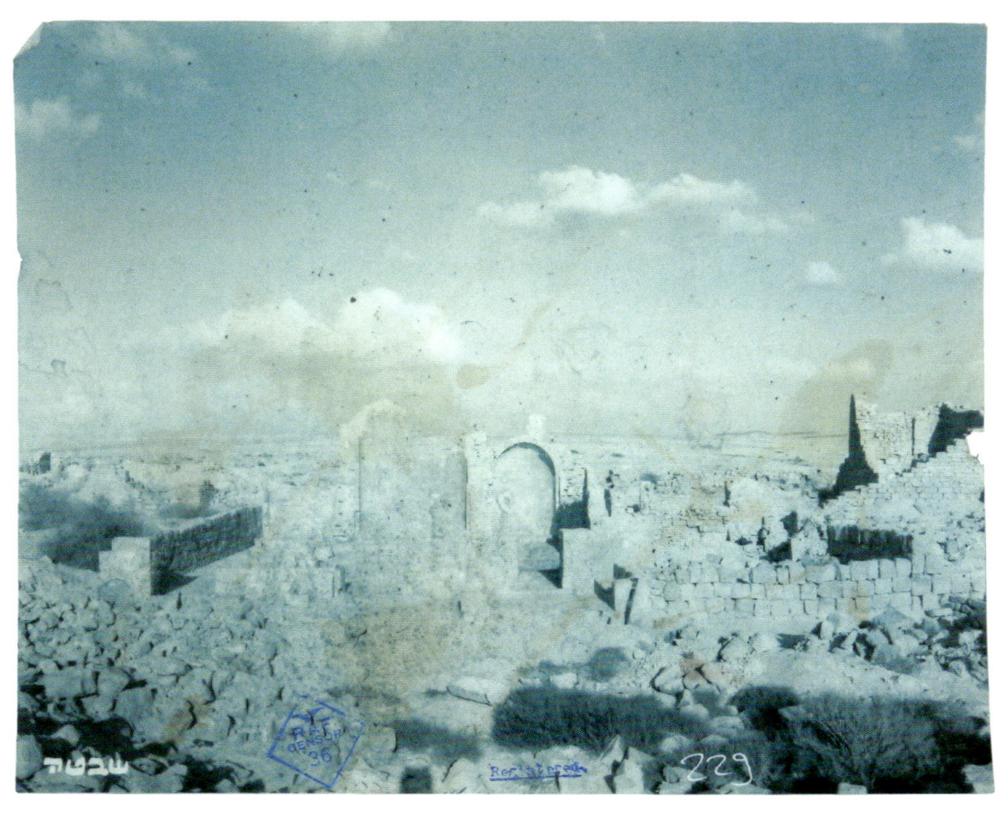

Shivta IV Palestine 1948 / 2016

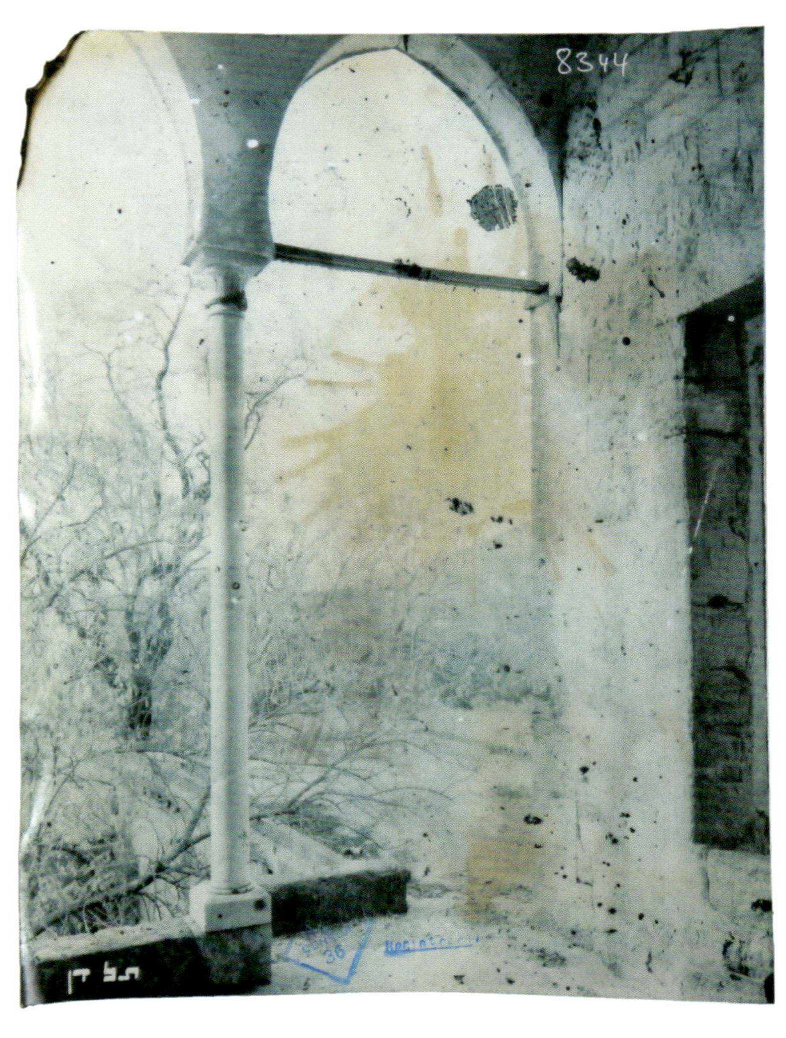

Tel Dan Palestine 1948 / 2016

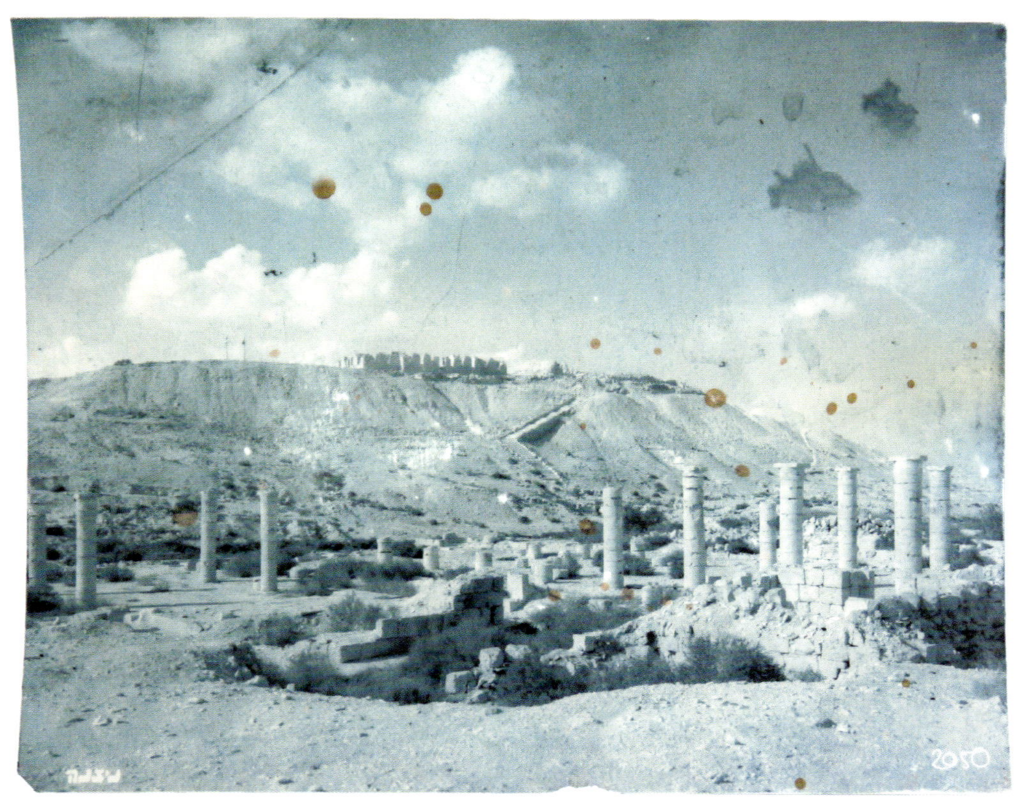

Nizzana Palestine 1948 / 2016

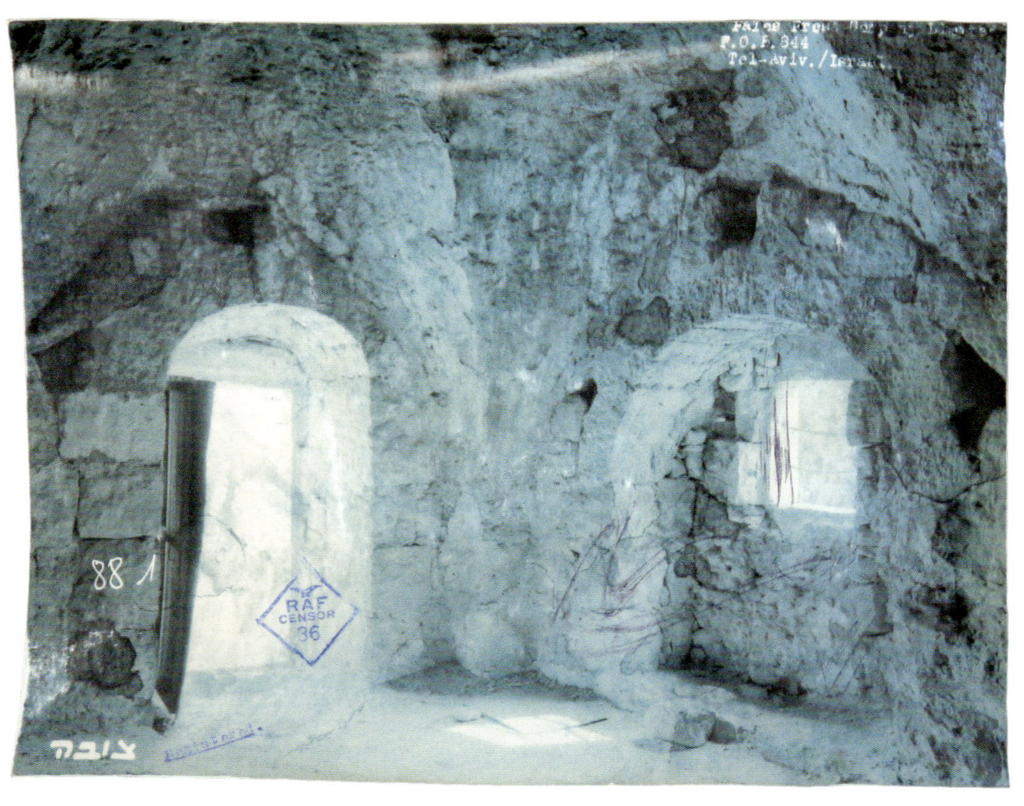
88 1
RAF
CENSOR
36
צובה

One Sky

Israel / Lebanon, 2015

One Sky I

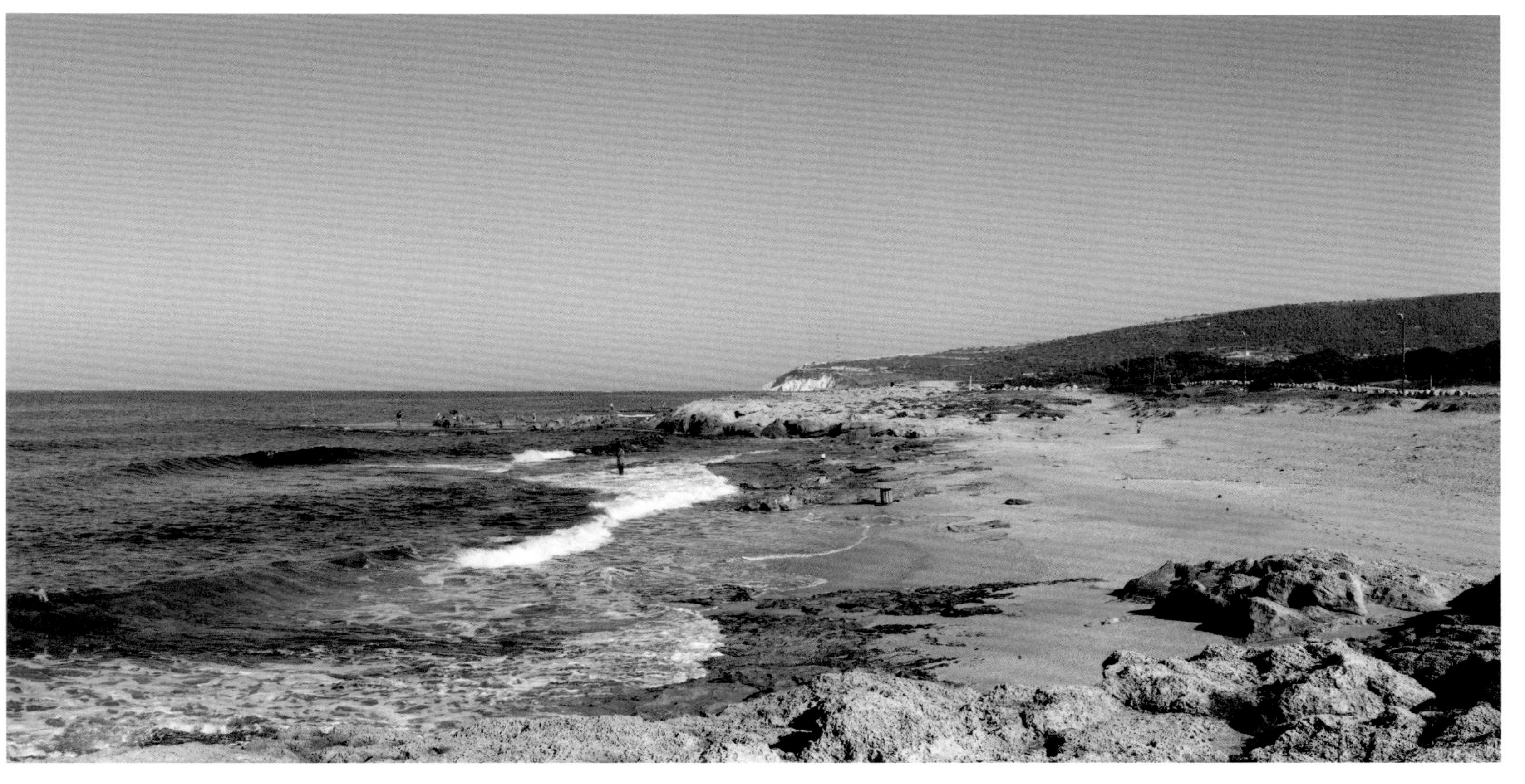

Liman Israel | 12-11-2015 | 9.00

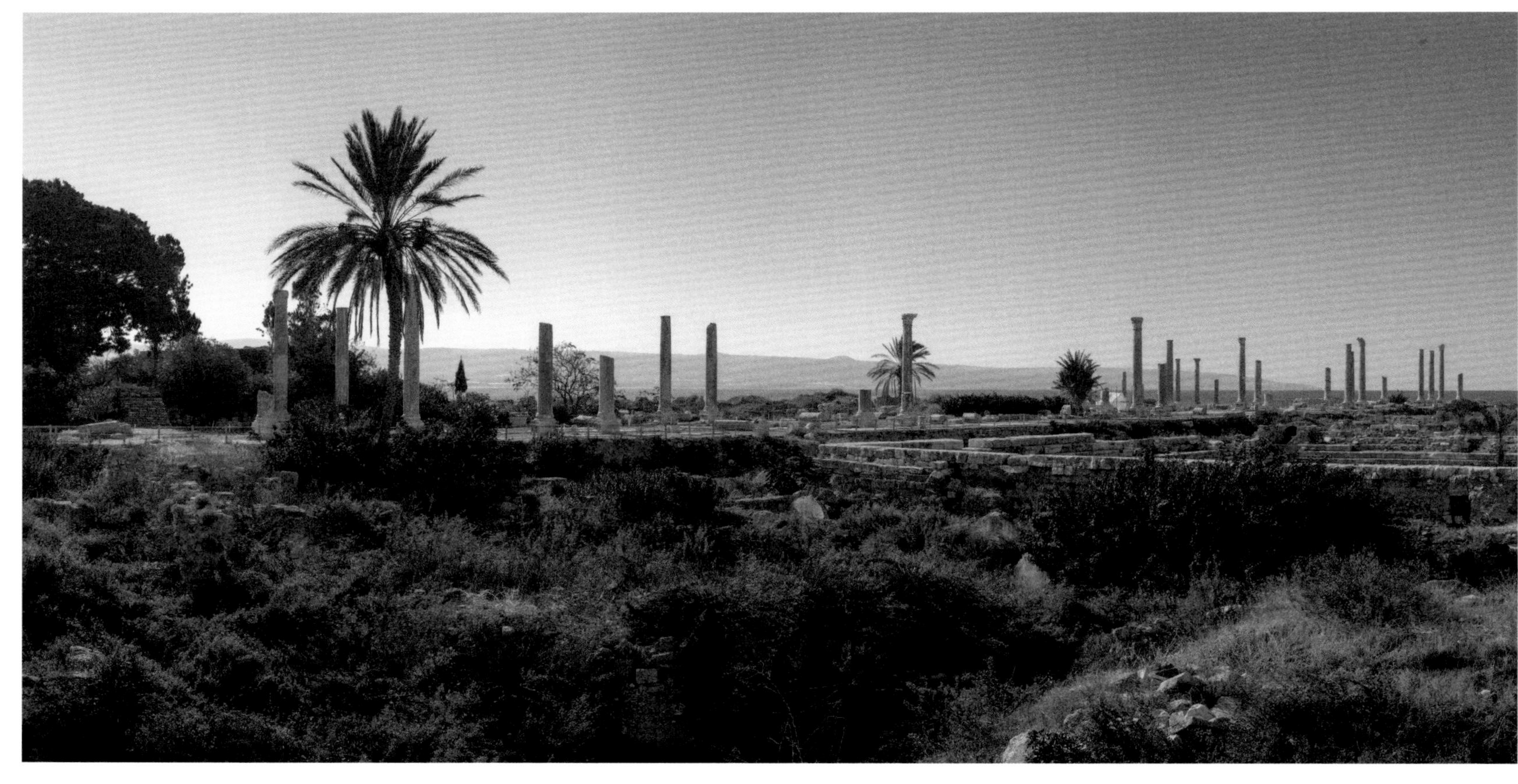

Tyre Lebanon | 12-11-2015 | 9.00

One Sky II

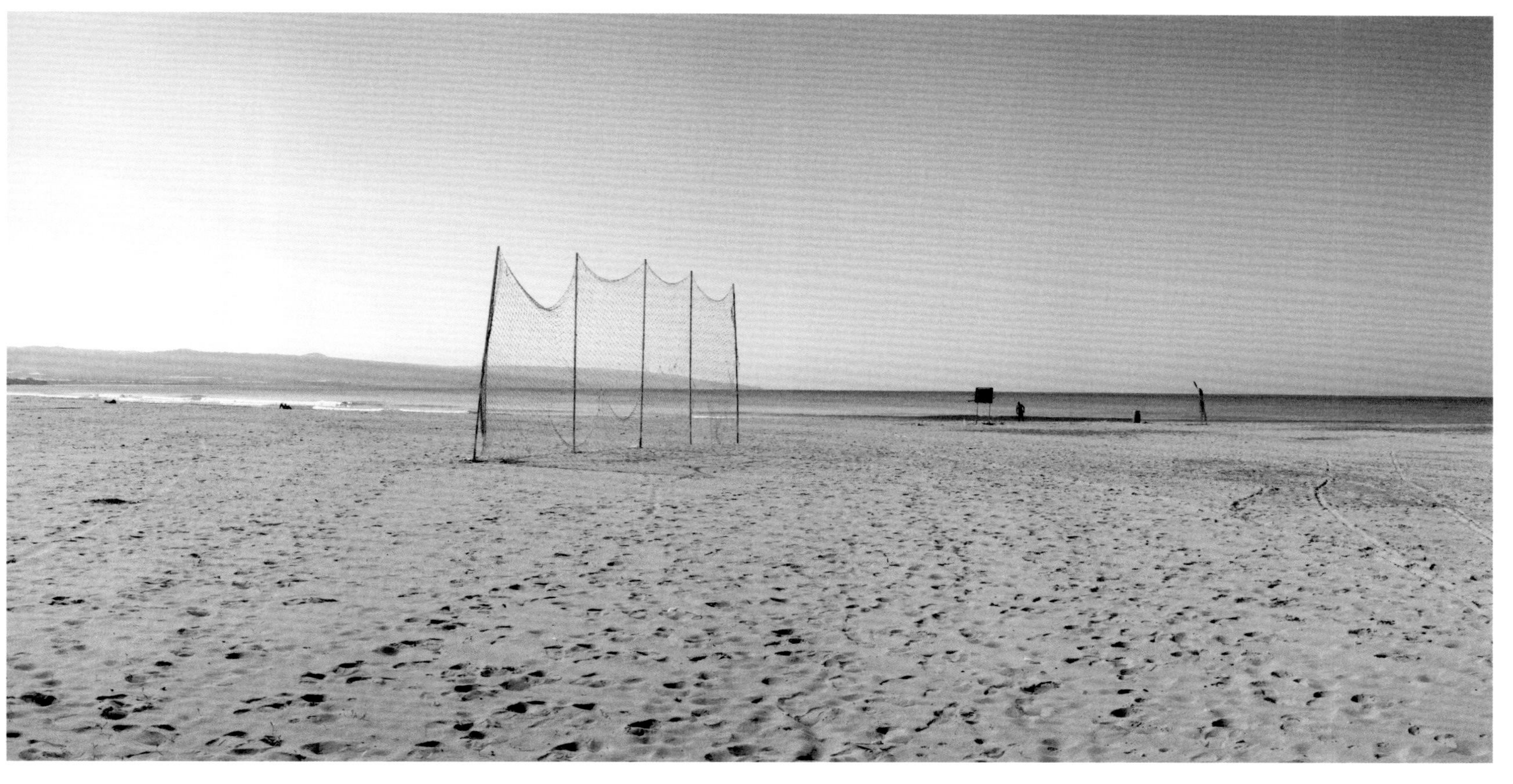

Sour Lebanon | 12-11-2015 | 10.00

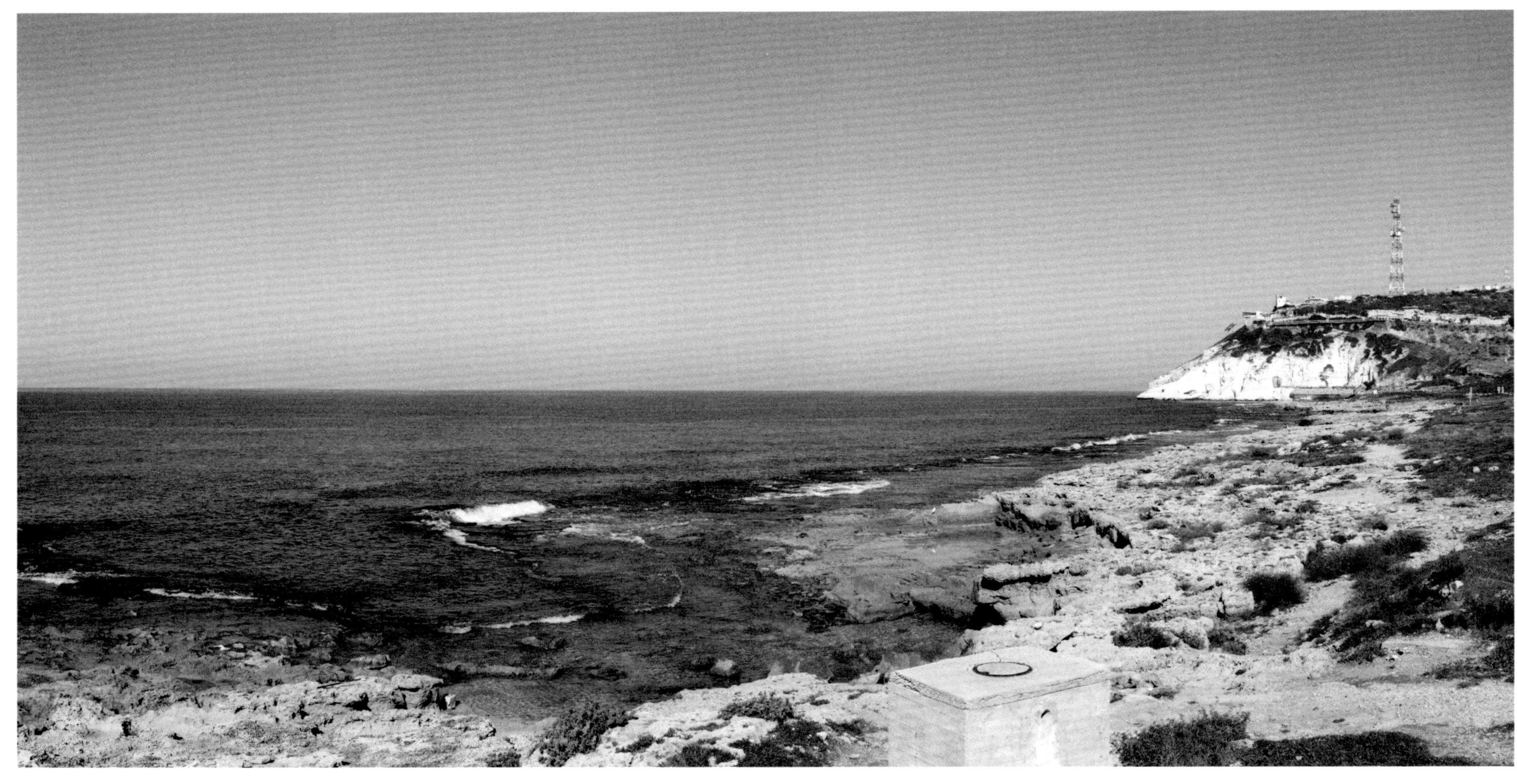

Rosch haNikra Israel | 12-11-2015 | 10.00

I.7

One Sky III

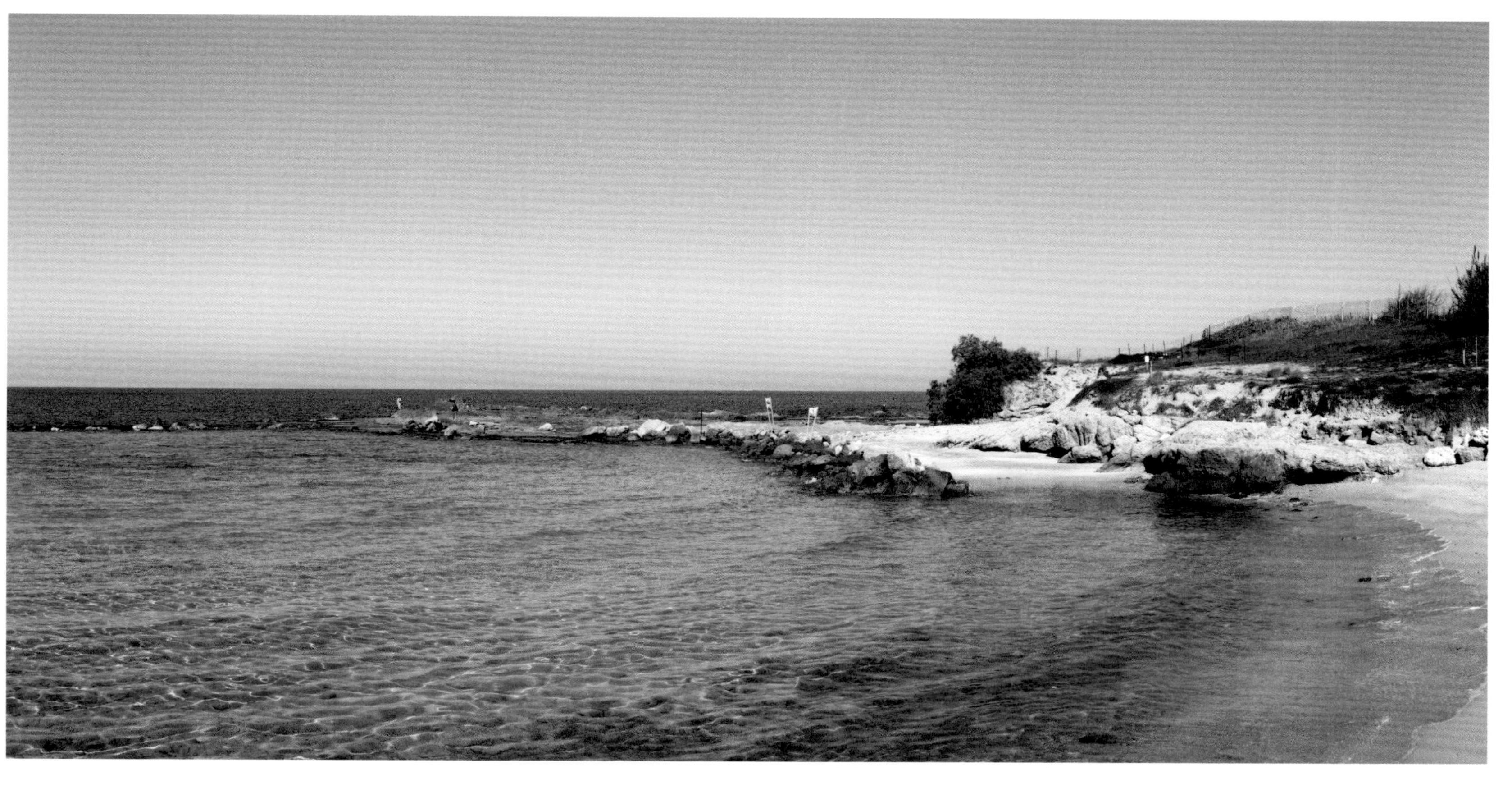

Liman Israel | 12-11-2015 | 11.00

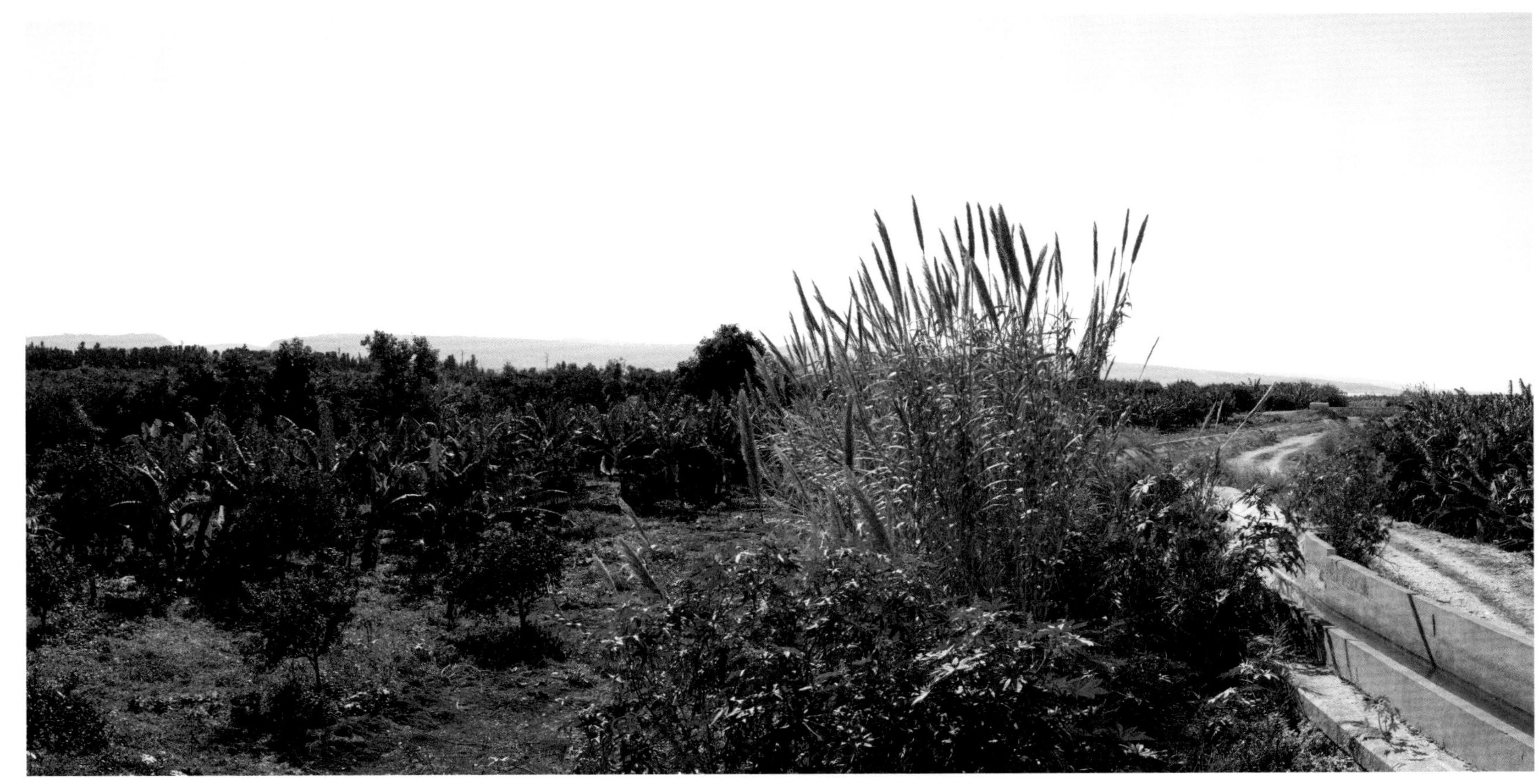

Rachidiyeh Lebanon | 12-11-2015 | 11.00

11.

One Sky IV

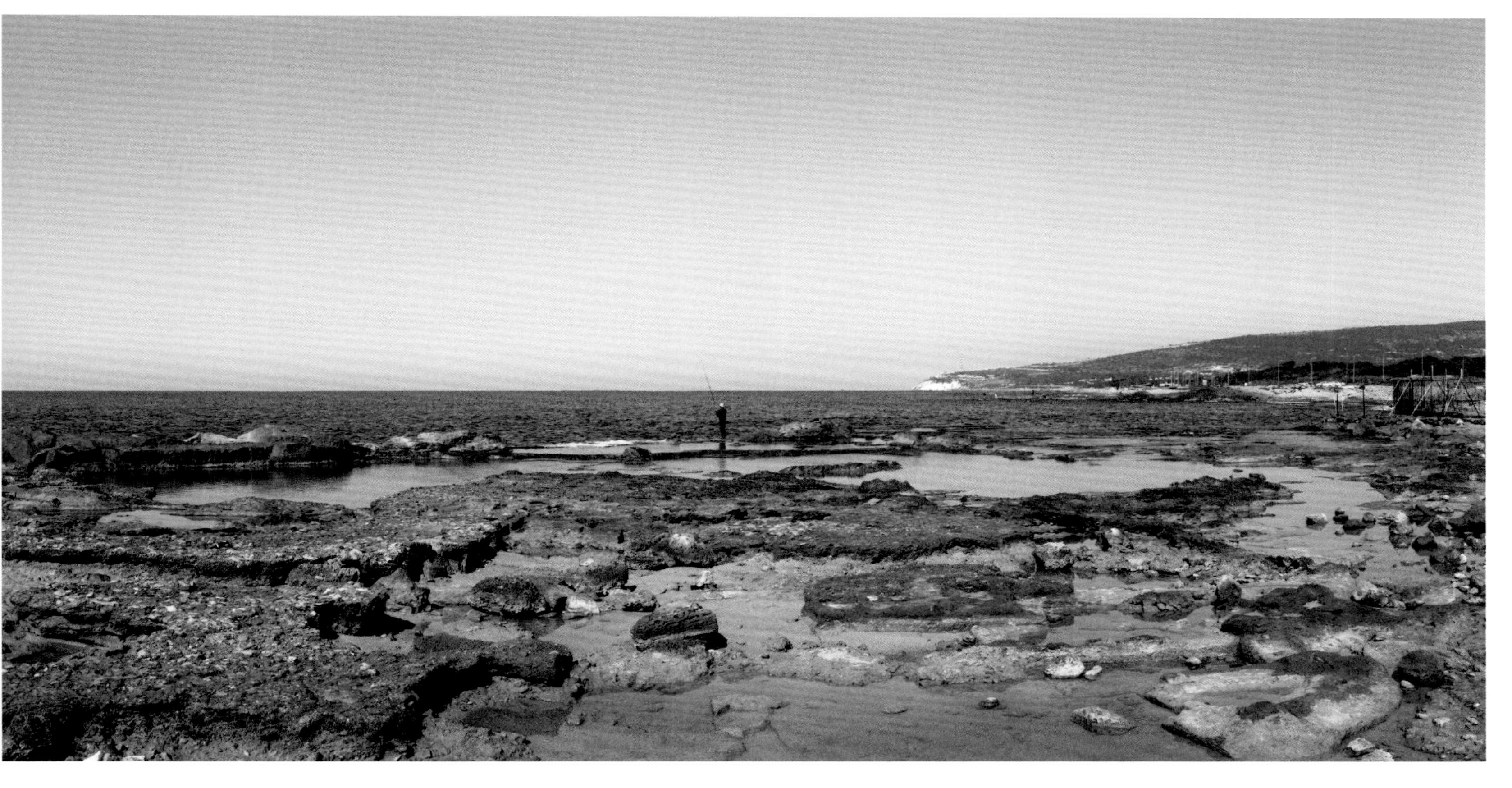

Liman II Israel | 12-11-2015 | 12.00

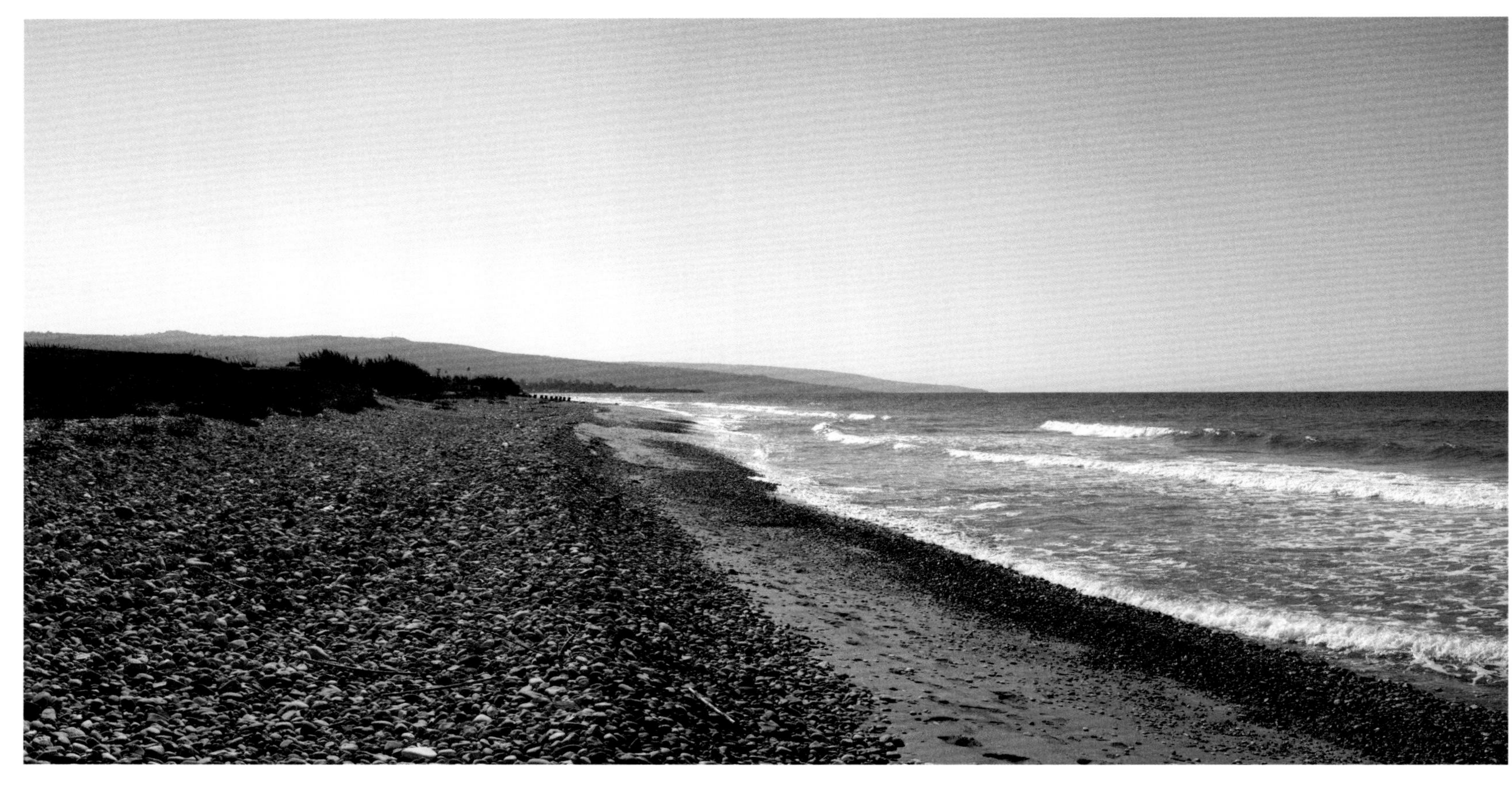

Rachidiyeh II Lebanon | 12-11-2015 | 12.00

One Sky VIII

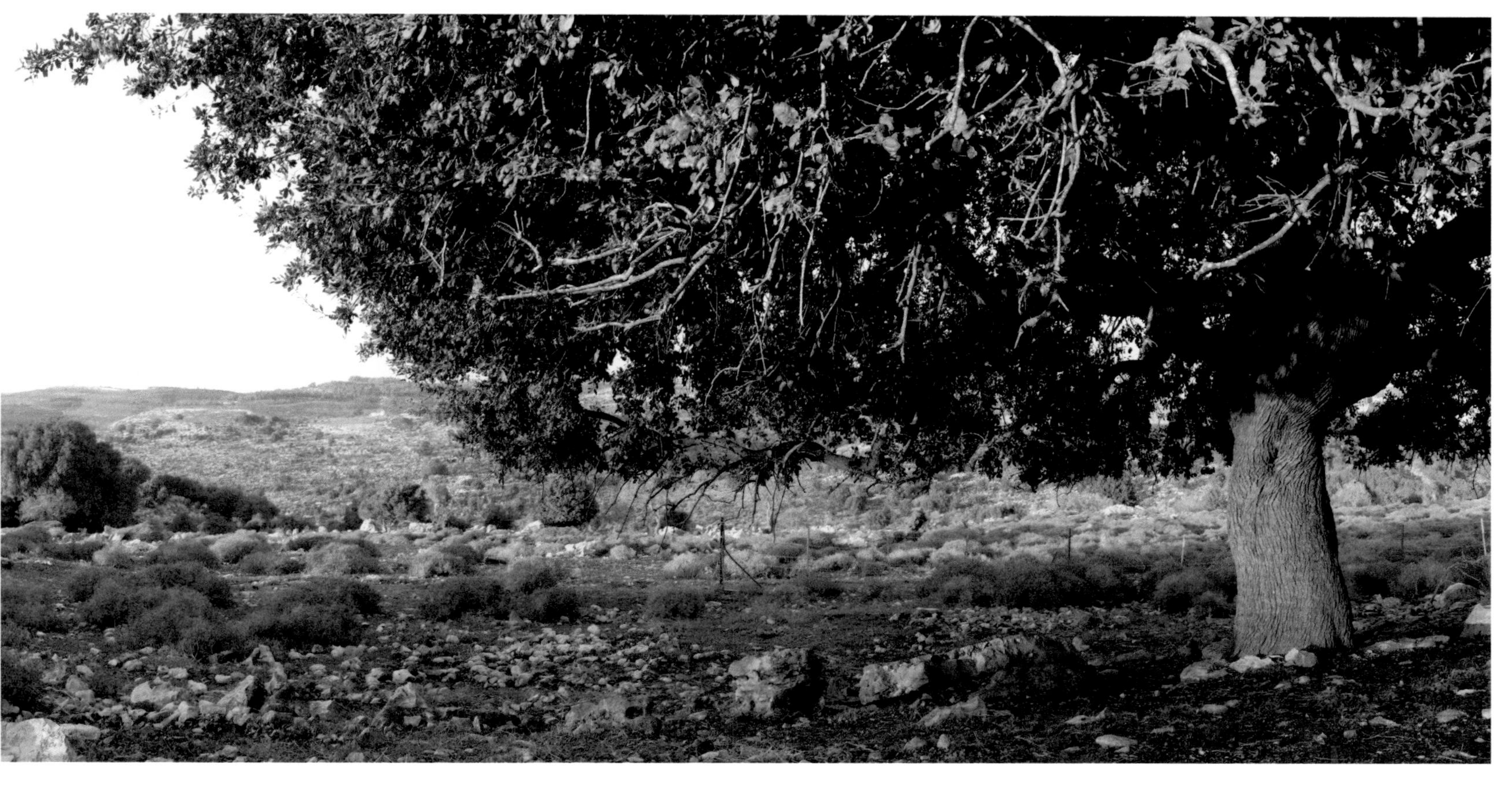

Arav Al AramSha Israel | 12-11-2015 | 16.00

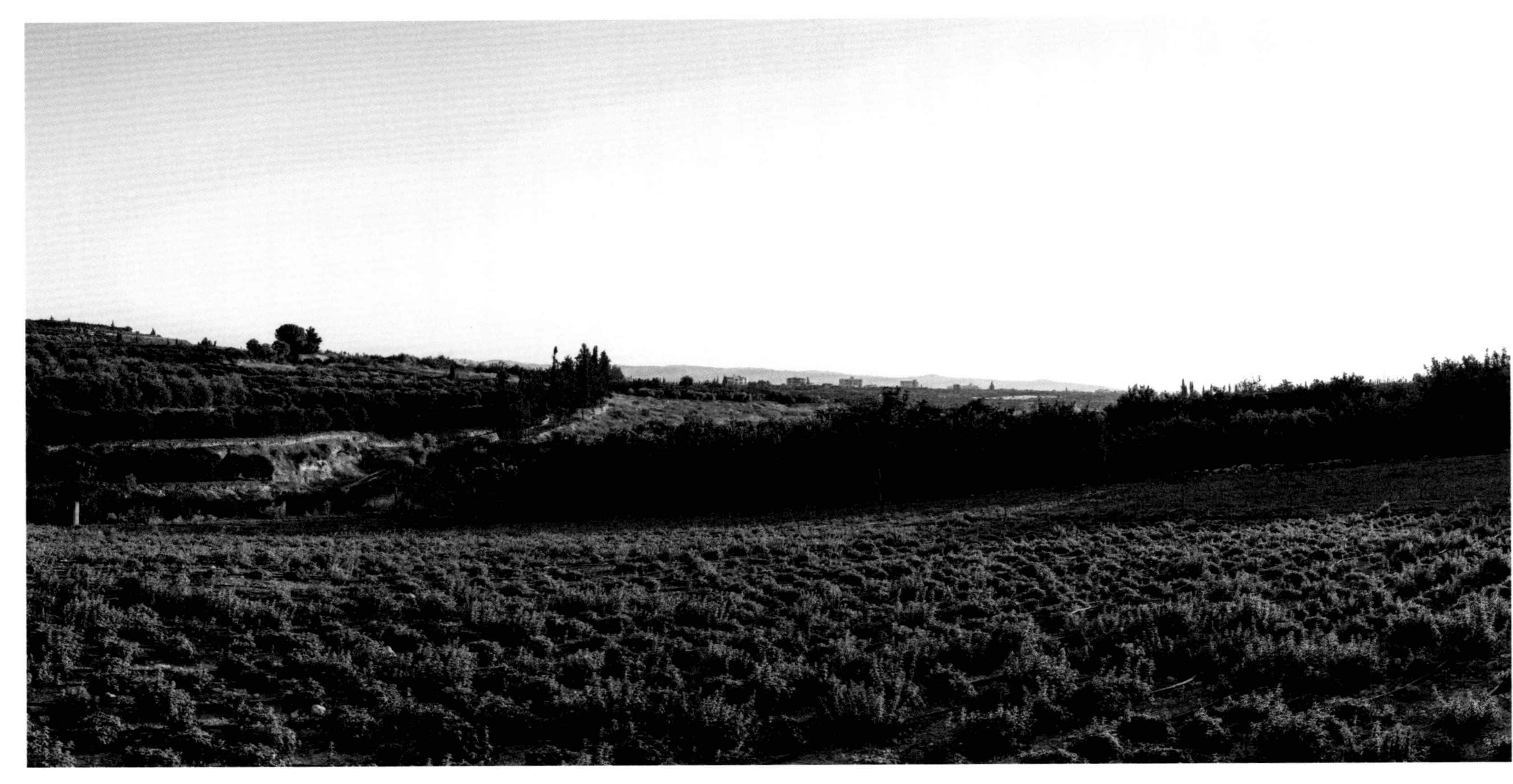

Bazouriye Lebanon | 12-11-2015 | 16.00

One Sky IX

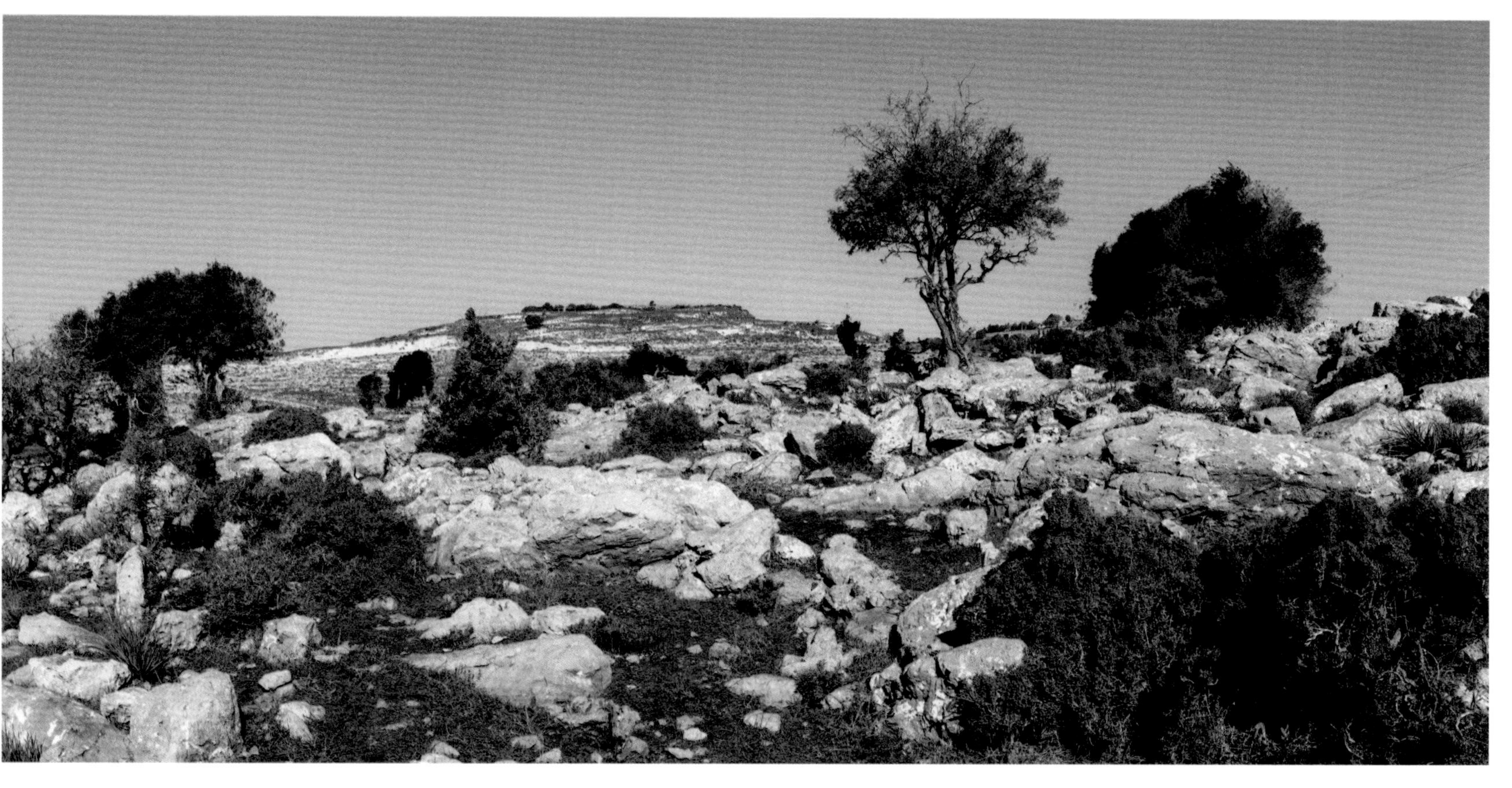

Adamit Israel | 13-11-2015 | 10.00

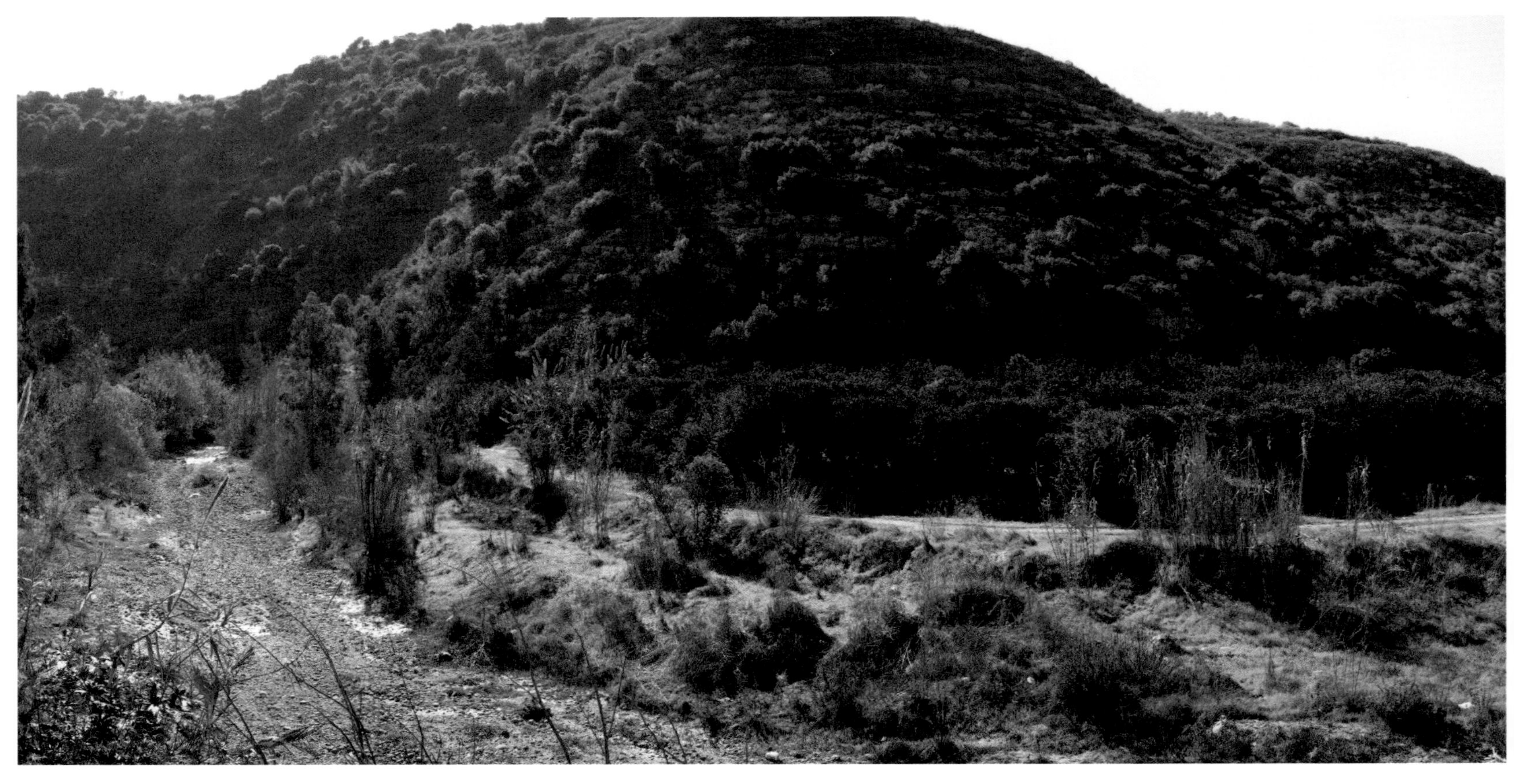

Zrariyeh, I Lebanon | 13-11-2015 | 10.00

One Sky XI

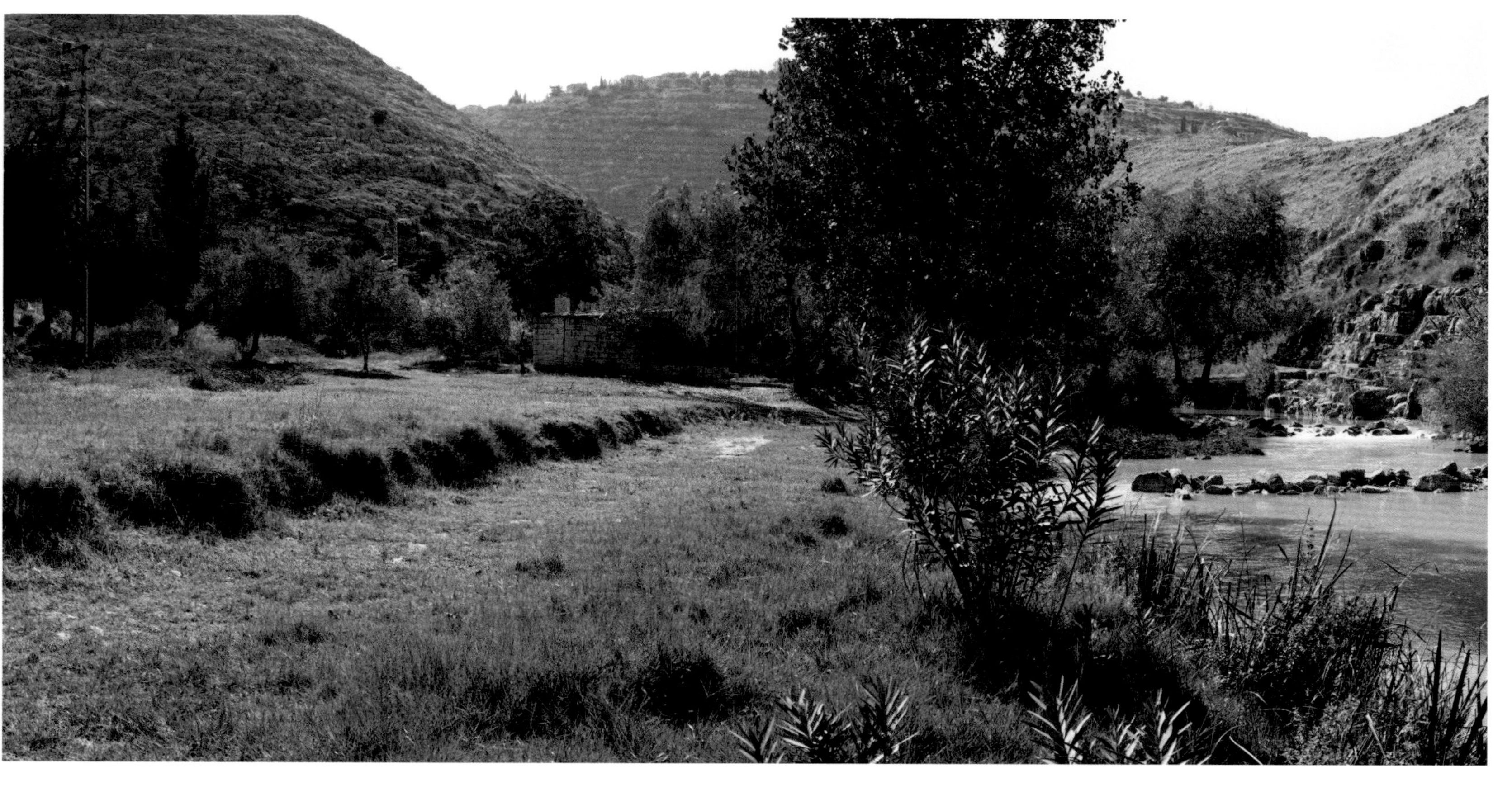

Sir El Gharbyeh Lebanon | 13-11-2015 | 12.00

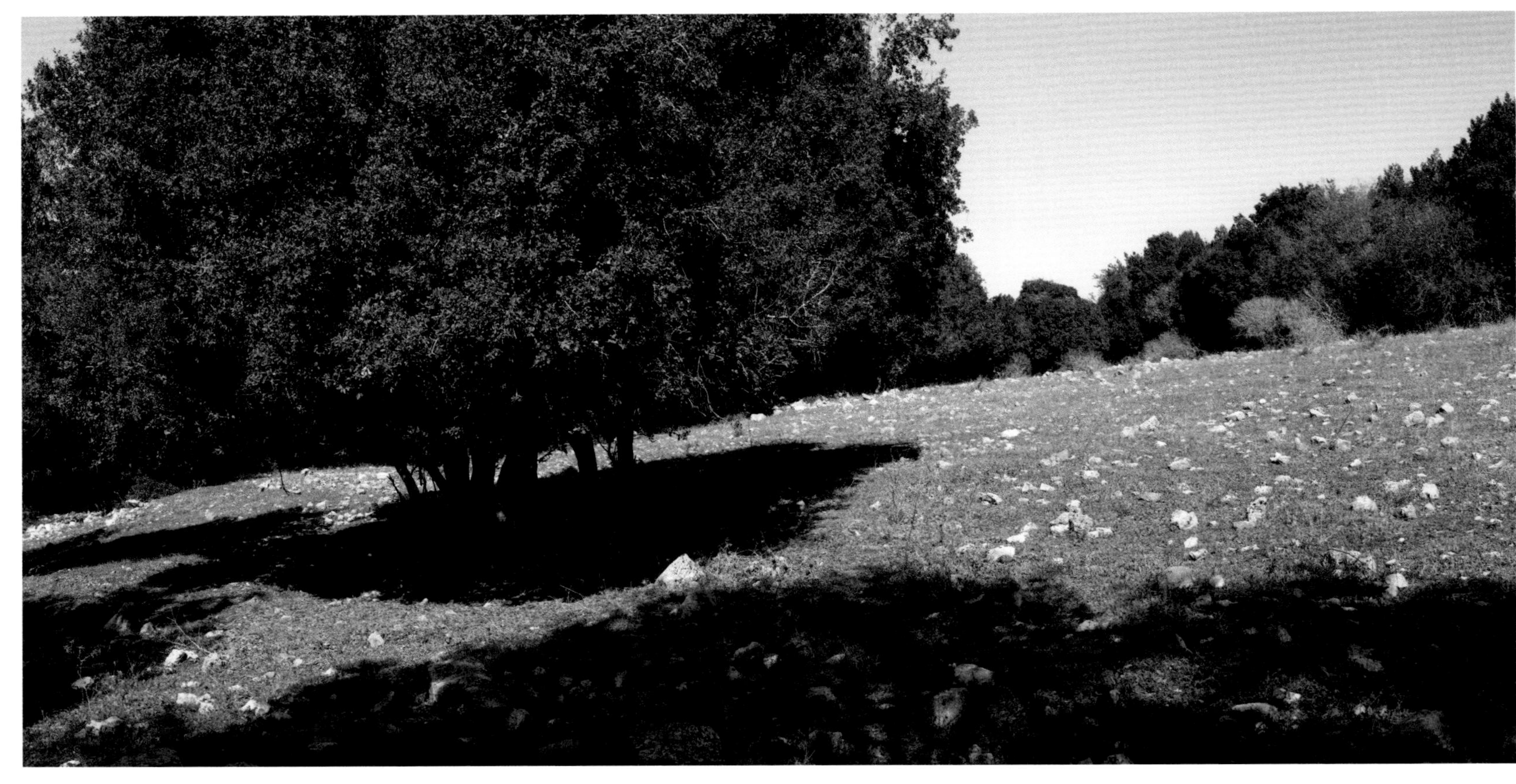

Even Menahem Israel | 13-11-2015 | 12.00

One Sky XII

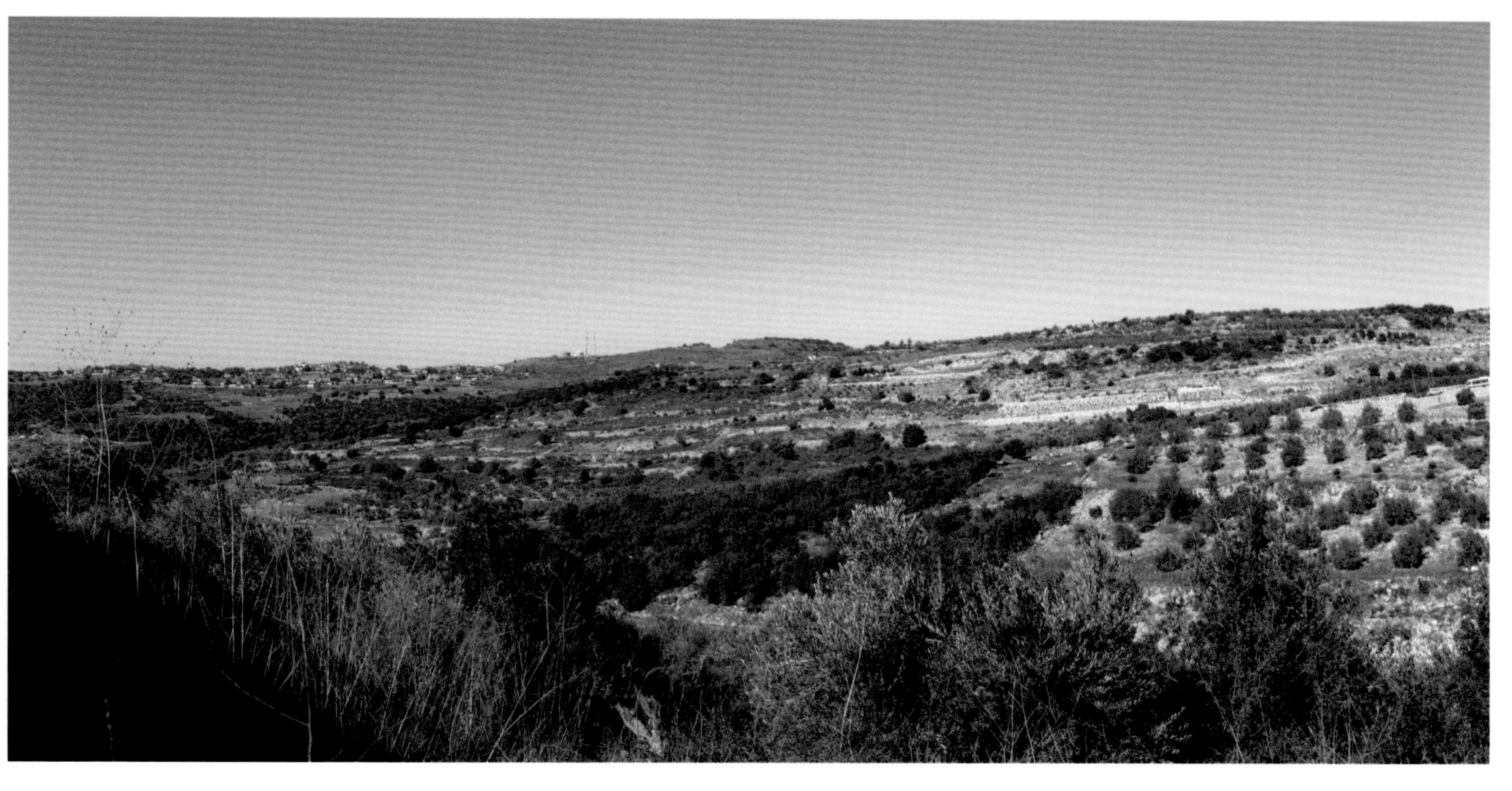

Netu'a Israel | 13-11-2015 | 13.00

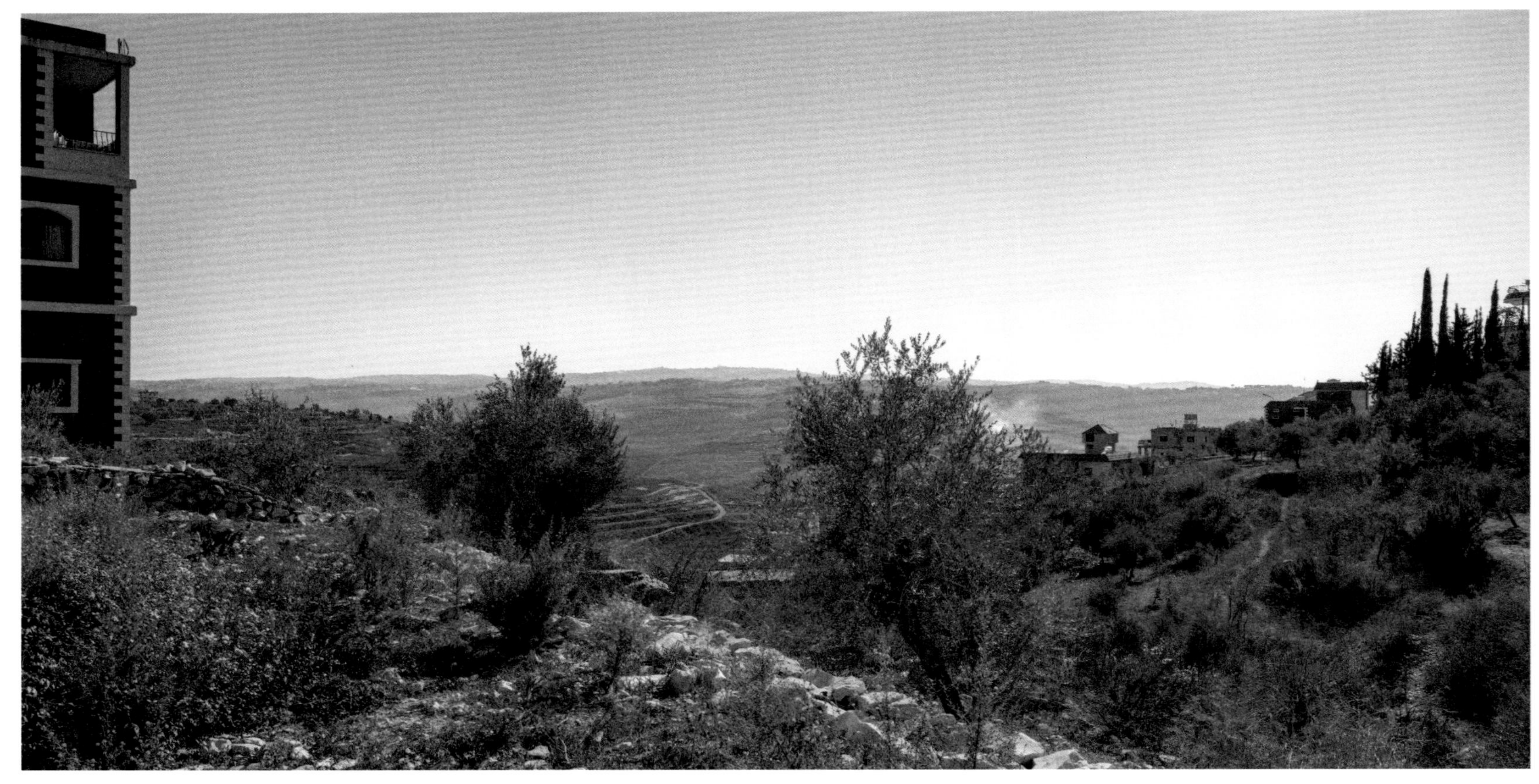

Kfar Sir Lebanon | 13-11-2015 | 13.00

One Sky XX

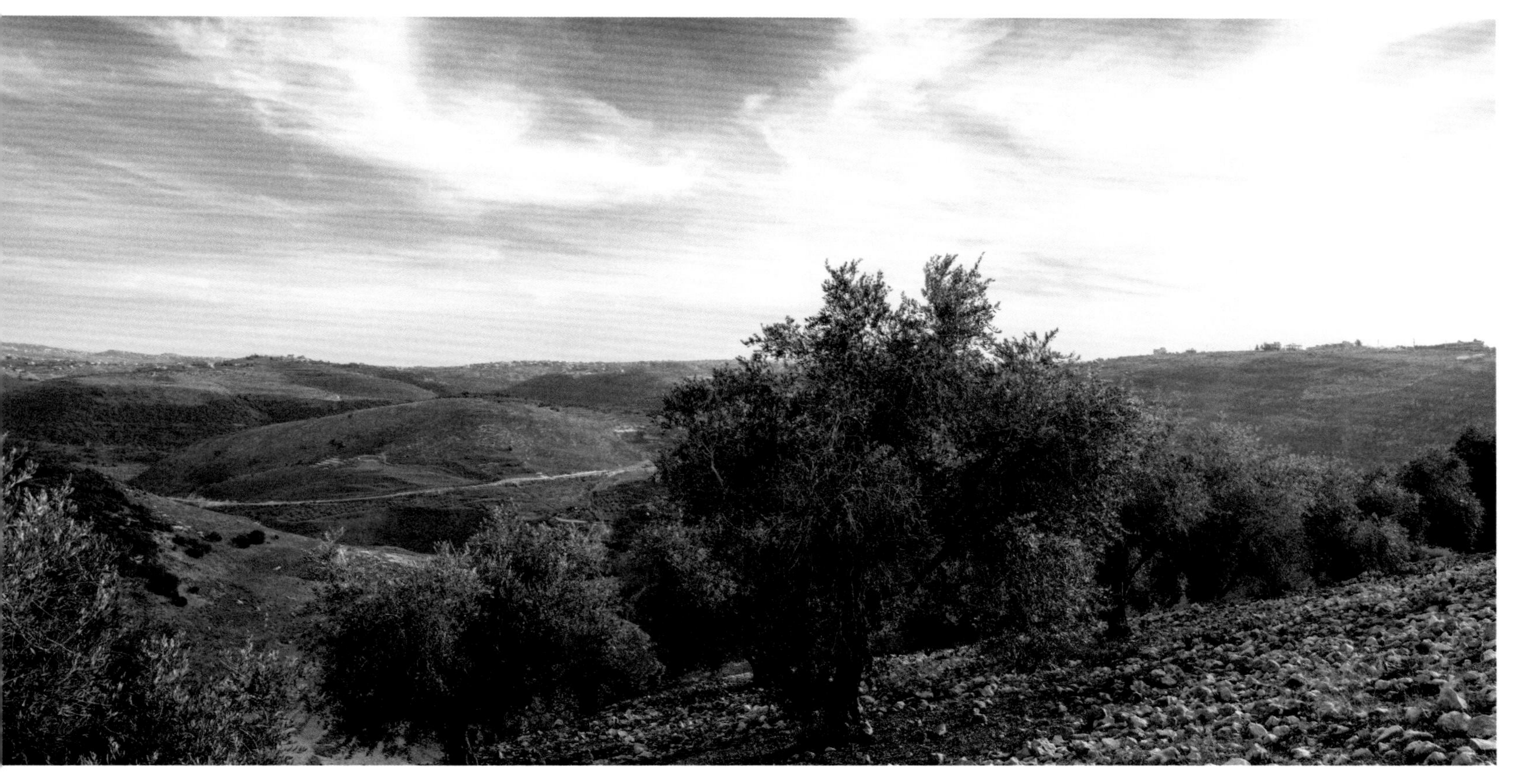

Froun Lebanon | 14-11-2015 | 15.00

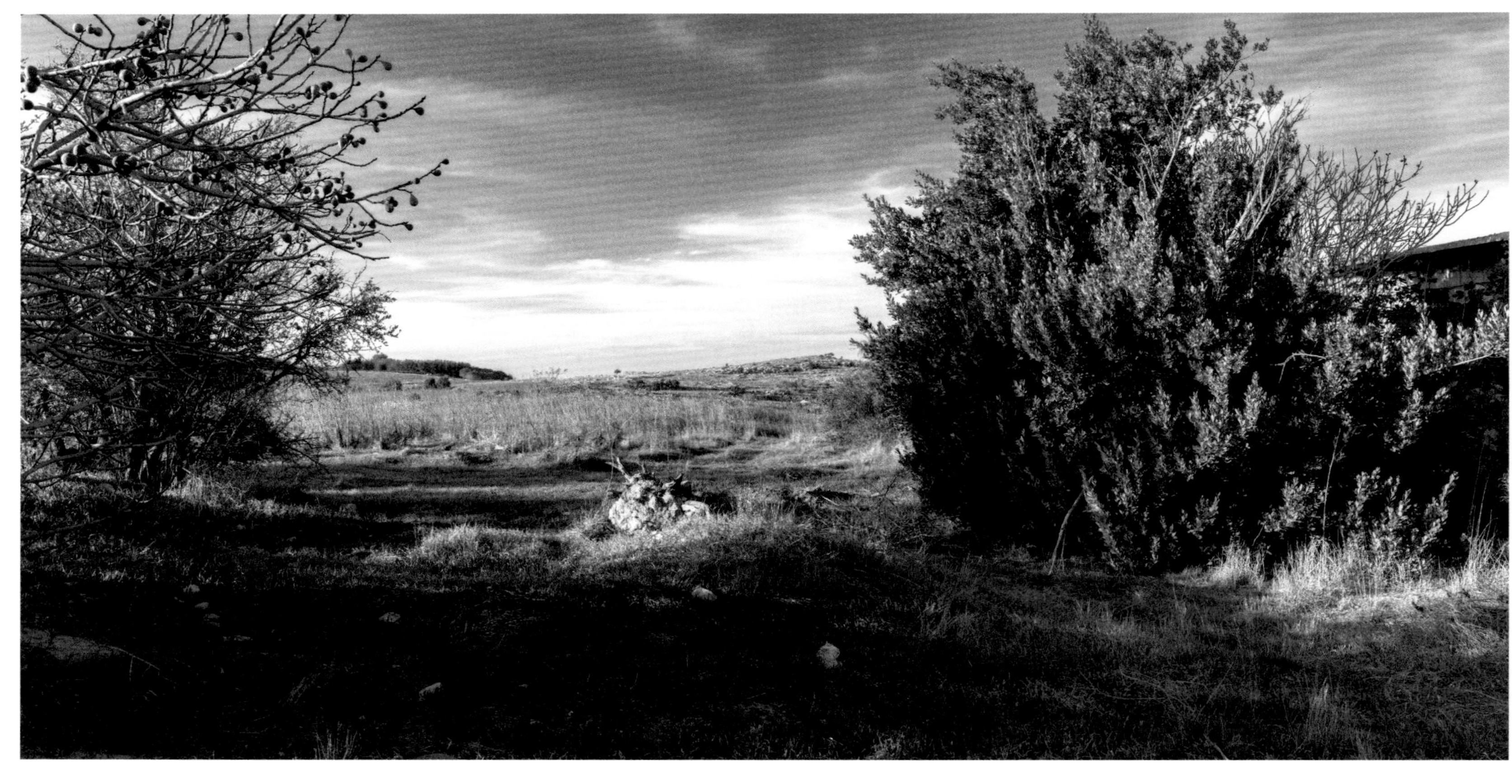

Elkosh Israel | 14-11-2015 | 15.00

مصر EGYPT

2011

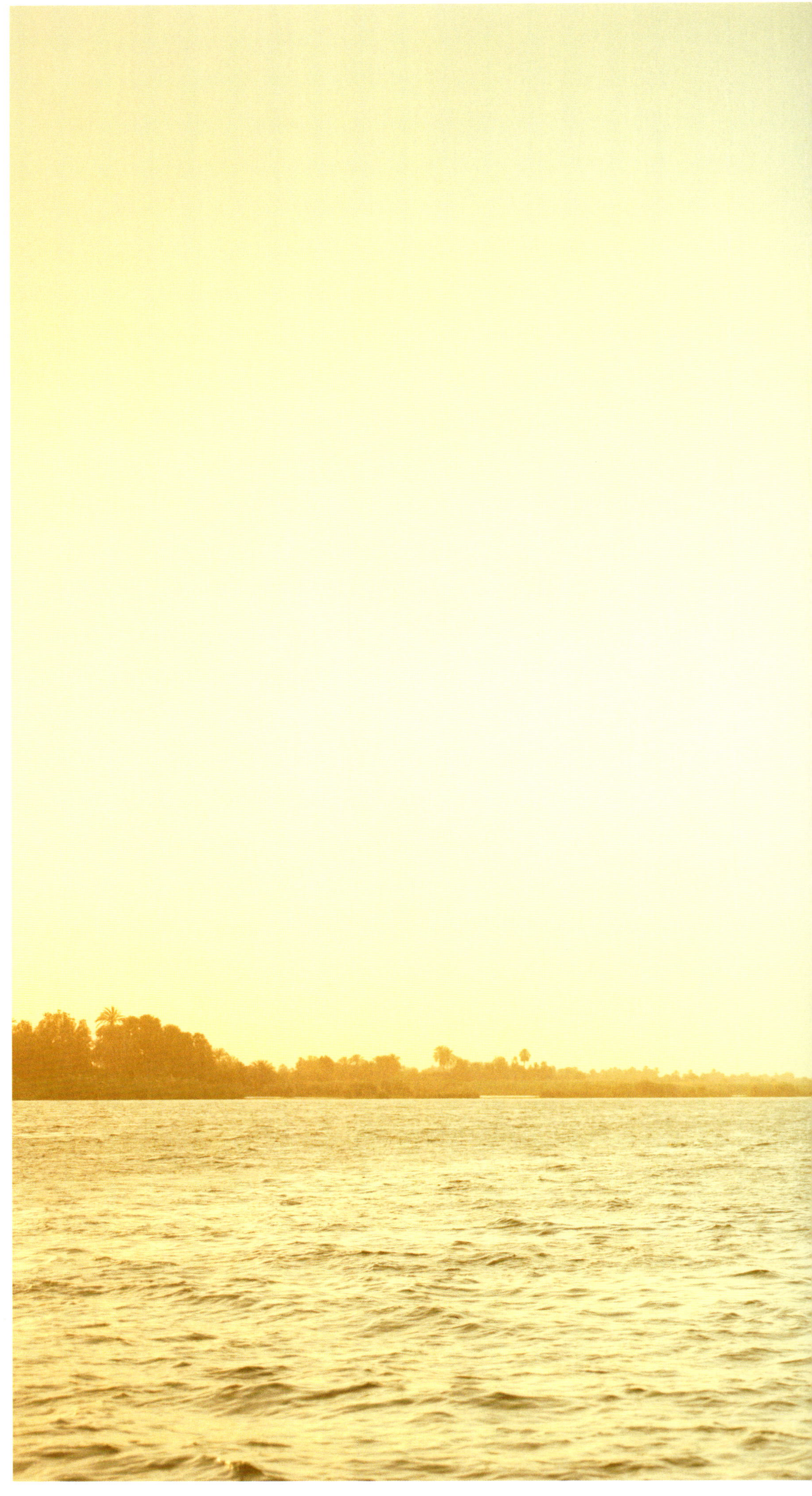

Nile I 2011

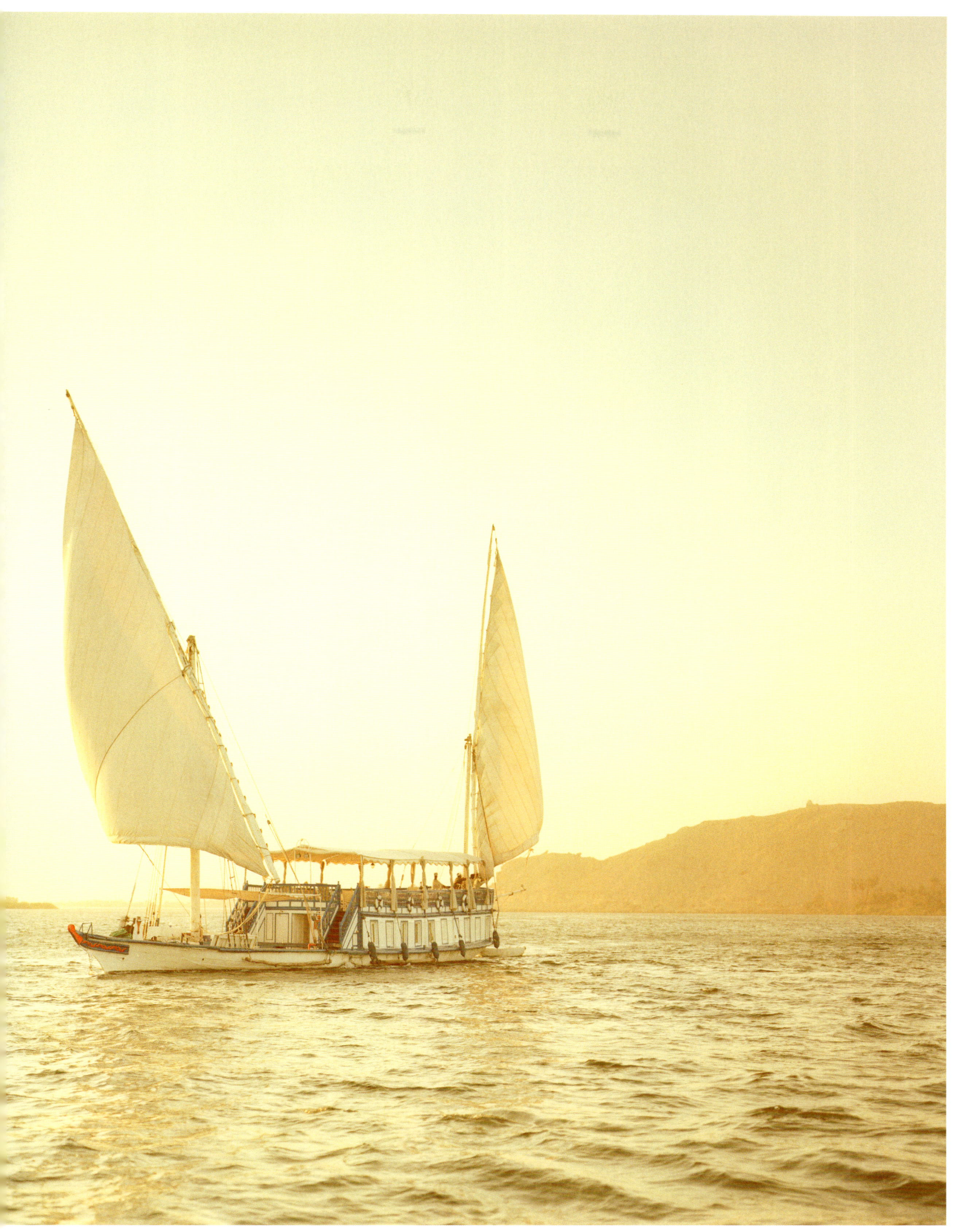

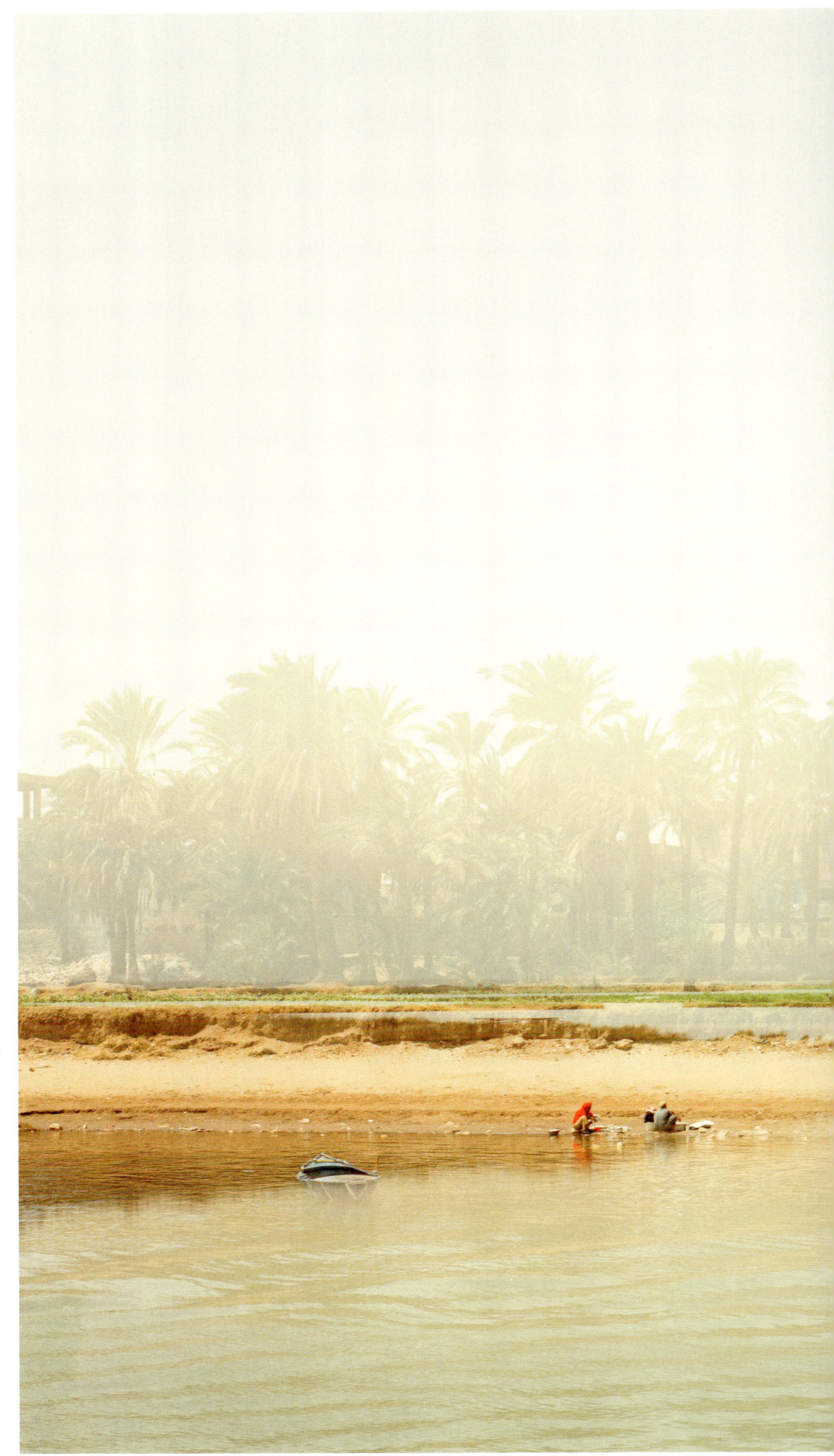

Fata Morgana 2011

١٤.

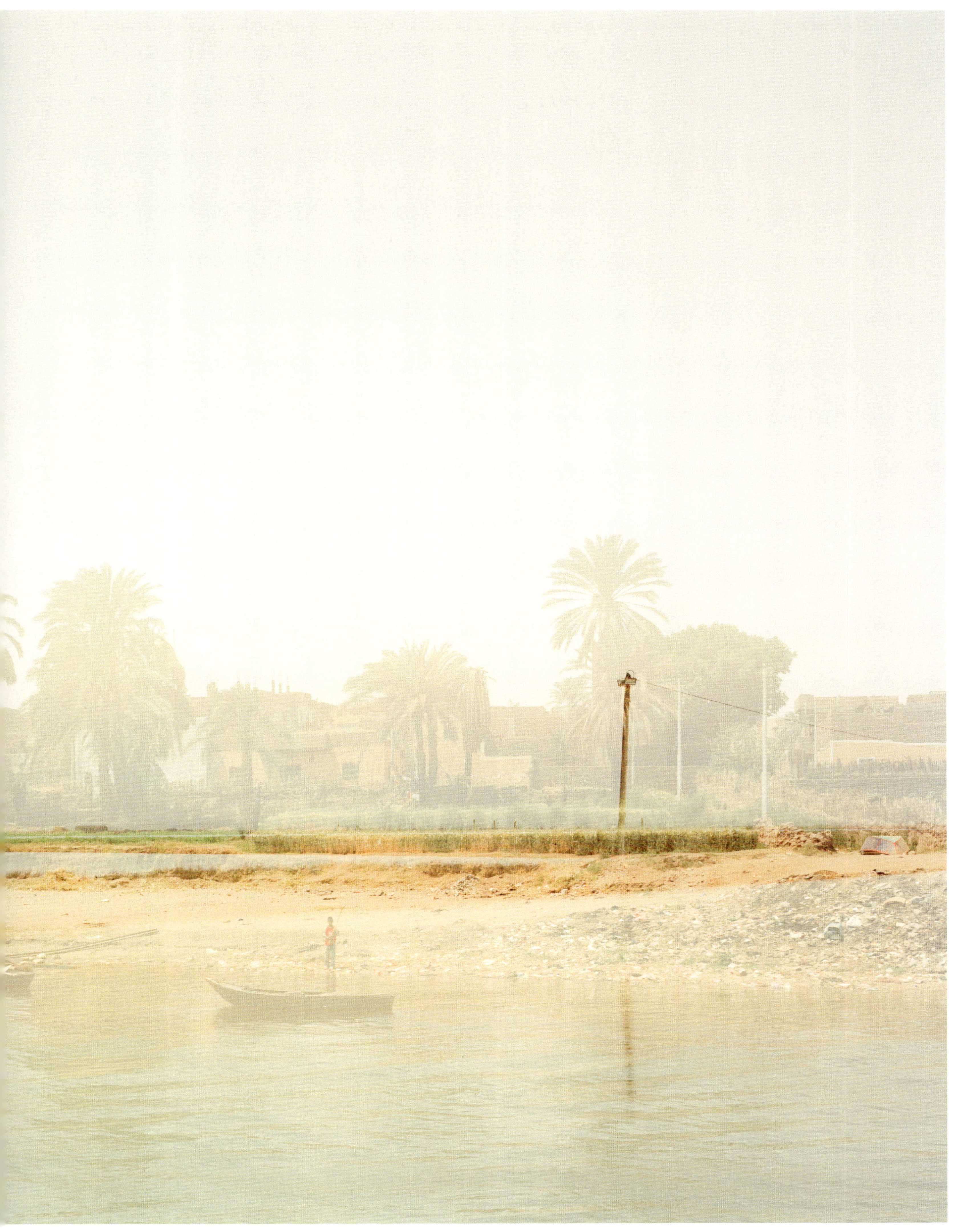

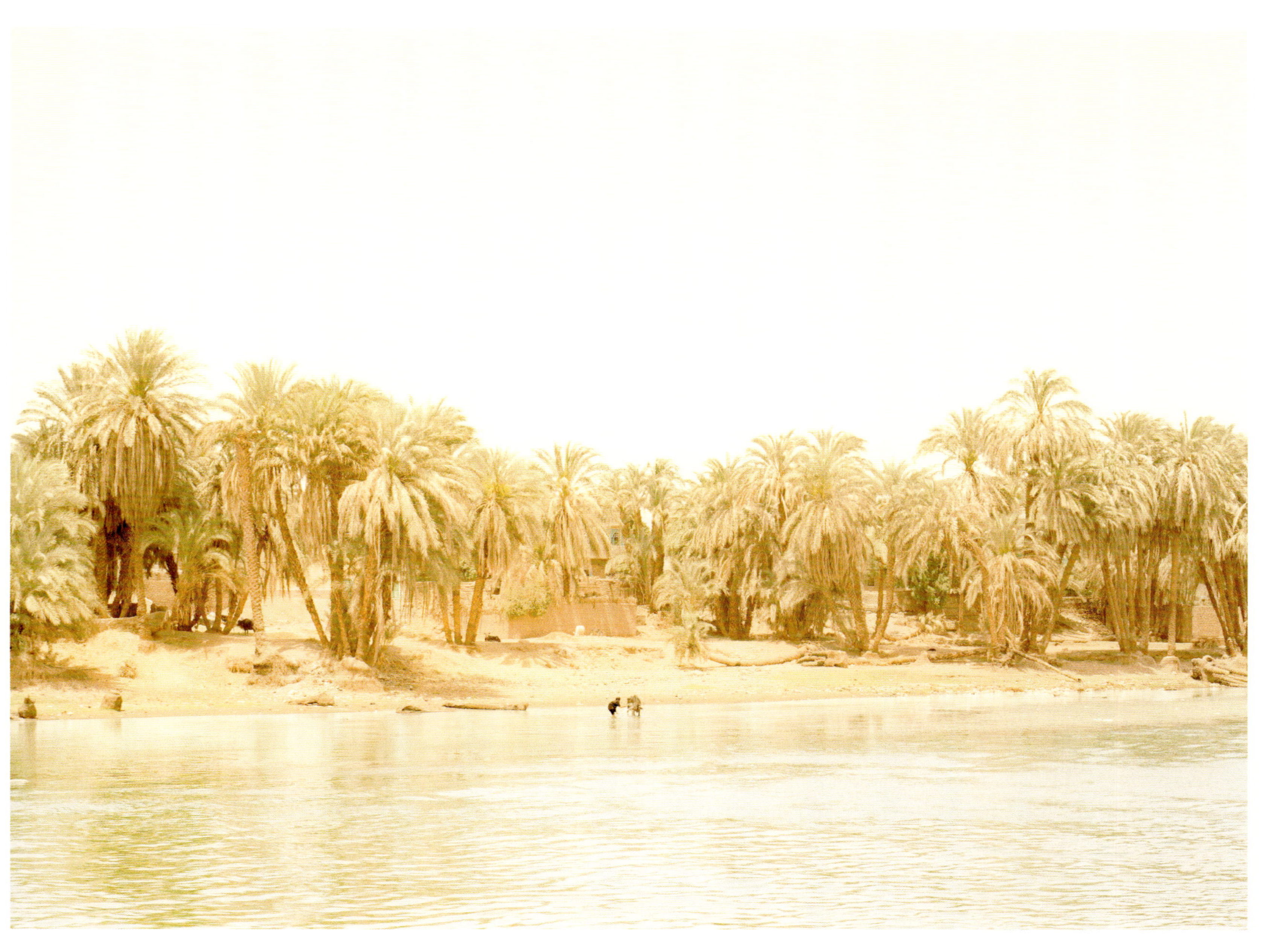

Armant II 2011

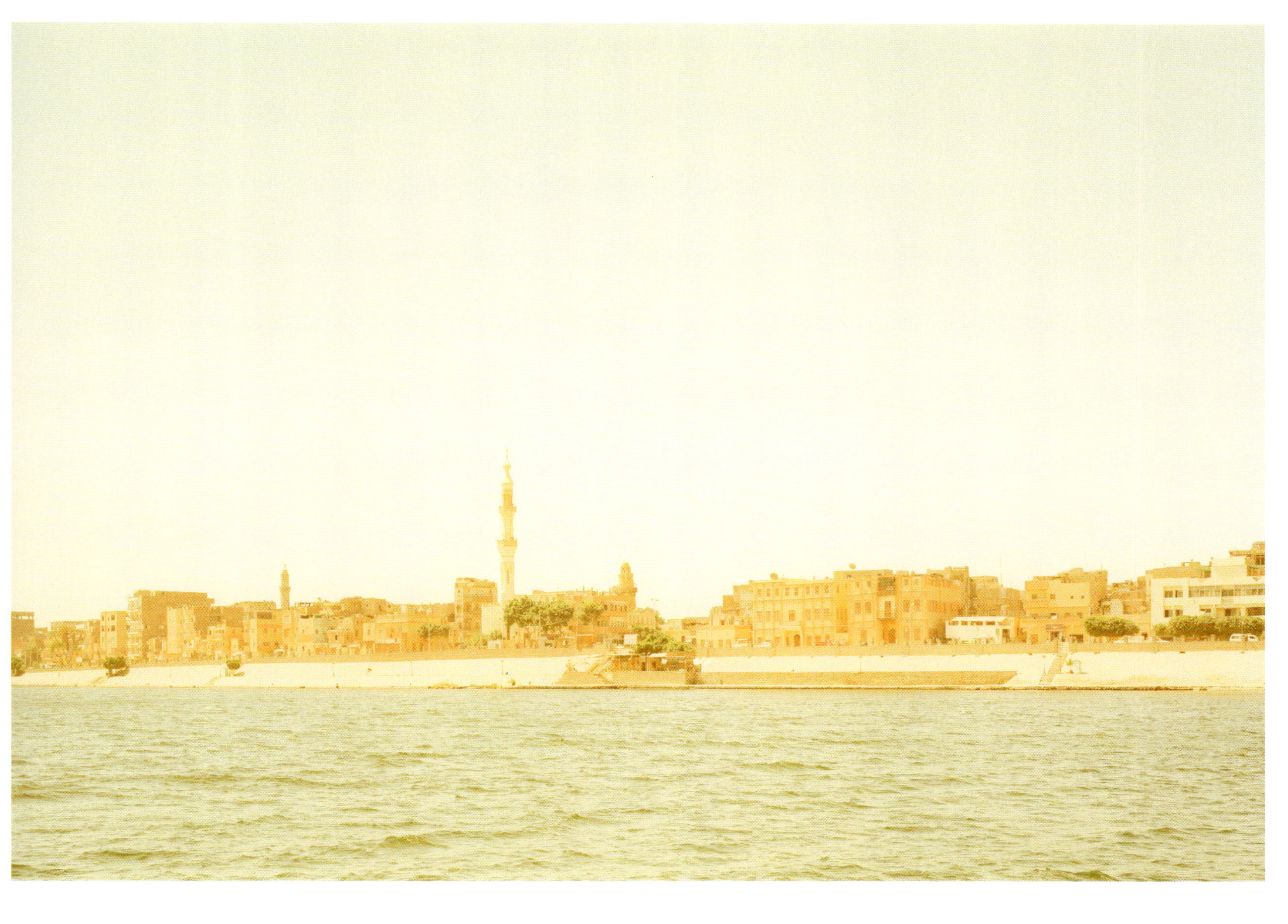

Esna I 2011

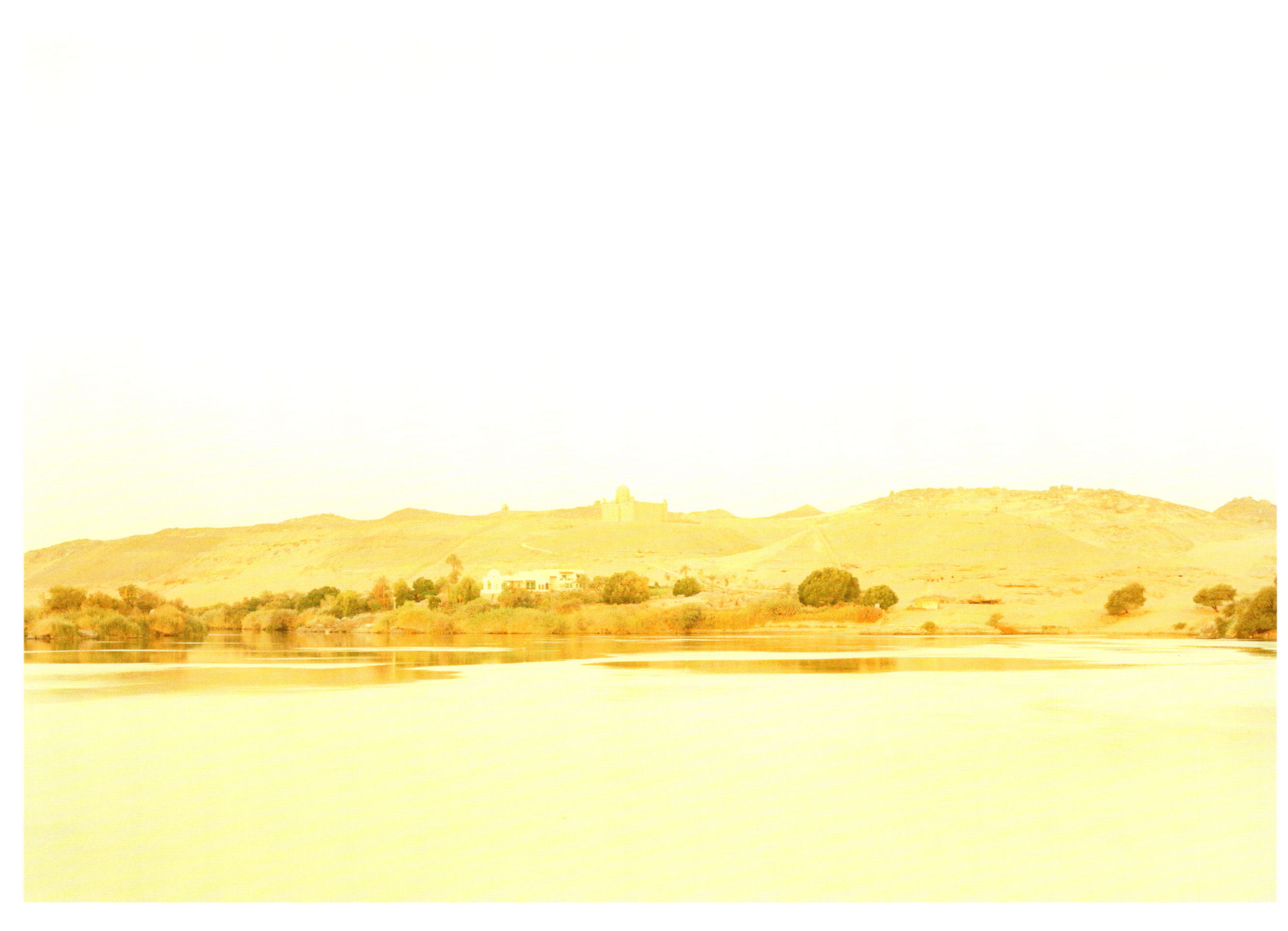

Aswan I 2011

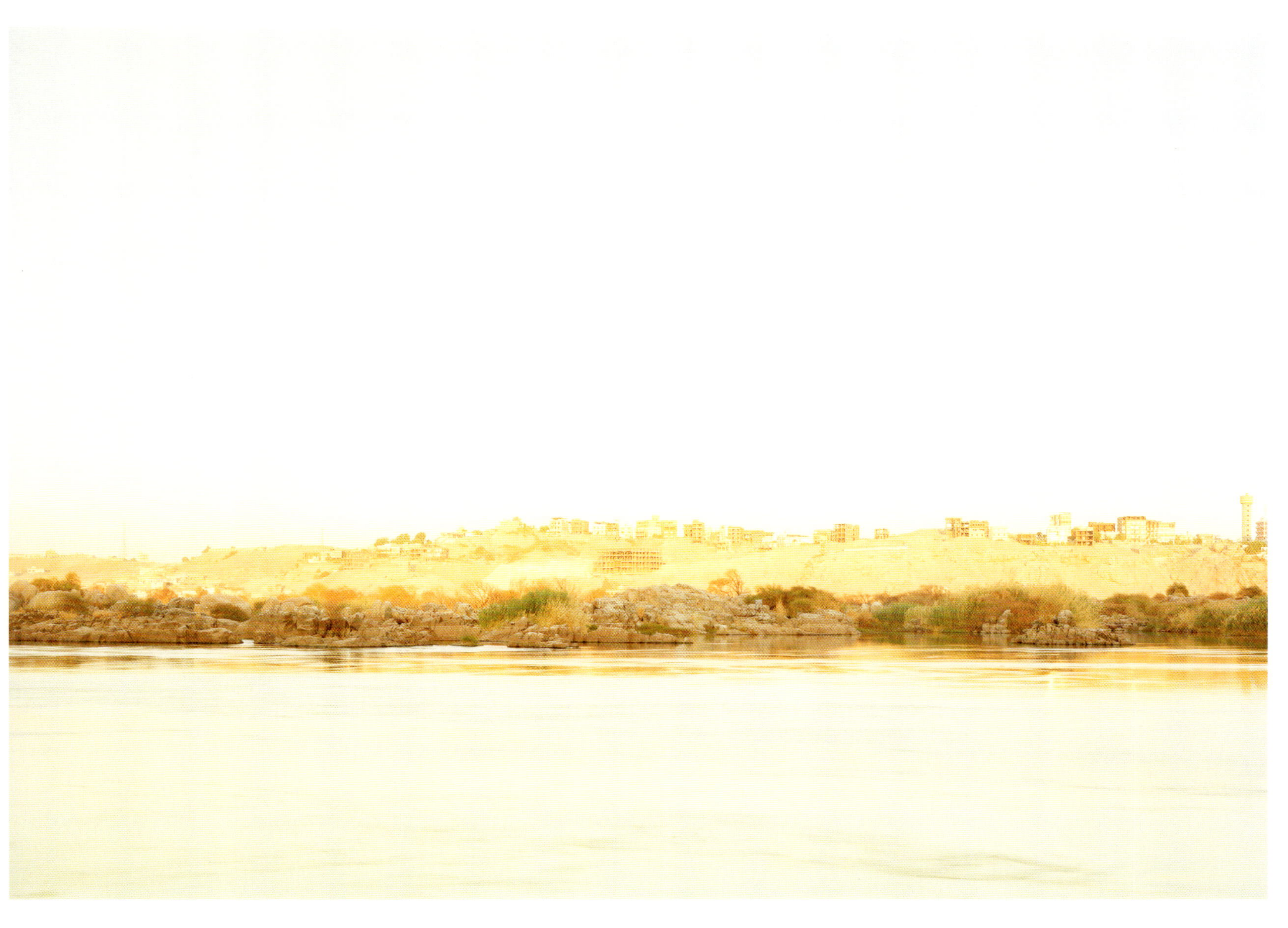

Aswan II 2011

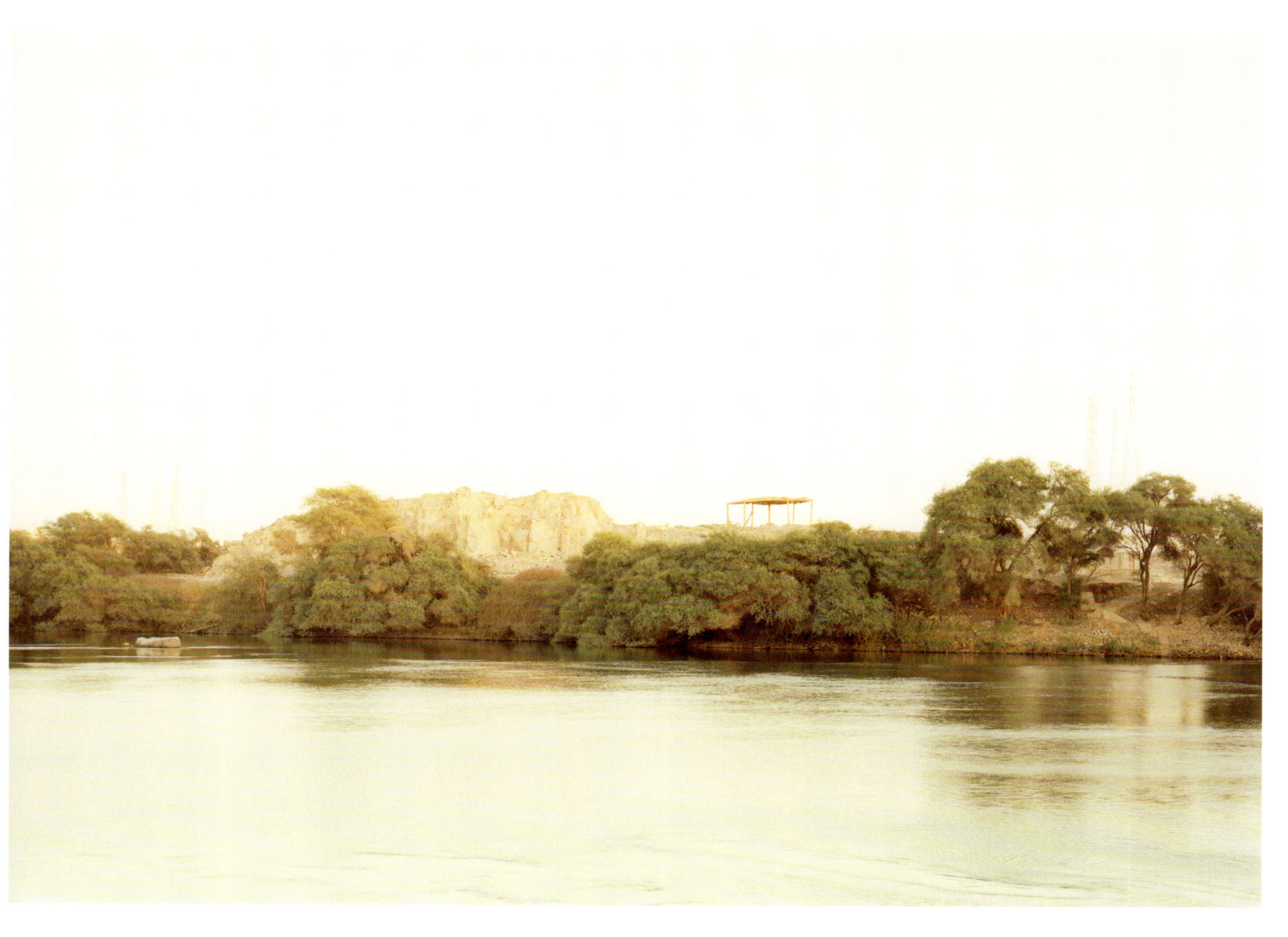

El Quarwad 2011

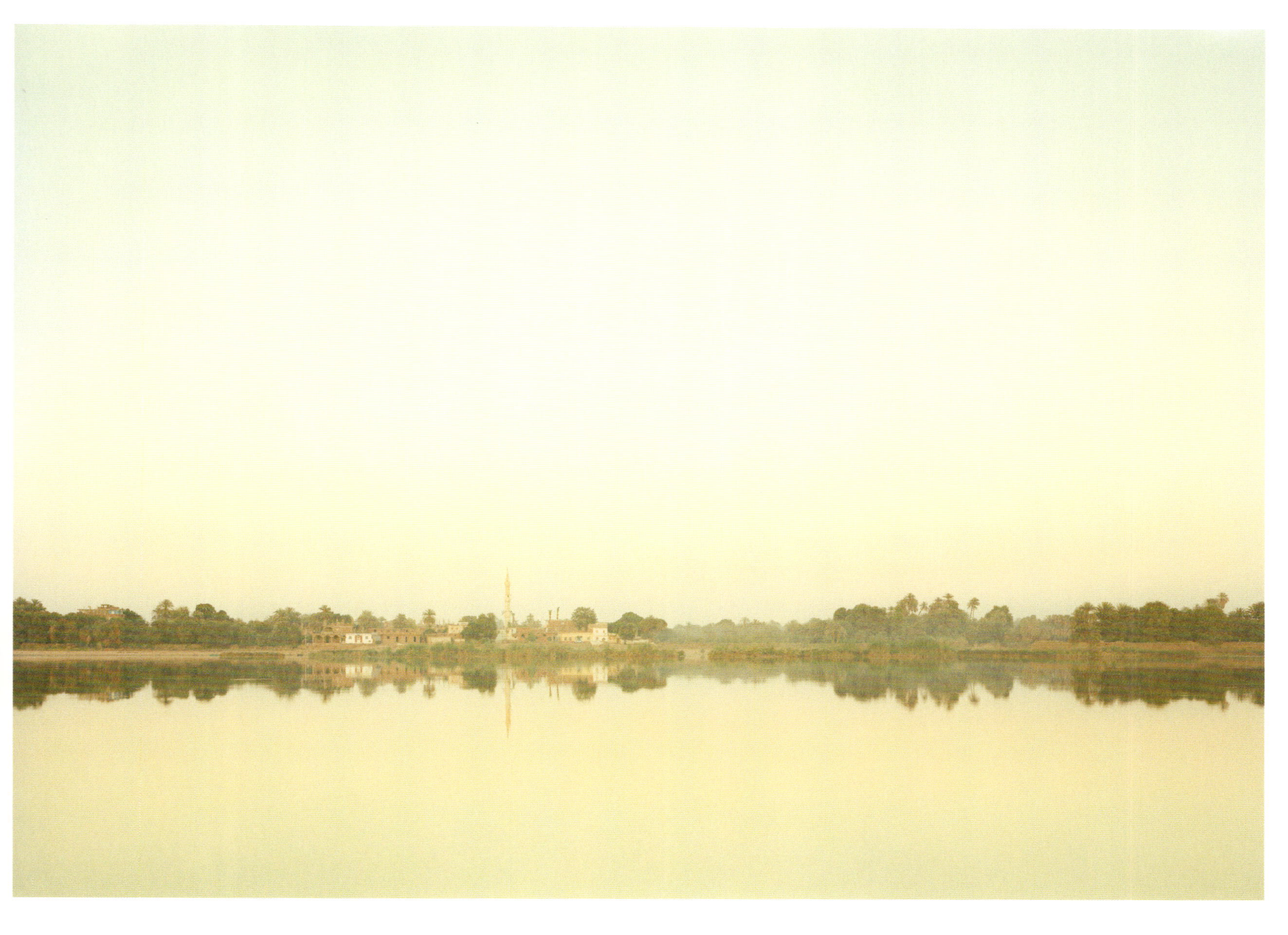

El Kab IV 2011

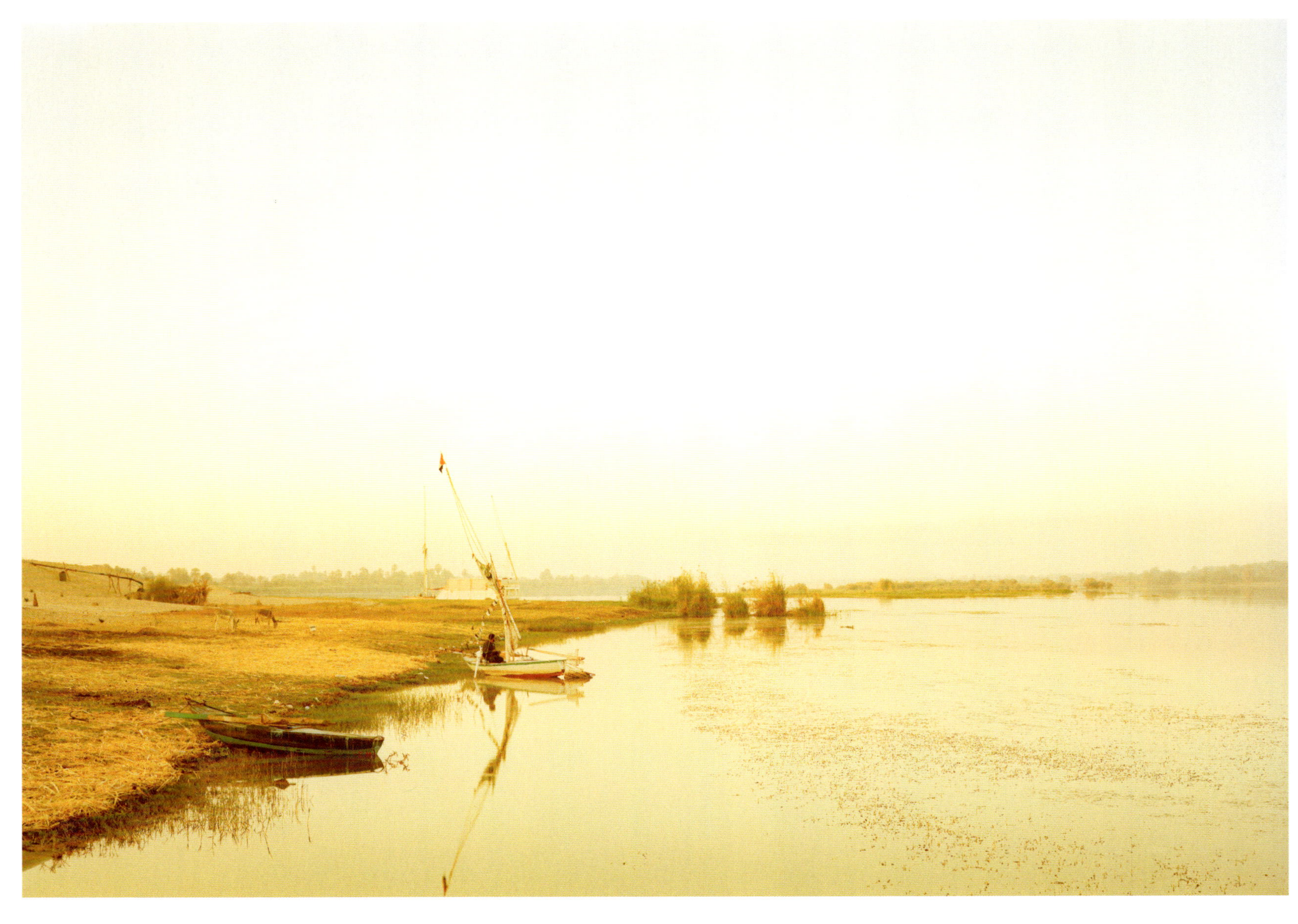

El Kab I 2011

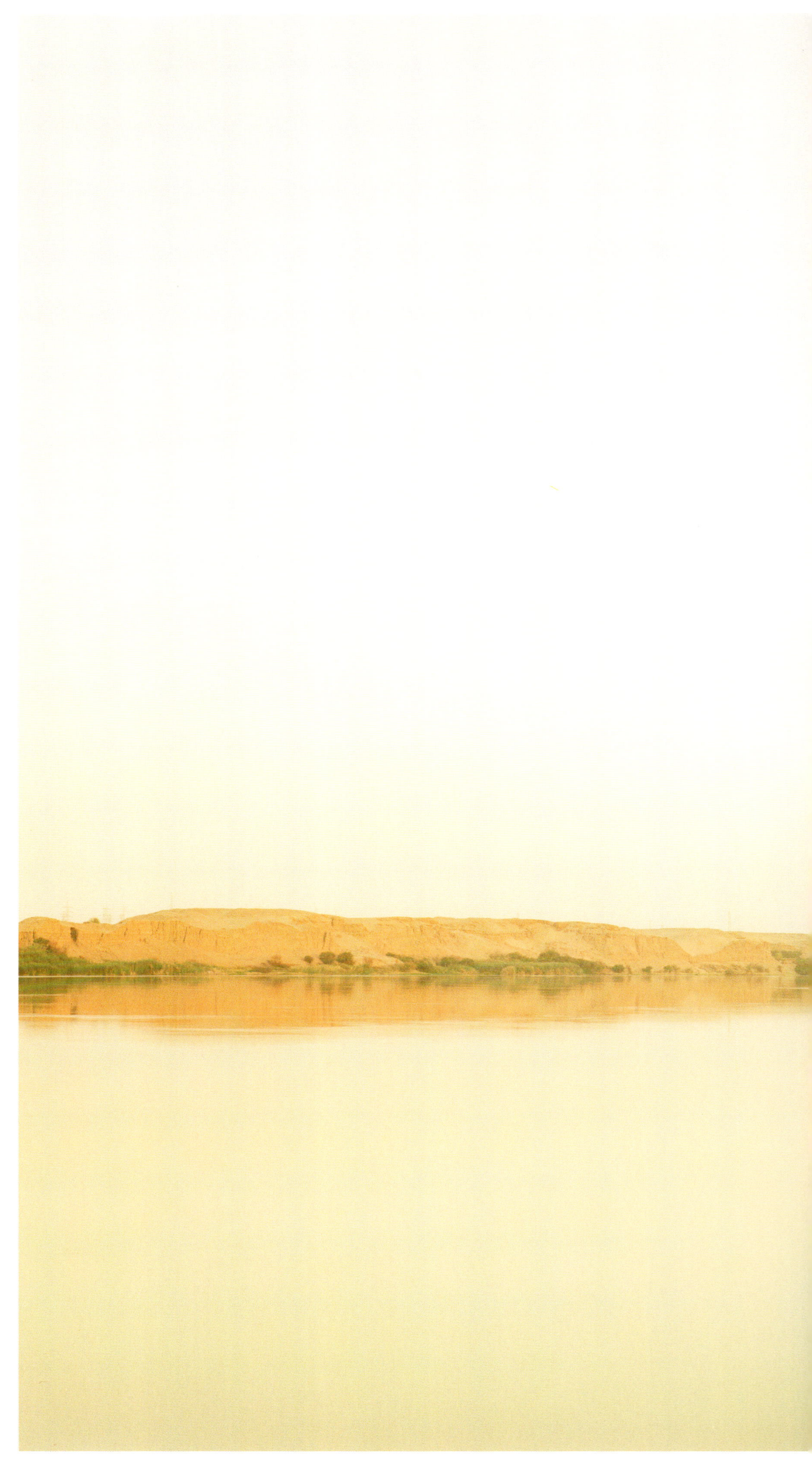

El Kab II 2011

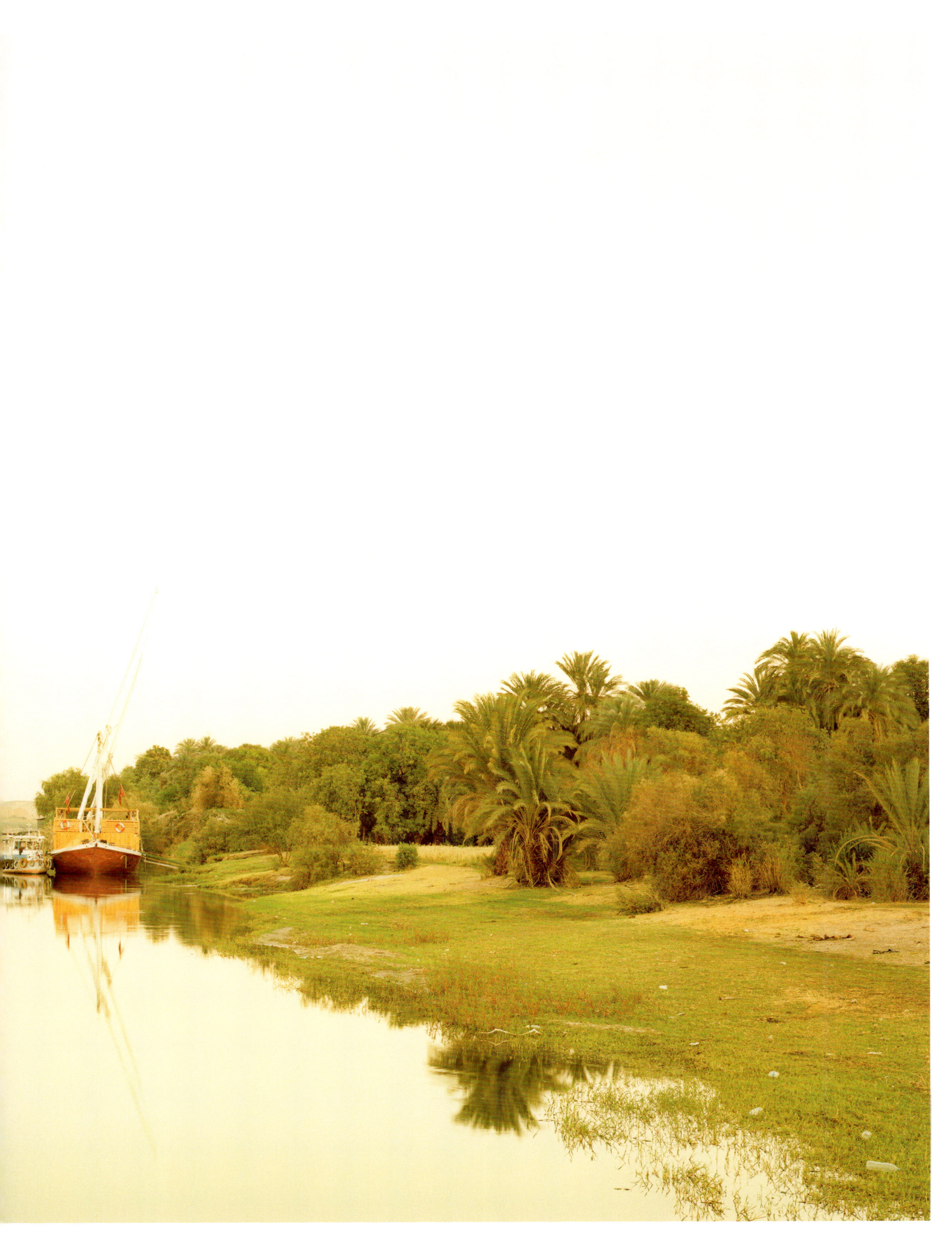

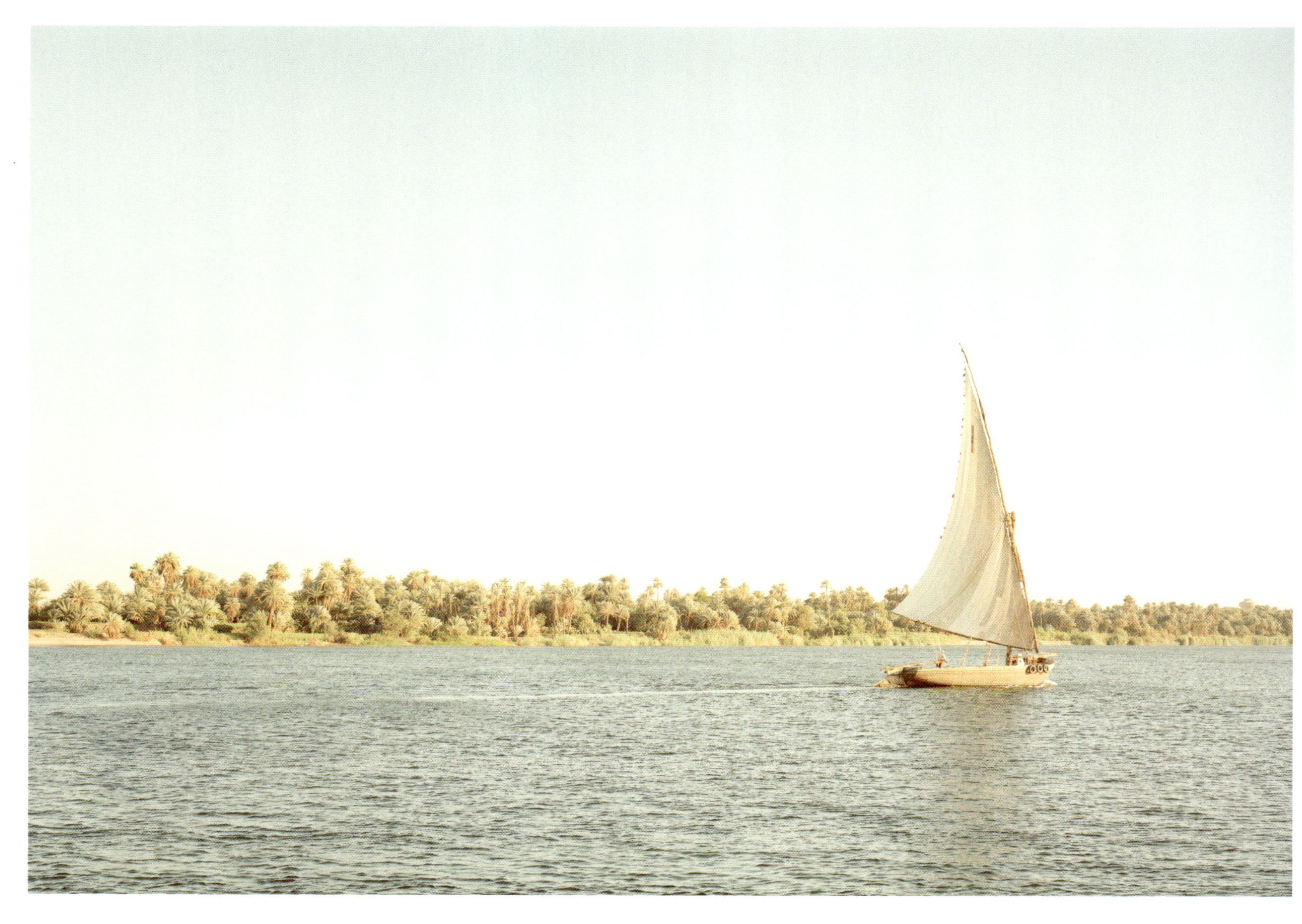

Salwa Bahry I 2011

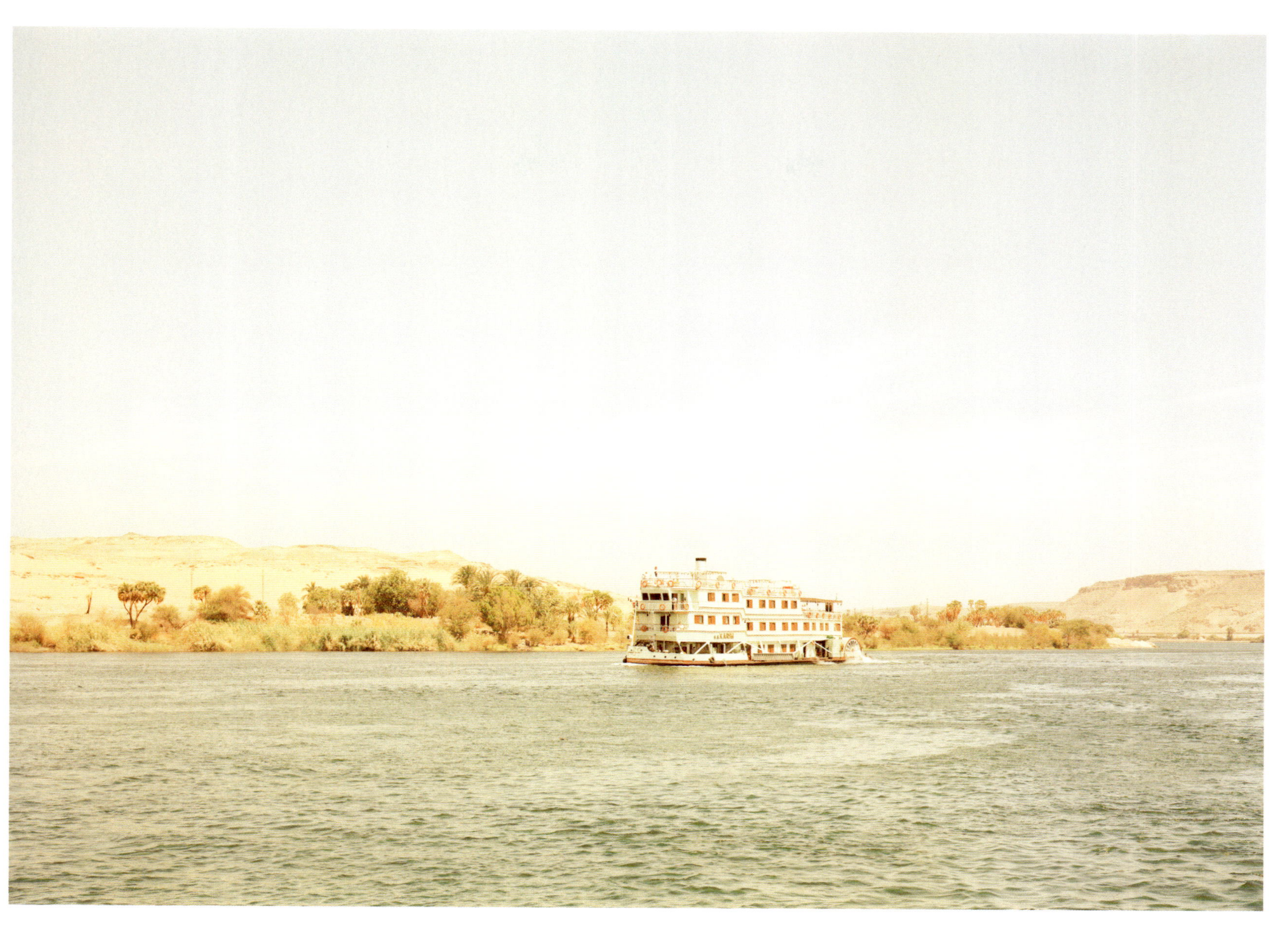

Salwa Bahry II 2011

APPENDIX

Translations / Übersetzungen

Der Orient im Orient

Elger Essers und Gustave Flauberts Perspektiven im Nahen Osten

ÖZKAN EZLI

„[...] ich probiere arabisches Brot, halbgebackenen Teig in Form runder Fladen. Ich passe so gut wie möglich auf mich auf, um mich nicht ungebührlich zu benehmen. Nach dem Mahl Spaziergang nach Abū-Mandūr auf dem linken Nilufer. – Gärten und Schilf (die einzige Nilstelle, wo ich welches gesehen habe, es kommt sonst kaum vor an den Nilufern) – pralle Sonne über dem Wasser.
Bei Abū-Mandūr macht der Nil einen Knick nach links (rechtes Ufer), nach jener Seite zu gibt es hohe Sandböschungen.
Eine Canja, einer Tartane ähnlich, gleitet über das Wasser: das ist der wahre Orient, melancholische und betäubende Wirkung; man ahnt hier schon etwas von dem Grenzenlosen, Erbarmungslosen, in dem man verloren ist.“ [1]

Es ist nicht das Brot, es sind nicht die arabischen Speisen, es ist auch nicht der heilige islamische Ort Abū-Mandūr und auch nicht der Nil. Es sind nicht diese Bilder und Eindrücke, die für Gustave Flaubert den „wahren Orient“ ausmachen, als er im Dezember des Jahres 1849 in Rashīd, nahe Kairo, im Nildelta spazieren geht. Obwohl dieses Wissen um die exotischen Details in der ersten Hälfte des 19. Jahrhunderts in Europa sehr wohl beschrieben, fotografiert, dokumentiert wird und ganz klar das Orientbild bestimmt, den Orient markiert.[2] Für Gustave Flaubert hingegen ist der „wahre Orient“ ein auf dem Wasser gleitendes Boot. Das Boot in Bewegung ist Orient, weil es eine bestimmte Stimmung, ein existentielles Ausgesetzt-Sein adrückt und eine anziehende Desorientierung verspricht. Bereits vier Tage zuvor, als Flaubert im Hafen von Alexandria zum ersten Mal Fuß auf „ägyptischen Boden“ setzt, fühlt er sich feierlich und voller Unruhe.[3] Der Orient: für Flaubert eine Erfahrung der Schwelle, die seine realistische, sezierende Beschreibung herausfordert. Denn natürlich weiß Flaubert seine Umgebung genau zu bestimmen und er könnte zweifelsohne wie ein gebildeter Tourist reisen, der *weiß*, was er sieht, der *zeigt*, was er sieht. Doch indem Flaubert den Orient im Orient entdeckt, macht er die Erfahrung einer Entgrenzung. Eine Erfahrung, die ihn zum Nachdenken über das Unterwegssein bewegt. Sie über-

1 Flaubert, Gustave (1996): *Reise in den Orient*, Frankfurt am Main: Insel Verlag, S. 42f.

2 Siehe hierzu: Said, Edward (2011): *Orientalismus*, Frankfurt am Main: Fischer Verlag, S. 235.

3 Flaubert (1996): S. 37.

setzt seine wissensgesättigte, genaue Beobachtung in einen reflexiven, existentiellen Gefühlszustand.

Woher aber kommt diese Erfahrung? Warum unterbricht er seine realistische Beschreibung? Sie kommt nicht einfach über ihn, weil er im Orient ist. Sein Verlangen war schon in Frankreich präsent, als Flaubert den eigentlichen Grund seiner Orientreise – der Fotograf Maxime Du Camp und Flaubert sind im Auftrag des Landwirtschafts- und Handelsministeriums unterwegs –, festhält: Er wolle aus seinem Ich herauskommen, „irgendwo und überall hin" fahren.[4] Darüber hinaus steht der Wechsel des erzählerischen Codes bei Flaubert auch in einem intertextuellen Zusammenhang. Rund dreißig Jahre vor Flaubert beschreibt auch der Orientalist Edward William Lane die Stadt Rashīd.[5] Doch anders als Flauberts mikrologische Darstellungen des Nilverlaufs schreibt Lane über den zurückgegangenen Schiffs- und Warenverkehr der Nil-Stadt und schätzt ihre Einwohnerzahl.[6] Er wählt eine ökonomische und makrologische Perspektive. Auch seine Erzählung rund um die Grabstätte Abū-Mandūr weicht entschieden von Flauberts Perspektive ab. Lane verweilt bei der heiligen Grabstätte des Sheykhs Abū-Mandūr und stellt anhand ihrer „mutmaßlichen" Wirkkraft Überlegungen zur Schicksalsgläubigkeit der Muslime an. Das Grab schütze nach muslimischem Glauben die Stadt vor Überschwemmungen und sei ein Ort von „talismanic influence".[7] Lanes Orient im Orient ist kein existentieller, sondern ein kultureller, der zwischen Orientalen und Briten unterscheidet: Der Orientale in Rashīd ist anders als der Brite abergläubisch, sehr religiös und autoritätsgläubig.[8] Der Orient, den Flaubert im Orient entdeckt, aber trennt nicht. Flaubert trennt ihn nicht von seiner Umgebung, sondern bindet ihn ein, in die Landschaft. Wo Lane seine faktenreiche Stadtbeschreibung mit religiösen Kategorien unterbricht und sich auf Mutmaßungen einlässt, dringt Flaubert real und imaginär in den Orient ein: mit den Assoziationen des gleitenden Bootes im Wasser und noch mehr mit allem, was ihn im Moment der Erzählung umgibt. Und tatsächlich verbringen Flaubert und sein Begleiter Du Camp nach einem mehrtägigen Aufenthalt in Kairo und nach einem Besuch der Pyramiden in Gizeh den wichtigsten Teil ihrer Reise auf einer Canja, fahren flussaufwärts von Bulak/Kairo über Assiut, Luxor, Esna, El-Kab, Assuan, über die Nil-Katarakte bis nach Wadi-Halfa.[9] Auch wenn sich dieser Teil ihres vierzehnmonatigen Aufenthalts (von Oktober 1849 bis Februar 1851) lediglich von Februar bis Mai 1850 erstreckt und sie danach Palästina,

4
Flaubert (1996): S. 15.

5
Flaubert war Lanes Reisebericht *Description of Egypt*, der im 19. Jahrhundert zu den wirkmächtigsten und mit am häufigsten rezipierten Werken zum Orient gehört, bekannt. Siehe hierzu: Said, Edward (2011): *Orientalismus*, Frankfurt am Main: Fischer Verlag, S. 236.

6
Lane, Edward William (2000): *Description of Egypt*, Cairo/New York: The American University in Cairo Press, S. 49f.

7
Ebd., S. 50.

8
Lane, Edward William (2000): S. 51.

9
Siehe hierzu Flaubert (1996): S. 83–179.

Syrien und den Libanon bereisen, bildet diese Fahrt auf dem Nil doch das Herzstück ihrer Reise.

In den Jahren 2005 und 2011 – also 160 Jahre nach Flaubert und Du Camp – hat der Fotograf Elger Esser dieselben Orte am Nil und dieselben Länder bereist, hat sie ebenfalls fotografisch festgehalten. Sein Buch *Morgenland* zeigt Fotografien aus Ägypten, Palästina, Israel und dem Libanon. Und wie in Flauberts Reisebeschreibung scheinen mir auch Essers Aufnahmen vom Nil der Schlüssel zu seinem Orient im Orient zu sein. Sein Verhältnis zum Orient ist – wie bei Flaubert – nicht von der kulturellen Leitunterscheidung eigen und fremd, modern und nichtmodern bestimmt, sondern vielmehr von der Unterscheidung Nähe und Distanz, von Teilsein und Nicht-Teilsein, von Morgen und Abend. Doch dazu später mehr. Denn um genauer greifen zu können, welches Morgenland die Bilder von Elger Esser zeigen, will ich mich in aller Kürze dem aufkommenden Orientalismus des 19. Jahrhunderts widmen, in dessen Zusammenhang Flauberts und Du Camps Orientreise steht. Danach möchte ich zeigen, worin sich Flauberts Orientbeschreibungen, mitunter auch Du Camps Fotografien, und Elger Essers Orientbilder ähneln, worin sie sich unterscheiden.

Wichtig ist es festzuhalten, dass die stärkste Differenz nicht zwischen den Orientreisenden des 19. Jahrhunderts (Flaubert und Du Camp) und dem heutigen Orientreisenden Elger Esser besteht. Es sind vielmehr die Beschreibungen Flauberts und die Fotografien Du Camps, die im Widerspruch zueinander stehen.[10] Dort wo Flaubert minutiös und ausführlich den Nil, Ägyterinnen, Ägypter, die Vegetation, Bootsanlegestellen, Tempel und Propyläen sozusagen in Nahaufnahmen beschreibt und dadurch ein äußerst heterogenes orientalisches Gefüge schafft, dominieren in Du Camps Fotografien die Monumente Ägyptens. Pyramiden, Tempel, Mausoleen, Moscheen und koptische Kirchen sind die Motive der 220 Fotografien, die Du Camp 1851 mit nach Frankreich bringt. Seine Aufnahmen stellen die Größe und Kolossalität der Monumente in den Vordergrund oder liefern Gesamtansichten.[11] Häufig ist auf den Aufnahmen auch Flaubert zu sehen, der neben den historischen Bauten als Maßstab fungiert. Flaubert beschreibt zudem, wie beschwerlich es jedes Mal war, die passende Anhöhe und den Ort für Du Camps Stativ zu finden.[12] Identische Standpunkte nimmt auch der bekannte englische Fotopionier Francis Frith auf seinen Reisen durch Ägypten und Palästina zwischen 1856 und 1859

10
Vgl. Stoll, André (1996): „Die Entführung des Eremiten in die Wüste". In: Flaubert (1996), S. 361–417, S. 391.

11
Siehe hierzu die Aufnahmen in den Publikationen: Flaubert (1996): „Bildteil". In: *Reise in den Orient*, von Gustave Flaubert, S. I–XXXII.

12
Flaubert (1996): S. 55.

ein. Seine Bilder aus Unterägypten, aus Theben und von den Pyramiden ähneln in ihren Motiven und Perspektiven den Fotografien Du Camps;[13] auch Frith baut Menschen als Maßstab ein und ebenso wie Du Camp ist er darum bemüht, im „‚perfekten Chaos der Ruinen' einen geeigneten Ort für die Kamera zu finden".[14] Die Suche nach einer alles umfassenden, panoptischen Perspektive zeigt sich eindrücklich in der Aufnahme des Isis-Tempels von Francis Bedford, eines weiteren britischen Fotografen, aus dem Jahr 1862.[15] Du Camp, Frith und Bedford dokumentieren die Größe der Monumente, stellen deren Repräsentationsmacht von Kultur und Geschichte dar. Fast könnte man meinen, das Licht aus dem Osten (der kulturelle Leitsatz der Römer) habe den Auslöser betätigt. Doch dieses Licht entspringt einzig den französischen und britischen Apparaturen, die den Orient im Orient auf spezifische Weise trennen. Die Orientalen selbst werden kaum in Relation zur Größe, Kultur und Geschichte ihrer Länder gesetzt. Sie werden (insbesondere in den Fotografien von Bedford) als Maßeinheit arrangiert und degradiert – sie wirken wie Kinder, die sich zufällig an diesen Orten getroffen haben.[16] Doch auch Fotografien, die sich dem Alltag der Orientalen widmen, weisen der einheimischen Bevölkerung weder einen natürlichen noch einen realistischen Ort zu. Sie entstehen, wie es der von Bernd Stiegler herausgegebene Bildband *Orientbilder. Fotografien 1850–1910* dokumentiert, „in den Ateliers der Großstädte", in Kairo und Alexandria. Für diese Aufnahmen wurden entweder die Studios mit Requisiten ausstaffiert oder man arrangierte ein entsprechendes Ambiente im Freien. In den Fotoateliers und Hinterhöfen wurde »ein regelrechtes Orient-Theater auf die Bühne gebracht, bei dem die Darsteller nacheinander verschiedene Rollen einnehmen konnten«; vom Derwisch über den Tarbusch zum Turbanträger, von der verschleierten zur entblößten Frau.[17] Dabei ging es nicht um die Darstellung von Individuen, sondern um Typen, die einer allgemeinen Kategorie angehörten und zeitlos waren.[18] Ein besonderes Kennzeichen des Orientalismus des 19. Jahrhunderts ist nach Edward Said, dass man die einheimische Bevölkerung nicht nur weniger wahrgenommen, sondern vielmehr durch sie hindurchgesehen, sie praktisch ignoriert hat.[19] Daher war es eher eine exotische Spielerei als eine befremdliche Angelegenheit, wenn sich Briten und Franzosen in orientalischer Kleidung ablichten ließen, wie es die Aufnahmen der genannten Fotografen zeigen. Dass sich ein „Orientale" in westlicher Kleidung abbilden ließ, war fotografisch undenkbar. Konzepte eines latenten Orientalismus wie die „Sinnlichkeit" der Orientalen, „ihr Hang zum Des-

13
Siehe hierzu: Stiegler, Bernd (2015): *Orientbilder. Fotografien 1850–1910*, Frankfurt am Main: Weissbooks, S. 41–47.

14
Aus: Ebd., S. 40.

15
El Hage, Badr / Gordon, Sophie (2014): *Cities, Citadels, and Sights of the Near East*, Cairo/ New York: The American University in Cairo Press, S. 32.

16
Siehe hierzu: El Hage / Gordon (2014): S. 53–55.

17
Stiegler (2015): S. 60. Siehe die Aufnahmen in: Ebd., S. 133–137; S. 149, S. 175 und S. 176.

18
Siehe: Stiegler (2015): S.61.

19
Said, Edward (2011): *Orientalismus*, Frankfurt am Main: Fischer Verlag, S. 237.

potismus, ihre Anomalie und ihre Rückständigkeit" setzten sich im Laufe des 19. Jahrhunderts fest und schufen ein Vorstellungssystem, das nach Saids Interpretation den Kolonialismus der Engländer und Franzosen Ende des 19. und Anfang der 20. Jahrhunderts legitimierte. Im Zentrum dieses französischen und britischen Orientalismus – so Said – stand die Annahme, dass der Orientale sich nicht aus eigener Kraft werde entwickeln können, dass der Westen diesen Modernisierungsprozess übernehmen müsse, um den Orient Schritt für Schritt zu okzidentalisieren. Nicht der Orientale habe Bezug zu den alten Hochkulturen des Ostens, sondern die Orientalisten des Westens. Solch großhistorische Trennungen sind nur möglich, wenn Beobachter eine Totalperspektive einnehmen und für sich als selbstverständlich beanspruchen. Diese ist, wie es Flauberts Reisebeschreibung zeigt, mit hohem körperlichem Aufwand, einer langen Suche nach dem besten Ort für das Stativ und die aufwendige technische Apparatur verbunden. Diesen Aufwand, diese Suche kaschieren die Aufnahmen aus der Panoramaperspektive. Für Said ist mit dieser Perspektive des Orientalisten das Ziel verbunden, „das ganze Panorama der Kultur, Religion, Mentalität, Geschichte und Gesellschaft" zu erfassen.[20] Wie lange diese Perspektive und dieses Vorstellungssystem überdauerten, zeigen auch literatur- und islamwissenschaftliche Forschungen zu schriftlichen Quellen aus dem arabischen und türkischen Raum. Von Anfang bis Ende des 20. Jahrhunderts lautete in vielen dieser Studien der Befund, dass weder arabische noch türkische Autoren und Reisende „wirkliche" Autobiographien und Reisebeschreibungen verfasst hätten. Für die Autobiographie fehle es ihnen an Introspektion, für die Reisebeschreibung die Fähigkeit, andere Kulturen in ihren umfassenden Zusammenhängen zu begreifen. Dafür gab es nach Ansicht der Forscher zwei Gründe: Entweder stünden den arabischen und türkischen Autoren ihre Körperlichkeit, ihre Sinnlichkeit und ihre Sexualität im Weg, oder es sei der Islam, der die Entwicklung des Individuums verhindere.[21] Aber schon Flauberts Orient im Orient scheint die orientalistischen Bestimmungen von Ost und West und von Edward Said zu konterkarieren. Irgendwann gehen ihm die ägyptischen Tempel „furchtbar auf die Nerven" und er fragt sich, ob es denn genauso wäre „mit den Kirchen in der Bretagne, den Wasserfällen in den Pyrenäen? Immer diese Notwendigkeit! Tun, was man tun muß; immer den Umständen entsprechend (auch wenn einen der Widerwille des Augenblicks von ihnen abhält) etwas sein müssen: wie ein junger Mann, ein Reisender, ein Künstler, ein Sohn, ein Staatsbürger usw. gerade sein

20
Ebd., S. 274. Doch hat Saids vielzitierte These nur eine bestimmte Reichweite. Besonders wenn man arabische, türkische Reisebeschreibungen und wissenschaftliche Reflexionen aus dem 19. und 20. Jahrhundert im Vergleich zu westlichen Texten im Vergleich betrachtet, was Said in seiner wichtigen Studie unterlassen hat. Denn gelingende und scheiternde Konstitutionen von Subjekt und Kultur gibt es in dieser Zeit mit unterschiedlichen Prägungen im westlichen, wie auch im nahöstlichen Kulturraum. Siehe hierzu: Ezli, Özkan (2012): *Grenzen der Kultur. Autobiographien und Reisebeschreibungen zwischen Okzident und Orient*, Konstanz: Konstanz University Press.

21
Siehe hierzu: Ezli, Özkan (2012): S. 19–40.

muß."[22] Flauberts Reisebeschreibung ist nicht von einem Sein in der Geschichte, sondern von einem Sein in der gegebenen Zeit bestimmt. Der erzählerische Prozess, der in Flauberts Reisebeschreibung stattfindet, ähnelt der Perspektive in den Fotografien von Elger Esser: beide übersetzen Geschichte in Zeit und Dauer. Träger dieses Prozesses sind bei beiden variierende Beobachterpositionen, die sie als in die Landschaft Eingebundene ausweisen.

Flaubert beschreibt den Orient aus unterschiedlichen Perspektiven, nimmt immer wieder andere Positionen ein, doch ein Erzählmodus kehrt immer wieder: Es ist eine schnappschussartige Bildabfolge, wie er sie zu Beginn seiner Reise wählt, als er auf der Canja an den Pyramiden von Sakkara vorbeigleitet. „Tanz der Matrosen. – Joseph an seinen Kochtöpfen. – Zur Seite geneigtes Boot. – Der Nil inmitten der Landschaft. – Wir befinden uns im Mittelpunkt. – Die Palmbüschel unterhalb der Pyramide von Sakkara sehen wie Brennesseln am Fuße von Gräbern aus."[23]

Wie in unserem Eingangszitat bindet Flaubert unterschiedliche Aspekte wie Sinnlichkeit, Essen, Dinge, Monumente der Geschichte und Fauna zu einer Landschaft zusammen, aus deren Konstellation keine Hierarchie erwächst. Die einzige Notwendigkeit ist das gleitende Boot. Ähnlich „demokratisch" fällt seine Beschreibung aus, als sie mit der Canja kurz vor Theben sind.[24] „Wir werden bald Theben erreichen. Vor uns rechts, hinter den Bergen, liegt das Tal der Könige; links vor mir befindet sich eine kleine Barke mit fischenden Männern. Sie stößt an ein weites Sandufer, an dessen Ende eine grüne Linie von Palmen ist. Der Wind nimmt jetzt wieder zu, wir kommen schneller vorwärts."[25] Würden wir uns bei dieser Bootsfahrt kurz vor Theben einen Touristen von gestern oder heute vorstellen, seine Blicke wären nur auf das Tal der Könige gerichtet. Flaubert jedoch bindet die Gräber der Könige mit einem fischenden Ägypter in einem Satz zusammen. Wer oder was hat hier Vorrang? Gibt es etwas, das ungebunden, monumental oder zeitlos wirkt? Wer ist kleiner und wer deshalb größer und wer steht für was? Flauberts Bruch mit der kolonialistischen Repräsentationspolitik ergibt sich aus seinem Orient im Orient. Zu einem Tempelbesuch in Koshtamna am Nil schreibt er: „Die Kolosse im Innern tragen auf dem Bauch, an der Stelle der Gürtelschnalle, einen Löwenkopf. Man ist ganz geblendet und betäubt von den Unmengen von Fledermäusen; sie schwirren und piepsen; unsere arabischen Kinder schwingen

22
Flaubert (1996): S. 126.

23
Ebd., S. 17.

24
Zum Zusammenhang von Demokratie und Erzählung siehe: Koschorke, Albrecht (2011): *Wahrheit und Erfindung. Grundzüge einer Erzähltheorie*, Frankfurt am Main: Fischer Verlag, S. 38.

25
Flaubert (1996): S. 96.

ihre Fackeln, eins stellt sich auf einen Tisch und hält seine Fackel in die Luft. Wenn die Fledermäuse zum Eingangstor hinausfliegen, sieht man die blaue Luft zwischen ihren dünnen, grauen Flügeln. An der Tür stand ein Esel, dessen Konturen sich im Licht abzeichneten; Himmel und Nil dahinter sind ganz blau; zwischen Himmel und Nil ein gelber Streifen, der Sand."[26]

Flaubert zeigt uns nicht einfach den Orient oder wofür er steht, sondern er lässt ihn uns sehen. Seine Bilder sind malerisch, setzen unsere Augen in Bewegung und lassen vor ihnen eine Landschaft erstehen, weil Monument, Fledermaus, Kind, Esel, Fluss und Sand aufeinanderfolgen und einen Zusammenhang herstellen. Diese realistische und zugleich piktoralistische Abfolge schafft für den Leser Dauer. Eine Dauer, die sich aus der Perspektive auf Augenhöhe entwickelt und somit eine Form des demokratischen Sehens ermöglicht. Wie bei Flaubert ist auch in den Fotografien Essers das gleitende Boot eine Art „Mittelpunkt". Das Subjekt, der Betrachter nimmt ebenfalls diesen Standpunkt ein, ist Teil der abgelichteten Umgebung. Mögen es die Aufnahmen im Süden oder im Norden des Libanon sein, in En Naqora oder die gestaffelten Bilder der Salinen in Enfeh – viele seiner Aufnahmen hat Esser vermutlich von einem Boot aus gemacht. Seine Fotografien zeigen im unteren Drittel die Wasser des Nils, dann folgen die Boote, an die sich im oberen Drittel des Bildes Küsten und Landschaften anschließen; Bootsanlegestellen und Flussbiegungen wie bei Flaubert. Es sind Bilder, die auf den ersten Blick Distanz zur gegenüberliegenden Küste schaffen, und doch ist der Fotograf, der Betrachter, ist der Blick, die Perspektive Teil der abgelichteten Landschaft. Der Betrachter steht nicht auf der anderen Seite des Flusses, er gehört nicht von vornherein zu einer anderen Kultur. Essers Fotografien sind nicht geprägt von einer identitätspolitischen Kategorie der Differenz. Seine Perspektive ist vielmehr von einer „hermeneutischen Distanznahme" bestimmt, wie sie die Literaturwissenschaftlerin Andrea Polaschegg für den deutschen Orientalismus des 19. Jahrhunderts herausgearbeitet hat. Diese trennt nicht das Vertraute vom Fremden, sondern bringt beides in eine dynamische Relation.[27] Eine annähernde Distanz, die sich auch in Essers libanesischem Tagebuch von 2005 zeigt, in dem wir ebenfalls die verbindende Logik Flauberts finden. Gebäude, Dinge, Tiere und Menschen werden in Zusammenhänge gebracht, das Auge des Beobachters wird in Bewegung versetzt.

26
Flaubert (1996): S. 136.

27
Siehe hierzu: Polaschegg, Andrea (2005): *Der andere Orientalismus. Regeln deutsch-morgenländischer Imagination im 19. Jahrhundert*, Berlin/New York: Walter de Gruyter, S. 43.

Auch die Einfarbigkeit, die Monochromie von Essers Fotografien trägt dazu bei, die Dinge zusammenzusehen und sie zugleich in ihren Positionen zu belassen. Wie das Bild hier im Bild entsteht, ist mit dem erzählerischen Verfahren Flauberts durchaus vergleichbar. Doch trotz aller Ähnlichkeit zwischen Flaubert und Esser besteht eine gravierende Differenz: Körperlichkeit und Vielfarbigkeit trennen beide Kunstschaffenden voneinander. Interessanterweise sind es genau diese Aspekte, die Said dazu veranlassten, Flaubert als Orientalisten zu bezeichnen.[28] Hat Elger Esser den Körper und die Farbe ausgeschlossen, um dem möglichen Orientalismus-Vorwurf zu entgehen?

Flauberts wie Essers Zugänge sind trotz aller Ähnlichkeiten in historisch-politischen Zusammenhängen zu sehen. Flauberts Reisebeschreibung ist eine realistische, fein ziselierte Form der Kritik an der westlichen Zivilisation und ihren kolonialistischen Bestrebungen. Für Esser ist das politische Assoziationsfeld des Orients und Okzidents ein anderes, das sich erst nach Saids Veröffentlichung globalpolitisch konstituiert hat. Denn ein Jahr nach dem Erscheinen seines Buchs *Orientalismus* kommt es 1979 im Iran zu einer Kulturrevolution islamischer Prägung. Bis Ende der 1990er Jahre macht sich die Rede vom islamischen Fundamentalismus breit.[29] Das orientalistische Assoziationsfeld, das Said noch mit einer Systematisierung von Sinnlichkeit, Despotie und Faulheit beschrieb, beginnt sich grundlegend zu verändern. Mit dem 11. September, mit al-Qaida und der Entstehung des „Islamischen Staats" ist der Orient faktisch und imaginär entweder in eigener Zerstörung begriffen oder stellt eine fremde und große Gefahr dar. An die Stelle der unterentwickelten, aber gastfreundlichen, sinnlichen, faulen Orientalen sind die gefährlichen getreten.[30] Jede Form der Körperlichkeit, das Ablichten von Minaretten oder Moscheen wäre in Essers Fotografien in diesem Assoziationsgeflecht gefangen. Ein echtes Sehen wäre unmöglich. Doch gerade in diesem Zusammenhang brechen seine Fotografien aus dem – hier nur sehr knapp skizzierten – aktuellen Diskurs aus, werden politisch im Flaubert'schen Sinne. Sinnlichkeit und Körperlichkeit liegen bei Esser nicht in den Fotografien selbst; vielmehr lösen sie im Betrachter selbst eine Körperlichkeit aus. Essers teilnehmende Perspektive macht den Betrachter zum Körper, der sich bewegen will. Ein Großteil seiner Fotografien lädt förmlich dazu ein, sich in die Szenen hineinzubewegen, den Kopf zur Seite zu drehen, um zu schauen, was da links vom Boot wohl noch liegen mag. Es ist diese

28
Saids Lektüre von Flauberts Reisebeschreibung missinterpretiert die politische Dimension der Körperlichkeit in *Reise in den Orient*. Denn die körperliche Disposition in Bezug auf Gewalt und Sexualität verbindet darin den Orientalen mit dem Okzidentalen mehr, als dass sie sie beide voneinander trennt.

29
Für viele: Heitmeyer, Wilhelm (1996): *Verlockender Fundamentalismus. Türkische Jugendliche in Deutschland*, Frankfurt am Main: Suhrkamp Verlag.

30
Siehe hierzu: Ezli, Özkan (2010): „Der ortlose Muslim. Das Prekäre als Niemandsland. Ein kulturwissenschaftlicher Kommentar zu Thilo Sarrazins *Deutschland schafft sich ab*", www.exzellenzcluster.uni-konstanz.de/ortlose-muslim-sarrazin.html (01.03.2017).

körperliche Mobilität, die Esser mit seinen Bildern auslöst, die über die Ausdehnung der Wahrnehmung hinausgeht. Man will wissen, was sich hinter oder neben den massiven Felsmauern von Akko in Israel befindet (Tafeln Seite 56–58). Man will in den Ruinen spazieren gehen, die Esser im Libanon fotografiert hat. Und genau im Auslösen dieser multiplen Körperbewegungen kommt Esser Flauberts Entdeckung vom Orient im Orient ganz nah, wenn dieser die Moschee in Rashīd zwar erwähnt, aber an ihr vorbeigeht und die im Wasser gleitende Canja erblickt. Dass der Orient wieder anziehend wird, ist Essers Perspektive zu verdanken, die ein angemessenes Verhältnis zwischen dem Betrachter und den Motiven schafft. Und was könnte heute politischer sein, als erneut einen Orient im Orient zu finden.

Literaturverzeichnis

El Hage, Badr / Gordon, Sophie (2014): *Cities, Citadels, and Sights of the Near East*, Cairo/New York: The American University in Cairo Press.

Ezli, Özkan (2012): *Grenzen der Kultur. Autobiographien und Reisebeschreibungen zwischen Okzident und Orient*, Konstanz: Konstanz University Press.

Ezli, Özkan (2010): „Der ortlose Muslim. Das Prekäre als Niemandsland. Ein kulturwissenschaftlicher Kommentar zu Thilo Sarrazins *Deutschland schafft sich ab*", www.exzellenzcluster.uni-konstanz.de/ortlose-muslim-sarrazin.html (01.03.2017).

Flaubert, Gustave (1996): *Reise in den Orient*, Frankfurt am Main: Insel Verlag.

Heitmeyer, Wilhelm (1996): *Verlockender Fundamentalismus. Türkische Jugendliche in Deutschland*, Frankfurt am Main: Suhrkamp Verlag.

Koschorke, Albrecht (2011): *Wahrheit und Erfindung. Grundzüge einer allgemeinen Erzähltheorie*, Frankfurt am Main: Fischer Verlag.

Lane, Edward William (2000): *Description of Egypt*, New York: The American University in Cairo Press.

Polaschegg, Andrea (2005): *Der andere Orientalismus. Regeln deutsch-morgenländischer Imagination im 19. Jahrhundert*, New York: Walter de Gruyter.

Said, Edward (2011): *Orientalismus*, Frankfurt am Main: Fischer Verlag.

Stiegler, Bernd (2015): *Orientbilder. Fotografien 1850–1910*, Frankfurt am Main: Weissbooks.

Unbequeme Landschaften

OSNAT ZUKERMAN RECHTER

„Heilige Landschaft", so nennt W. J. T. Mitchell die Landschaft Israels, wobei er vorzieht, von Israel/Palästina zu sprechen. Mitchell stellt die These auf, dass die vorherrschende visuell-bildliche Darstellung von Landschaft im Diskurs der westlichen Kunstgeschichte sogar eine Idealisierung der vernarbten Landschaft Israels ermöglicht, indem sie jedwede Anzeichen von Gewalt daraus tilgt.[1] Eine Bildoberfläche ist von sich aus dazu angetan, stereotypen Mustern Vorschub zu leisten, die zur Verschleierung von Geschichte beitragen und unsere Fähigkeit, sie zu interpretieren, außer Kraft setzen. Israel/Palästina, ein für die drei bedeutenderen Religionen, die auf der Bibel beruhen, heiliges Territorium, so Mitchells These, kann zu einer Illusion unschuldiger Natur werden, obwohl doch seine Landschaftsoberflächen deutlich die Anzeichen von Kriegen und Machtkämpfen sowie archäologische Ausgrabungen aufweisen. Betrachtet man diese Landschaft unter dem Aspekt des Bilderverbots –, worunter gegenständliche Darstellungen und Skulpturen oder Ähnlichkeiten fallen – wie es das (nach angelsächsischer Zählung) Zweite Gebot ausspricht, so kann diese Landschaft paradoxerweise selber zu einem Idol werden. Verwandelt in eine ideologische Darstellung, stellt die heilige Landschaft als Idol Machtbeziehungen als natürliche dar und ist als solche, so argumentiert Mitchell, Gegenstand einer falschen Selektivität der Erinnerung.

Die Landschaftsbilder, die Elger Esser während eines dreiwöchigen Besuchs in Israel im Herbst 2015 aufgenommen hat, können beim Betrachter diese Illusion unschuldiger Natur begünstigen, auf die Mitchell anspielt. In Essers Arbeiten wird den Landschaftsoberflächen eine malerisch/postkartenähnliche visuelle Darstellung zugestanden, die den Konventionen des aufs Malerische bedachten Schauens westlicher Touristen-Pilger entspricht. Die Fotografien legen den Gedanken nahe, dass Esser die Möglichkeit, die Landschaft könne selbst ein heiliges Idol sein, als Bezugspunkt nimmt. Auf allen Bildern, die in Israel aufgenommen wurden, wie auch auf den meisten seiner Fotos überhaupt sind die abgebildeten Orte menschenleer und die Merkmale ihres Hier und Jetzt ausgeklammert. Das

1
W. J. T. Mitchell, *Landscape and Power*, Chicago: University of Chicago Press, 1994, S. 5–34.

hat zur Folge, dass wir, wie Simone Schimpf in einem Essay angemerkt hat, den sie zu einem früheren Buch Essers geschrieben hat, zwar wissen, wo und wann die Bilder gemacht wurden, doch wir können die Zeit, in die sie unserem Gefühl nach gehören, nicht bestimmen.[2]
Essers Landschaftsfotografien und insbesondere seine Veduten stellen sich als der Zeit enthoben oder zeitlos dar, während sie doch eigentlich absichtsvoll die Zeit verschleiern und so verhindern, dass der Betrachter der Illusion von Unschuld erliegt. Das Bemühen, das darauf verwandt wird, die Landschaft von den Charakteristika des Hier und Jetzt zu reinigen und sie als idyllisch zu präsentieren, schafft Verfremdung, und ähnlich fragil wie die Spiegelung einer Landschaft in ruhigem Wasser legt es den ephemeren Charakter der auf ein Idol fixierten Illusion bloß, die sich ihr hätte zuschreiben lassen. Darüber hinaus wird bei einigen dieser Fotografien der einzelne Blickpunkt vervielfältigt. Auf diese Weise folgen sie nicht dem panoptischen Muster eines dominierenden Blickpunkts, einem seinem Wesen nach überwältigenden und kolonialistischen Muster, wie es typisch ist für die Tradition bildlicher Darstellung im Westen. Diese beiden technischen Maßnahmen – also die Tarnung von Zeit mit verschiedenen Mitteln und die Vervielfältigung des Blickpunkts – erzeugen in dieser Werkreihe ein komplexes und mehrdeutiges Verhältnis zu Wahrheit, Authentizität, Geschichte und Erinnerung. Trotz solcher Komplexität bleibt dieses Verhältnis jedoch treu gegenüber den Bewegungen, von denen die Oberfläche wimmelt, und treu der Fotografie als einem Medium zur Darstellung von Oberflächen statt von Tiefentheorien (wie beispielsweise der Psychoanalyse).
Die Arbeiten, die Esser in Israel gemacht hat, bilden drei Gruppen: eine Anzahl von großformatigen Landschaftsaufnahmen, sodann die Fotos *Palestine 1948* und die Serie *One Sky*. In jeder dieser Gruppen wie auch in den Beziehungen zwischen ihnen gehen Verheimlichung, Sichtbarkeit und glättende Bearbeitung ein raffiniertes Rollenspiel ein.

I.

Die großen Landschaftsfotografien wurden mit einer analogen Kamera an verschiedenen Orten in Israel aufgenommen. Die Bilder von Akko, dem See Genezareth und Jisr az-Zarka zeigen vorherrschend Wasser, ein typisches Motiv in vielen von Essers Fotografien. Für Betrachter, die sich auskennen mit der Geschichte dieser Orte und dem, was sie politisch und gesellschaftlich heute in Israel bedeuten, enthalten Essers quasi-pastorale

2
Simone Schimpf, „In Combray und anderswo“, in *Elger Esser: Eigenzeit*, München: Schirmer/Mosel, Kunstmuseum Stuttgart, S. 146–149.

Einstellungen, in denen die Zeit angehalten scheint, ein stilles Unbehagen. Das antike und malerische Akko hat eine gemischte Bevölkerung, und aufgrund sozialer Spannungen kommt es hin und wieder zu Ausbrüchen. Der See Genezareth, der einzige See Israels, ist ein Symbol für die nationalen Ängste hinsichtlich von Wasserknappheit; der Wasserstand wird täglich gemessen und in der Presse veröffentlicht. Und Jisr az-Zarka, die am schlimmsten benachteiligte arabische Gemeinde in Israel, liegt in der Nähe von Caesarea, einer der reichsten Städte Israels. Bis zum heutigen Tag ist kein einziger israelischer Künstler, der sich mit Jisr az-Zarka als Thema auseinandergesetzt hat – und das waren nicht wenige –, auf die Idee gekommen, den Blick von Armut und Gewalttätigkeit, die den Ort übel prägen, abzuwenden und lediglich auf das Meer zu richten. Das heißt, seine Verkommenheit mittels des einzigen gemeinsamen Nenners zu kaschieren, der ihn nicht nur gleichberechtigt mit dem begüterten Nachbarn verbindet, sondern auch mit den Ländern des gesamten Mittelmeerbeckens und, ein zusätzlich bereichernder Bezugspunkt, mit der Levante unserer Zeit und früherer Epochen.

Die anderen Arbeiten aus dieser Gruppe sind Abend-/Nachtbilder von Montfort und Shivta, aufgenommen mit einer Belichtungszeit von eineinhalb bis zwei Stunden. Sie spannen eine imaginäre geographische Linie zwischen Montfort, einer archäologischen Stätte im Norden Israels mit Ruinen einer mittelalterlichen (13. Jh.) Kreuzritterburg, und Shivta in Israels südlicher Wüste, das aus den Ruinen einer auf das erste bis neunte Jahrhundert zurückgehenden nabatäischen Stadt besteht. Zusammen mit der geographisch-imaginären Linie ziehen die Fotos dieser beiden Stätten, die zwei große vergangene Zivilisationen miteinander verbinden, die Jahrhunderte auseinanderliegen und sich in ihren archäologischen Überresten verkörpern, auch eine zeitübergreifende Linie. Durch die Wahl dieser beiden besonderen alten Stätten im Norden und im Süden entsteht der Eindruck einer Verdichtung von historischer Zeit und physischem Raum, unter anderem aufgrund des Effekts der langen Belichtungszeit.

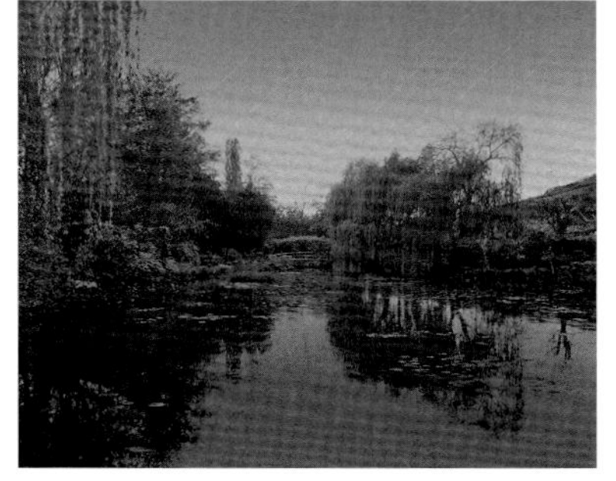

Elger Esser
Giverny I
Frankreich, 2010

Die Fotos von Montfort und Shivta stehen in einem Dialog mit der Gruppe von Nachtaufnahmen, die Esser auf Claude Monets Landsitz in *Giverny* (2010) machte. Bei beiden Serien stand die technische Entscheidung einer langen Belichtungszeit im Vordergrund. Bei *Giverny* betonte die verlängerte Aufzeichnung des Lichts, das von leicht über die Filmplatte dahingleitenden Blättern und Wasser reflektiert wurde, die gemäldeartigen Eigenschaften dieser „Nachtstücke“. Zugleich ließen diese Arbeiten die Unterschiede zwischen der Erfahrung von Zeitlosigkeit, wie sie von Essers Aufnahmen hervorgerufen wird, und der Motivation der impressionistischen Malerei hervortreten, welche den Schwerpunkt auf prävisuelle menschliche Wahrnehmung und die Erfahrung des Augenblicks/Jetzt legte – eine Erfahrung, die unter anderem ihren Ausdruck in den *Seerosen* findet, die Monet in dem von ihm angelegten quasi-natürlichen Garten gemalt hat. Bei den Aufnahmen von Montfort und Shivta bringt die lange Belichtungszeit andere Bedeutungen hervor als bei denen von *Giverny*. Die lange Belichtungszeit schrieb den Partien des Himmels bei diesen Fotografien Linien von Licht ein, als erweckten Sternschnuppen eine statische Urlandschaft aus dem Schlaf und setzten sie in Bewegung. Das Ineinanderfließen von Zeiten und Epochen, das schon die Fotos der historischen Stätten kennzeichnete, wurde auf diese Weise zusätzlich mit der Kreisbewegung der Erde verbunden und mit der ewigen kosmischen Konstellation, deren Teil sie ist.

II

Die Gruppe von Arbeiten mit dem Titel *Palestine 1948* umfasst 16 relativ kleine Fotografien verschiedener Orte in Israel/Palästina: Lifta, Caesarea, Maale Sdom, Beit She'arim, Tel Dan, Hirbet Tzunam, Nimod, Shivta und Arab al-Aramshe. Die Abzüge sind versengt, fleckig und mit verschiedenen Stempeln versehen, darunter dem eines Zensors. Der Name des fotografierten Ortes ist auf dem unteren linken Rand einer jeden Aufnahme in hebräischen Buchstaben angegeben. Der naive Betrachter könnte sie für Archivbilder halten. In Essers Ausstellung in den Galerieräumen von Loushy Art & Projects in Tel Aviv, wo die Arbeiten zum ersten Mal gezeigt wurden, trugen sie den Titel *Das Geheimarchiv des Livi Benjamin*, womit auf die Anwesenheit eines Geheimnisses angespielt wurde, bei dem Verheimlichung und Zensur eine Rolle spielten.

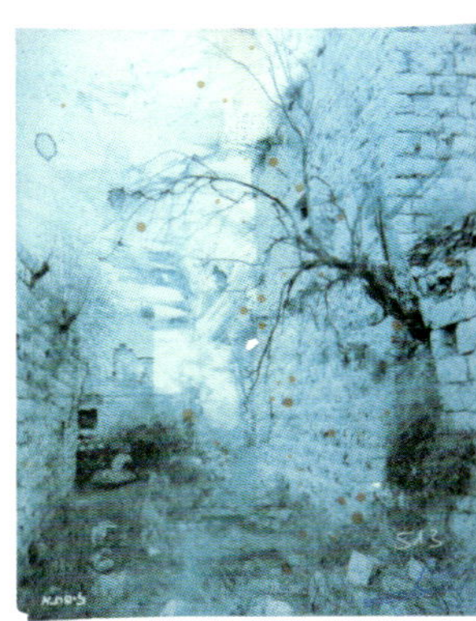

Elger Esser
Das Geheimarchiv des Livi Benjamin, Palestine 1948, Lifta VII, 2016

Die bearbeiteten Fotos, die von Esser 2015 an verschiedenen Orten in Israel aufgenommen wurden, maskieren sich als Archivaufnahmen aus dem Jahr 1948, dem Jahr, in dem Israel gegründet wurde. Die Verwendung von archivarischen Zusätzen wie Beschriftung, Flecken und Stempel bringt unser gewohntes „Lesen" der Bilder durcheinander, da sie zwar die Zeit, aber nicht den Ort, an dem sie aufgenommen wurden, verschleiert. Würde die Wahrheit offenbar und das Geheimnis gelüftet werden, ginge unser Vertrauen in diese Werkgruppe als Darstellung historischer Wahrheit und als authentisches Dokument verloren. Und damit auch unser Vertrauen in ihren Schöpfer – den Landschaftsfotografen, der es uns ermöglicht hat, in eine zeitlose Landschaft einzutauchen, uns mit dem Urheber eins zu fühlen, und der sich plötzlich als ein listiger und betrügerischer Demiurg entpuppt, der Kunstgriffe anwendet, um uns irrezuführen.

Die Werkgruppe *Palestine 1948* ist ein authentisches, einzigartiges Dokument, wenn auch nicht immer in vorhersagbarem und direkt historischem Sinne. Es ist eine Sammlung von Fotografien, die Esser in seinem Labor hergestellt und individuell bearbeitet hat und die deshalb von ihrem Status des reproduzierenden Bilds abweichen. Diese Sammlung nimmt für sich – in Walter Benjamins Worten – die Aura eines Originals in Anspruch. Wie die „Täuschung", die darin besteht, den Landschaften die Charakteristika des Hier und Jetzt zu nehmen, ist die „Vortäuschung" eines historischen Archivs eine konzeptuelle Entscheidung, die eigentlich lehrt, sich in Acht zu nehmen vor dem, was wir sehen, und nicht blindlings den Mustern des Denkens und Sehens zu gehorchen. Bezeichnenderweise sind Ausdrücke wie „exposure" (Belichtung) – ein Wort, das zugleich Entblößung und Bloßstellung bedeutet – und „ans Licht bringen" Begriffe, deren moralische Bedeutung mit der grundlegenden Abhängigkeit vom Mechanismus des Sehens und der Fotografie als ein auf Licht reagierendes Medium zusammenhängt. Essers fiktives Fotoarchiv unterdrückt nicht irgendein historisches oder politisches Geheimnis; deshalb hat Zensur hier keine Bedeutung. Auf der anderen Seite sind es eben unsere von besagter archivarischer Konvention freigelegten historischen Denkmuster und Betrachtungsweisen in Bezug auf Israel/Palästina 1948, die uns überraschen und schockieren könnten und die auch der Grund für Zensur wären. Das identische Format der Abzüge, die gleichförmige Beschriftung, mit der Orte benannt werden, und die direkte und detaillierte Bearbeitung, die jedes Bild erfährt, geben den fotografierten Orten den gleichen Stellenwert, trotz der Verschiedenheit ihres jeweiligen historischen, geographischen und demographischen Status. Das von Esser geschaffene Archiv ist ein Akt der Demokratisierung mittels einer Fotografie, deren Absicht es ist, die herrschende Wirklichkeit zu tarnen und zu verwischen, um die Existenz einer anderen, in höherem Maße respektvollen und egalitären Möglichkeit zu signalisieren, und sei es nur für den Blick.

III.

Den dritten Teil dieser Werkreihe, die Serie *One Sky*, bilden vier versilberte Kupferplatten mit Tintenstrahldrucken von Landschaftsaufnahmen. Auf

jeder Platte befinden sich zwei verschiedene Fotos: acht insgesamt, eine auf jeder Seite. Die technische Maßnahme, beide Seiten zu bedrucken, zwingt den Betrachter, sich zwischen beiden Seiten der Platte, die wie ein Hindernis im Raum steht, hin und her zu bewegen, um beide Ansichten zu sehen, die nicht zusammen betrachtet werden können.
Die Bilder wurden simultan zu beiden Seiten der Grenze zwischen Israel und dem Libanon und in deren unmittelbarer Nähe aufgenommen: ein Foto auf israelischem Gebiet mit Blick nach Norden zum Libanon, das andere auf libanesischem Gebiet Richtung Süden nach Israel. Zwei Digitalkameras wurden simultan eingesetzt und waren in einem fixierten und zuvor festgelegten Winkel ausgerichtet, diagonal zur Landschaft und gen Himmel zielend. Der Umstand, dass es sich um zwei verfeindete Staaten handelt, und die unruhige Grenze verhinderten jeglichen Austausch der beiden Fotografen untereinander. Die Landesgrenze erzwang Einschränkungen der Bewegung und der Kommunikation, die sich in Beschränkungen von Körper und Blick umsetzten. Im Verlauf der fotografischen Aktivitäten, die mehrere Tage in Anspruch nahmen, bedeutete das Fehlen von Kommunikation einen Verlust an Kontrolle. Wenn es einen Dialog gab, dann war er imaginär und beruhte auf Abmachungen und Entscheidungen, die vorab getroffen worden waren. Im Gegensatz zu dem panoptischen Blickpunkt musste Esser auf die Verfügungsgewalt über den Sucher verzichten, was mit sich brachte, dass ein anderes Auge über manche Einstellungen entschied und der Blickpunkt des Anderen ins eigene Werk einging. Bei *One Sky* wurde die Landschaft in ihrer Eigenschaft als Bedeutungsträger zu einem Akt der Kommunikation zwischen Menschen (und dem Fehlen einer solchen), statt nur ein Akt der Kommunikation zwischen dem Menschlichen und dem Nicht-Menschlichen (der Kamera, der Natur) zu sein.

In Elger Essers Werk geht es immer wieder um Fragen der Tarnung. Tarnung bedeutet nach Ayelet Zohar nicht, nicht gesehen zu werden, sondern nicht interpretiert zu werden.[3] Tarnung verbirgt nicht etwas, das nicht existiert, sondern glättet und assimiliert visuelle Information, die existiert, so dass wir sie falsch interpretieren. Deshalb ist Tarnung in allererster Linie ein Verteidigungsmechanismus, wie Tarnfarben in der Natur oder die Verhaltensmuster bestimmter Tiere, die angesichts von Gefahr erstarren und so tun, als seien sie tot. Die Fotografie ist ein Medium, das seit seinen Anfängen immer wieder mit dem Vorwurf vorgebli-

3
Ayelet Zohar, „Strategies of Camouflage: Depersonalization, Schizoanalysis and Contemporary Photography", Kap. 8, in: Ian Buchanan und Lorna Collins (Hrsg.), *Deleuze and the Schizoanalysis of Visual Arts*, London: Bloomsbury Books, 2014, S. 173–201.

cher Realität, des Einfrierens und der Todesstarre belegt wurde. Bei Essers Landschaftsaufnahmen geht es nicht um das, was wir sehen, weil es existiert, sondern um das, was wir nicht sehen, obwohl es existiert, wie die Erinnerung. Und so wie die sichtbaren Elemente von Tarnung unsere Wahrnehmung irreführen und verbergen, was existiert, verbirgt die auf den Fotos offenbarte Landschaft, was in ihr existiert und worum es dabei geht – um Erinnerung. So jedenfalls verstehe ich Essers Nachvollzug von Marcel Prousts *Suche nach der verlorenen Zeit* in seiner Fotoserie *Combray* (2007–2009).

In einer Vorlesung, die er vor Studenten in Israel hielt, erwähnte Esser eine Kindheitserinnerung, bei der es um Venedig ging. Im Alter von etwa zehn Jahren baute er im Hof ein Baumhaus, stürzte ab und fiel auf den Kopf. Die Folge war eine Gehirnerschütterung, der Familienurlaub in Italien wurde abgebrochen, und man kam nicht bis nach Venedig. Diese Erinnerung, zu der sich später die Erinnerung an die häufigen Arbeitsaufenthalte seiner Mutter in Venedig gesellte, während er in der Familienwohnung in Rom zurückblieb, und an die kleinen Geschenke, die ihm seine Mutter von dort mitbrachte, führten dazu, dass Esser Venedig mit einem Gefühl der Abwesenheit gleichsetzte. Und trotz der vielen Reisen, die ihn als Erwachsener nach Venedig führten, blieb es, wie er sagt, für ihn unerreichbar. „Venedig ist reine Reflexion, im Wasser wie im Himmel", sagt Esser, und jeder Besuch in der Stadt gleicht dem ersten Mal. „Venedig ist überall, und am meisten sogar in uns selbst. Es ist unser steingewordenes Portrait. Stärker als Rom, als die Levante, als Konstantinopel und natürlich stärker als die Neue Welt."[4] Essers Landschaften und Veduten sind Portraits des Menschlichen. Nicht solche von einer Person oder einer Stadt, sondern von Menschen und ihren Mühen auf Erden, wie sie sich durch die Linse der Erinnerung im Wasser und im Himmel spiegeln.

In seiner Fotoserie der Levante *(Morgenland)* richtet Esser seinen Blick von Venedig nach Osten – zum Libanon, nach Ägypten und Israel, hin zu der Region, deren Name auf den Sonnenaufgang zurückgeht und die Brennpunkt ständiger Spannungen und Krisen ist, welche in den letzten Jahren das Gesicht Europas zu verändern drohten.[5] „Levante" ist eine geographisch-kulturelle Organisationkategorie, deren Grenzen sich im Laufe der Geschichte verschoben haben und die den Blick festlegt, der von dort, von Europa, hierher gerichtet wird. Wenn ich Essers Fotografien des Libanon und Ägyptens betrachte – Länder, die ich zu meinem tiefen Bedauern niemals besucht habe und die zusammen mit Israel Teil dieser levanti-

4
Elger Esser im Shenka College of Engineering, Design and Art, 16. November 2016. Titel der Vorlesung: „It is always the first time" („Es ist immer das erste Mal").

5
Venedig, das seine Stärke als Seemacht seinen Handelsbeziehungen mit den Ländern des Mittelmeerbeckens verdankte, bildete jahrhundertelang einen bedeutenden Bezugspunkt für Kultur und Handel im Hinblick auf die Levante, das Morgenland.

nischen Trilogie bilden –, erwacht in mir, einer gebürtigen Israeli, einer Jüdin osteuropäischer Herkunft, vor allem das Gefühl einer Existenz „zwischen den Welten". Jacqueline Kahanoff, eine Israeli, die in Ägypten geboren wurde und aufgewachsen ist und auf Englisch schrieb, hat dieses Gefühl treffend in Worte gefasst:

In Wirklichkeit gab es eine dritte, äußerst unbequeme Kategorie menschlicher Wesen, zwischen den Rosigen und den Braunen, Menschen wie wir, Juden, Griechen, Syrer, Christen, Armenier, Eingeborene in gewissem Sinne und Europäer in anderer Hinsicht, die „Levantiner" genannt wurden, und die Juden schienen die schlimmsten von allen zu sein, so sagten manche Kindermädchen, obwohl doch alle doppelgesichtige Wesen waren, die niemals die Wahrheit sagten. Wie schwer es war für diese Zwischenmenschen, Menschen wie wir, zu wissen, für was man sich entscheiden sollte, wem man ähneln wollte und für wen man sein sollte – die Briten oder die Eingeborenen![6]

Diese Zwischenmenschen, deren gespaltene Identität, mutierte Kultur und deren Leben zwischen den Welten Kahanoff beschreibt, teilen sich offenbar dasselbe Meer, den einen Himmel und dieselben irritierend unbequemen Landschaften, von denen Essers Fotografien im Sinne Prousts Zeugnis ablegen.

6 Jacqueline Kahanoff, „The Blue Veil of Progress", 11.6.1967. Zitiert mit Genehmigung von Laura d'Amade und Unterstützung des Archivs für Hebräische Literatur am Heksherim Forschungsinstitut der Ben-Gurion Universität Negev – Prof. Yigal Schwartz und Ilan Bar-David.

LEBANON

8
Raouché II
Lebanon 2005
C-Print, DiaSec Face
142 × 184 × 5 cm

11
Jbail
Lebanon 2005
C-Print, DiaSec Face
136.5 × 184 × 5 cm

13
Enfeh I
Lebanon 2005
C-Print, DiaSec Face
142 × 184 × 4 cm

15
Enfeh II
Lebanon 2005
C-Print, DiaSec Face
142 × 184 × 5 cm

17
Enfeh III
Lebanon 2005
C-Print, DiaSec Face
184 × 240 × 5 cm

18
En Naqoura I
Lebanon 2005
C-Print, DiaSec Face
140 × 184 × 5 cm

19
En Naqoura II
Lebanon 2005
C-Print, DiaSec Face
140 × 184 × 5 cm

20
Saida II
Lebanon 2005
C-Print, DiaSec Face
184 × 242.5 × 5 cm

23
Raouché I
Lebanon 2005
C-Print, DiaSec Face
140.5 × 184 × 5 cm

24
Saida I
Lebanon 2005
C-Print, DiaSec Face
125 × 162 × 5 cm

33 – 53
Lebanese Daybook 4 – 11 December 2004
Mixed Media: wood, glass, acrylic paintings on cedar wood, C-print on aluminium
Each:
100 × 160 × 14 cm

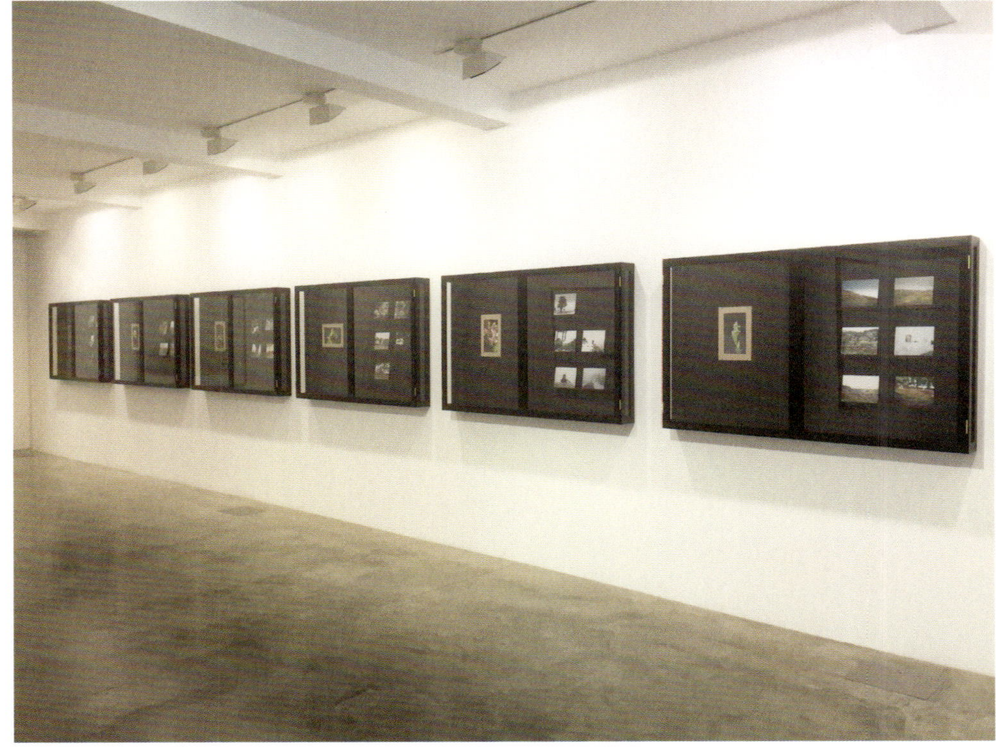

Lebanese Daybook Elger Esser. Morgenland. Parasol unit foundation for contemporary art, London 29 March – 21 May 2017.

ISRAEL

56
Akko IV
Israel 2015
C-Print, Diasec Face
138 × 184 × 5 cm

58
Akko III
Israel 2015
C-Print, Diasec Face
154.5 × 184 × 5 cm

59
Akko II
Israel 2015
C-Print, Diasec Face
154.5 × 184 × 5 cm

61
Jisr az-Zarqa I
Israel 2015
C-Print, Diasec Face
146 × 183.5 × 5 cm

62
Ma' Agan Micha' el I
Israel 2015
C-Print, Diasec Face
138 × 184 × 5 cm

63
Ma' Agan Micha' el II
Israel 2015
C-Print, Diasec Face
138 × 184 × 5 cm

65
Môle de Césarée
Palestine / Israel
2007, C-Print,
handcoloured
184 × 255 cm

67
Shivta
Israel 2015
C-Print, Alu-Dibond
184 × 228.5 × 4 cm

69
Sea of Galilee I (See Genezareth I)
Israel 2015
C-Print, Diasec Face
184 x 230 x 5 cm

70
Sea of Galilee II (See Genezareth II)
Israel 2015
C-Print, Diasec Face
184 x 217.7 x 5 cm

72
Montfort
Israel 2015
C-Print, Alu-Dibond
184 × 229.8 × 4 cm

81 – 97
The Secret Archive of Livi Benjamin, Palestine 1948
Israel 2015
Each vitrine:
Silver gelatin print, coloured
29.3 × 37.5 cm

99 – 134
One Sky
Israel / Lebanon 2015
Mixed Media:
Silver-coated copper-plate, directprint, black painted board, white painted pedestal
91 × 45,4 cm (copper-plate)
148,5 × 114 × 30 cm (with pedestal)

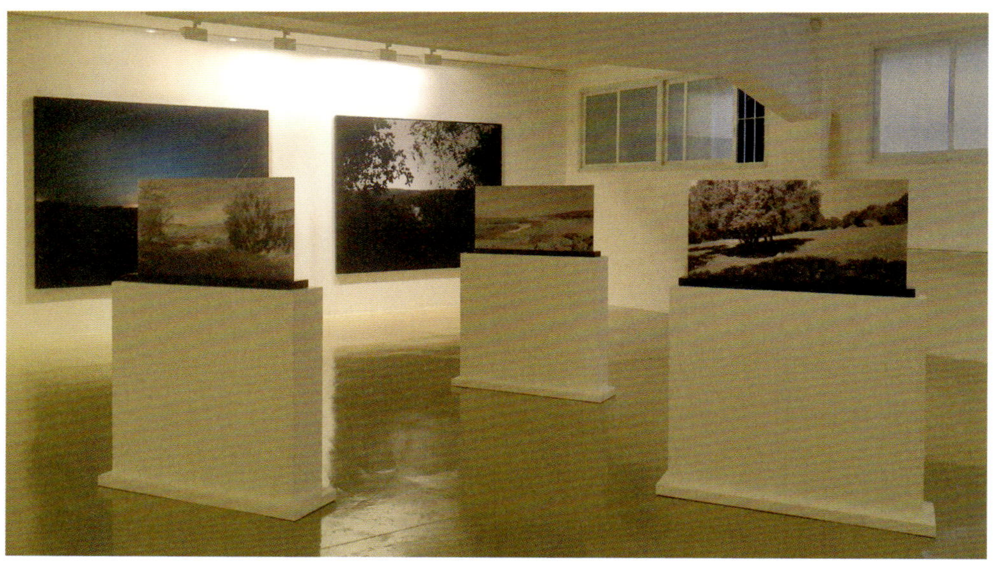

One Sky Elger Esser. from Shivta to Lifta. Loushy Art & Projects, Tel Aviv. November 2016.

EGYPT

138
Nile I
(Nil I)
Egypt 2011
C-Print, Diasec Face
184 × 242 × 5 cm

140
Fata Morgana
Egypt 2011
C-Print, Diasec Face
184 × 240 × 5 cm

143
Armant II
Egypt 2011
UltraChrome Print
70 × 82 × 3.5 cm

145
Esna I
Egypt 2011
C-Print, Diasec Face
138 × 184 × 5 cm

146
Aswan I
(Assuan I)
Egypt 2011
C-Print, Diasec Face
184 × 236 × 5 cm

147
Aswan II
(Assuan II)
Egypt 2011
C-Print, Diasec Face
184 × 243 × 5 cm

149
El Quarwad
Egypt 2011
C-Print, Diasec Face
141 × 184 × 5 cm

152
El Kab I
Egypt 2011
C-Print, Diasec Face
142 × 184 × 5 cm

154
El Kab II
Egypt 2011
C-Print, Diasec Face
184 × 239.5 × 5 cm

156
Salwa Bahry I
Egypt 2011
C-Print, Diasec Face
97 × 124 × 4 cm

157
Salwa Bahry II
Egypt 2011
C-Print, Diasec Face
140.5 × 184 × 5 cm

Imprint

CREDITS

Concept: Elger Esser, Monika Malsy
Graphic Design and Typesetting:
Monika Malsy, Düsseldorf
Reproductions: NovaConcept, Berlin
Production: Schirmer/Mosel München
Printing and binding: Printer Trento, Italien
Translations: Den Essay von Osnat Zukerman Rechter übersetzte Jörg Trobitius aus dem Englischen.
Özkan Ezli's essay was translated from the German by Ehren Fordyce.

ISBN 978-3-8296-0797-1
www.schirmer-mosel.com

THANKS TO

Thaddaeus Ropac
Ziba Ardalan and the team of Parasol Unit
Meir Loushy
Adar Segalit
Galit Julia Aloni
Didier Caille
Osnat Zuckerman Rechter
Özkan Ezli
Bernd Stiegler
Malte Bruns
Magdalena Spitlbaur
Dorothea Kartmann
Mara Wallat
Justus Kewenig
Barbara Huttrop
Jule Kewenig
Michael O. Kewenig (in memoriam)
Rose Shoshana
Arne Ehmann
Elena Bortolotti
Benédicte Burrus
Antonio Homem
Monika Malsy
Lothar Schirmer
Martje Esser
Nathalie Khoury
Bernard Khoury
Khaled Sleem
Andrée Sfeir-Semler
Ulrich Semler
Rana Nasser-Eddin
Neila Kunigk
Martine Landat and
Jan-Peter Tripp